Follow the Angels

The Path of Dedication

All Glories to Sri Guru and Gauranga

Follow the Angels

The Path of Dedication

Swami B.R. Sridhara

MANDALA
publishing group

For philosophical inquiries please contact:

Śrī Nārāsiṅgha Caitanya Maṭha
P.O. Box 21, Sri Rangapatna - Karnataka-571 438, India
E-mail: gosai@gosai.com
Web site: http://www.gosai.com/chaitanya/
or
Śrī Caitanya Sarasvata Maṭha
Kolerganj, P.O. Navadvīpa, Dist. Nadia, West Bengal, 741302 India

Senior Editors:
Tridaṇḍi Gosvāmī Śrī Śrīpāda
Bhakti Gaurava Nārāsiṅgha Mahārāja
and
Tridaṇḍi Gosvāmī Śrī Śrīpāda
Bhakti Bhāvana Viṣṇu Mahārāja

Assisted by numerous ever–aspiring servants
of Śrī Śrī Guru and Gaurāṅga

To order this and other books by
Gosai Publishers and Mandala Publishing Group contact:

Mandala Publishing Group
2240 B 4th St., San Rafael, Ca. 94901, U.S.A.
e-mail: mandala@mandala.org
web site: http://www.mandala.org/
Phone: 1-800-688-2218

All photos: Courtesy Mandala Archives

First printing: 2001 limited edition 3,000 copies

Printed by Srinivas Fine Arts (P) Ltd., Bangalore, India
for the Mandala Publishing Group
ISBN 1-886069-30-1

Contents

Preface

To have even the slightest touch with Divinity is our greatest fortune. This becomes possible when, by the will of the Supreme, one is drawn into connection with the Lord's agent, the bonafide spiritual master.

The finite *jīva* soul will find all that is necessary to nourish his innermost spiritual necessity in the agent of the Supreme Lord. Enthused by the words and association of the spiritual master, one easily makes progress on the path of dedication.

In *Follow the Angels,* Śrīla B. R. Śrīdhara Deva Gosvāmī Mahārāja illuminates the path of dedication by describing in detail many of the finer points of understanding required for our advancement in spiritual life.

Śrīla Śrīdhara Mahārāja speaks to his readers from the depth of his subjective experience of the Absolute Truth. The guidance we receive in *Follow the Angels* is indeed of incalculable value in the soul's march toward Eternity. We therefore pray that those who are greatly fortunate to read this book will hear His Divine Grace with the greatest care and attention—for as it is said in learned circles, "When wisemen speak, wisemen listen."

Introduction

Follow the Angels is indeed a timely publication that will certainly enthuse all sincere souls who are in search of the highest plane of truth. *Śrīmad Bhāgavatam,* the most exalted scripture ever to see the light of day assures us that if one wants to make advancement in spiritual life that it is necessary to follow in the footsteps of the devotees of the Supreme Lord.

bhāvanti puruṣa loke mad-bhaktas tvaṁ anuvrataḥ
bhāvan me khalu bhaktānāṁ sarveśāṁ pratirūpa-dhṛk

"Those who follow your example will naturally become My pure devotees. You are the best example of My devotee, and others should follow in your footsteps." (*Bhāg.* 7.10.21)

In *Follow the Angels* the author Śrīla B. R. Śrīdhara Deva Gosvāmī Mahārāja, the illustrious Guardian of Devotion, guides the readers on the path of dedication shown by our predecessor *ācāryas* such as Śrīla Bhaktivinoda Ṭhākura and Śrīla Bhaktisiddhānta Sarasvatī Ṭhākura Prabhupāda. To follow the path of the previous *ācāryas* is indeed the way of success in spiritual life, whereas to obscure the path of the previous *ācāryas* or to create a method of spiritual practice of our own fancy certainly implies failure.

In part one of *Follow the Angels* Śrīla Śrīdhara Mahārāja discusses the Kṛṣṇa Conception as the highest plane of truth attainable for a living entity. The basis of this conception is that Absolute beauty, affection, love and harmony are the highest goals ever discovered and that these exist in Kṛṣṇa to the fullest degree. It is Kṛṣṇa alone who can satisfy the innermost hankering of the soul. "Awake, arise! Search for your fortune!"

Śrīla Śrīdhara Mahārāja explains that this requires a proper connection with a real agent or *guru* who has a direct connection with Kṛṣṇa. The *guru* assures our future in spiritual life. The *guru* and Vaiṣṇavas are the agents of the Supreme Lord and Śrīla Śrīdhara Mahārāja explains that such agents are higher than the scripture and that all success can be achieved by service to such higher agents.

One must acquire an earnest desire to know the truth, which in due course will mature into pure spiritual attraction. Then a real taste for the truth will manifest—will be awakened in our heart. And all attraction for sense pleasure, fame, name, and money will vanish. When this spontaneous taste for the truth awakens within us, we are safe, but not prior to that.

In Kali-yuga the service of the Holy Name has especially been recommended, but first the name must be taken from a bonafide *guru*, and it should be chanted in the association of the *sādhu* or saint. In the acme of dedication there is only love, Vraja Vṛndāvana *bhāva*. And there is preaching—preaching is *saṅkīrtana*—the most effective way of chanting. Preaching is real service to the Holy Name, not just counting beads. These and many more illuminations on the Kṛṣṇa conception are revealed in part one of *Follow the Angels.*

From part two of *Follow the Angels,* the title of the book has been drawn. Here we find that we have come to the fulfillment of our innermost demand, but a measure of caution is given, "Fools rush in where angels fear to tread." In part two, Śrīla Śrīdhara Mahārāja advises that one should follow the angels and not make offense by rushing ahead when one is not actually qualified.

"One must go step by step. If we omit any step, we will be nowhere. We should be mindful of every step, and automatically that will take us in the right direction. Don't ever try to run very hurriedly. Try to remain a little down and back. That will forcibly take you to the goal, naturally. The higher Vaiṣṇavas will take you there. You can't go there on your own."

For the greatest success in our spiritual life a proper posing in the relativity of the Absolute Truth is required. Don't try to rush ahead—do not become an offender. Stay a little distant and below. That will draw the greatest fortune for you. *Pūjala rāga-pātha gaurava-bhaṅge,* try to keep at a respectful distance. Keep the highest goal always above your head. Don't rush towards that position. It is not that cheap.

Śrīla Śrīdhara Mahārāja says, "Śrīla Bhaktisiddhānta Sarasvatī Ṭhākura, has especially given this caution, *Pūjala rāga-pātha gaurava-bhaṅge.* Śrī Caitanya Mahāprabhu has distributed what He experienced in His deep trance, but we must be ready to pay for it. Sarasvatī Ṭhākura came for that purpose. *Pūjala rāga-pātha*—don't go hurriedly. Fools rush in where angels fear to tread. Don't commit offenses. This is the highest prospect of your life after many lifetimes. We should always move expressly towards the goal of having the temperament of a servant. We should not venture to tread on the highest plane. Fools rush in where angels fear to tread. Don't be a fool; become an angel. Try to follow the angels." This is a fragment of the valuable advice given by Śrīla Śrīdhara Mahārāja in part two of *Follow the Angels.*

In part three, Higher Talks, Śrīla Śrīdhara Mahārāja reveals the highest ideal of *guru-tattva*: Gaura-Gadādhara in *mādhurya-rasa,* and Rādhārāṇī in *Kṛṣṇa-līlā.* If we raise our head a little higher and look up, then we shall find Rādhārāṇī and Gurudeva. It is Rādhārāṇī who is instrumental in accomplishing the function of Gurudeva from behind. The source of grace for the *guru* is coming from the original source of service and love.

Śrīla Śrīdhara Mahārāja says, "We are requested not to see *guru* as limited in his ordinary personification, but as the transparent mediator of the highest function in his line. If only our vision is deep, we can see that according to the depth of our *śraddhā,* our vision, *guru-tattva* is very peculiar, very noble, very broad, wide and very deep."

As an example of the higher vision of *guru,* Śrīla Śrīdhara Mahārāja relates how his *guru* (Śrīla Bhaktisiddhānta Sarasvatī Ṭhākura) saw Gadādhara Paṇḍita and Svarūpa Dāmodara in Bhaktivinoda Ṭhākura and Gaura Kiśora dāsa Bābāji respectively. Śrīla Śrīdhara Mahārāja then carries his readers away with an unparalleled description of Gadādhara Paṇḍita as a shadow of Mahāprabhu running after Him as if his heart had been stolen. Like a shadow, he is moving after Mahāprabhu. Śrīla Śrīdhara Mahārāja compares Gadādhara Paṇḍita to Rukmiṇī. "So when Mahāprabhu plunders the spirit of Rādhārāṇī, the rebellious *vāma* nature, what remains is comparable to Rukmiṇī—a passive seer, without any power to assert, only an onlooker. An onlooker, tolerating everything, a very pitiable condition that elicits kindness and sympathy from everyone." This and other higher talks one will find in part three of *Follow the Angels.*

It is with great happiness that Gosai Publishers present this publication and we trust that it will be well received by the devotional community for it contains the most valuable wisdom for progress in our spiritual lives.

Śrīla Śrīdhara Mahārāja is renowned throughout the world as a saint and self-realized pure devotee of the Supreme Lord—we therefore bow down to his lotus feet and humbly beg forgiveness for any mistake that we may have made in our attempt to serve him.

Svāmī B. G. Nārāsiṅgha

Completed on
13 October, 2000
First Day of Kārttika Māsa
Śāradīya Pūrṇimā, Gaurābda 514
Śrī Nārāsiṅgha Caitanya Maṭha

About the Author

Śrīla Bhakti Rakṣaka Śrīdhara Deva Gosvāmī Mahārāja was born in Hapaniya, West Bengal, India in 1895. His pastimes of youth were spent in learning and he naturally excelled in every subject that he took up. From his very childhood his tendency was towards the culture of the orthodox section, the *Vedas, Upaniṣads,* etc.—faith in God and all such things. He received his sacred thread in the family tradition when he was fourteen years old and his affinity for the divine world kept on increasing. In his early years he was especially attracted to Lord Rāmacandra. Later, when he came in contact with the doctrine of Śrī Caitanya Mahāprabhu, he began to read *Bhagavad-gītā* and developed an attraction towards Lord Kṛṣṇa.

After completing his primary and secondary education Śrīla Śrīdhara Mahārāja entered Krishnanath College at Baharampur [District Mushirabad], Bengal. In his fourth year of studies he graduated with a Bachelor of Arts degree in philosophy. For some time Śrīla Śrīdhara Mahārāja was searching for a *guru* from whom he could take initiation, but he could not find anyone to his liking. Then by the grace of the Almighty he met his eternal guide and preceptor Śrīla Bhaktisiddhānta Sarasvatī Ṭhākura and in 1927 Śrīla Śrīdhara Mahārāja became an initiated disciple.

In 1930 Bhaktisiddhānta Sarasvatī Ṭhākura awarded Śrīla Śrīdhara Mahārāja *sannyāsa* and bestowed upon him the name Bhakti Rakṣaka meaning "Guardian of Devotion." Bhaktisiddhānta Sarasvatī Ṭhākura saw in Śrīla Śrīdhara Mahārāja the ability to perfectly protect the Gauḍīya Vaiṣṇava line from misrepresentation and misconception. After reading Śrīla Śrīdhara Mahārāja's Sanskrit compositions glorifying Bhaktivinoda Ṭhākura, Bhaktisiddhānta Sarasvatī Ṭhākura remarked, "Now I am satisfied that, after I leave, there will be at least one man who can represent my conclusions (*bhakti-siddhānta*)."

Sometime after the passing away of Bhaktisiddhānta Sarasvatī Ṭhākura in 1936, Śrīla Śrīdhara Mahārāja established his own temple, Śrī Caitanya Sarasvata Maṭha, on the banks of the sacred Ganges in Navadvīpa-dhāma, the holy land of Śrī Caitanya Mahāprabhu. Having deeply assimilated the teachings of Śrī Caitanya, Śrīla Śrīdhara Mahārāja began composing original texts. His first work, *Śrī Śrī Prapanna-jivanāmṛta,* was a comprehensive scriptural study of *śaraṇāgati* (surrender). Śrīla Śrīdhara Mahārāja composed numerous songs, prayers, and commentaries in Bengali and Sanskrit. Among these important works are his commentaries on Bhaktivinoda Ṭhākura's *Śaraṇāgati,* Bengali translations of *Bhagavad-gītā* and *Bhakti-rasāmṛta-sindhuḥ,* and his own original Sanskrit poem summarizing *Caitanya-līlā, Prema-dhāma-deva Stotram.* An outstanding contribution to the *Rūpānūga Gauḍīya Saṁpradāya* is Śrīla Śrīdhara Mahārāja's commentary on *gāyātrī mantra* in the line of *Śrīmad Bhāgavatam.*

At an advanced age, in his fully matured stage of realization, Śrīla Śrīdhara Mahārāja spoke extensively on the teachings of Bhaktisiddhānta Sarasvatī Ṭhākura, and the great predecessor *ācāryas.* Those talks were recorded on audio/video and continue to be published by Śrī Caitanya Sarasvata Maṭha and by Śrīla Śrīdhara Mahārāja's many followers and admirers.

During the last days of his manifest pastimes, Śrīla Śrīdhara Mahārāja remained always absorbed in deep moods of devotional separation and hankering for the divine service of Śrī Śrī Rādhā-Govinda. Then in 1988 on *Amāvāsya* (the dark moon night), in the month of July, Śrīla Śrīdhara Mahārāja withdrew his manifest presence from this earthly plane to enter the *nitya-līlā* (eternal pastimes) of the Supreme Lord.

After his passing away Śrīla Śrīdhara Mahārāja was succeeded by his most affectionate and qualified disciple Śrīpāda Bhakti Sundara Govinda Mahārāja. At present the teachings of Śrīla Śrīdhara Mahārāja are being spread throughout the world via the noble efforts of his many loyal and dedicated followers.

Part One

The Krsna Conception

The Kṛṣṇa Conception

The grand tone, the divine tone, the call comes from the higher quarter, the divine quarter: "Awake, arise! Search for your fortune!" And you cannot but have that; it is your birthright, it is the wealth of your own soul. It is there, the relationship with the Highest Divinity. It cannot but be within you! You are His creature; you exist in His connection and relationship. You must have some connection within you. Don't be afraid of your present position; don't be disappointed. In this way, you are to preach to the world at large. "All come! You want *rasaṁ ānandaṁ,* the mellow of delight, the differentiated personification of Kṛṣṇa in Vṛndāvana, and that is very magnanimously distributed in Navadvīpa, the birthplace of Śrī Caitanya Mahāprabhu."

The Kṛṣṇa conscious conception is the highest conception: the Absolute good, the Absolute beauty, the Absolute autocrat, the Infinite. Vaikuṇṭha in its fullest conception is Goloka. Vaikuṇṭha has no *kuṇṭha,* that is, no limitation. That is Vaikuṇṭha, the conception of the Infinite. When it is consonant with the Kṛṣṇa conscious conception, it is considered the highest goal, the Absolute, the autocrat, and the beauty. The good, the beautiful, *raso vai saḥ. Akhila rasāmṛta mūrti.* All conceptions of *rasa* are harmonized. The Kṛṣṇa conception of the Absolute harmonizes different varieties of *rasa. Raso vai saḥ. Akhila rasāmṛta mūrti.* That is not intelligible by our present senses.

In the Vṛndāvana proposal, the Infinite is closest to the finite: *aprākṛta. Aprākṛta* is where the Infinite has come nearest to the finite beings, as though one of them. When He is so close, so near, no one can easily recognize whether He is infinite or not. Mahāprabhu has suggested to us, "Try for your fortune in Vṛndāvana. There is such a wonderful process: Nanda and Yaśodā, Kṛṣṇa's father and mother, have captured the Absolute and He is crawling in their compound (*aham iha nandaṁ vande yasyālinde paraṁ brahma*). Try to secure a position there, however negligible it may be. Try your fortune." We are in search of such a fortune, where all other proposals are eliminated.

kaṁ prati kathayitum īśe samprati ko vā pratītim āyātu
go-pati-tanayā-kuñje gopa-vadhūṭī-viṭaṁ brahma

"To whom can I tell it, and who will believe it, that the Supreme Absolute, Param Brahman, the paramour of the damsels of Vraja, is enjoying in the groves on the banks of the Yamunā?" (*Padyāvalī,* 98)

It is inconceivable that the Brahman, the greatest, the Absolute, has come to search for the least love of the *gopī* damsels of the cowherd class. He has approached in such a near and close way, and in such an ordinary, rural style. Try your fortune there.

We are out to do just that, under the guidance of Śrī Caitanyadeva, Who is understood to be the combination of the positive and negative aspects of the Absolute. The positive is busy distributing Himself to others. Mahāprabhu is that infinitely and inconceivably generous aspect of the Supreme. Śrī Caitanyadeva is both Rādhā and Kṛṣṇa combined. He is Kṛṣṇa in the mood of Rādhā, searching for Himself. He is both the positive and the negative aspects of the Absolute.

The Śaṅkara school and other impersonalists claim that when the positive and negative combine, the result is a kind of equilibrium. But according to the Vaiṣṇava philosophy, the combination is dynamic. His nature becomes that of searching for Himself—searching for His own positive self, in the mood of the negative. In that search, He distributes Himself to others. The negative attracts the positive, and the positive is thus distributed to the public. This is the essence of Śrī Caitanya Mahāprabhu. The intimate associates of the Lord have revealed such a conception, and we shall be able to conceive it according to the intensity and degree of our faith.

Necessity of a Real Agent

A real agent of Kṛṣṇa is necessary to save us, and also to help others. Hegel, the German philosopher, said that the idea is first, then the movements of the mind and body follow. His philosophy is called Ideal Realism. First we conceive of doing something, and then the movements of the mind and the body begin, so the idea leads us. The idea is all-important. Whatever idea we may follow, then the mind, the body, everything will follow.

Divya darśana, divanbhūti, a divine arrangement must be made, and we must have the help of the *sādhus,* the saints, who are His bonafide agents. There may be many sham agents also—pseudo agents, *sahajiyā* agents, imitationists. We must go to the real agent. And with his help, by his grace, we will gradually attain our end. *Naiṣāṁ matis tāvad urukramāṅghriṁ, spṛśaty anarthāpagamāyād arthaḥ.* Prahlāda Mahārāja said: So long as one's mind does not come in contact with the divine feet of the Lord, it is indispensable to get the help of His devotees, His agents, for the elimination of the undesirable elements within us.

Anarthāpagamāyād arthaḥ. Mahīyasāṁ pāda rajo'bhiṣekaṁ, niṣkiñcanānāṁ na vṛṇīta yāvat. Our divine life does not really begin as long as we do not come to the feet of the real master. There it begins: our real progress, real life. Our real advancement towards divinity begins when we get recognition from the agent of the Lord. Some might say, "This is a monopoly, and an autocratic system. God is for everyone, why should some mediator be necessary at all? He is open to all; He knows us all. If we only desire Him sincerely, He will come directly." That may be their conception.

A Proper Guardian Assures Our Future

We are unsettled, running hither and thither with no principle in our life, and our position is very sad. This kind of life is very troublesome. To think, "I cannot put my faith anywhere," means that I cannot find a friend anywhere. I am friendless, moving amongst foreigners or perhaps even enemies.

But I must have a friend, or at the very least, some friendly atmosphere. I must come into such company in whom I can rest all my faith, in whom I can believe and trust. Without this, my life is miserable. By God's infinite grace, some *śraddhā* (faith) should come to us: "It is not that I can only trust and believe, but it is this: I cannot but show my regard to a personality of the higher position, *gurum evābhigacet.*"

When we suffer from uncertainty to the extreme, we shall hanker for connection with the *guru,* the spiritual master. We cannot only put an enquiry to him with faith and trust, but *guru* is a guardian who is our well-wisher, more so than we are to ourselves. The guardian is a friend who thinks more of us than we think of ourselves. He knows more about our welfare than we do. That is what it is like to have a guardian, a friend, a *guru.* If one commits *Vaiṣṇava-aparādha* or *Nāma-aparādha,* offenses against the Vaiṣṇava or the Holy Name, one may be detained again and again. It is not such a cheap thing. Still, there is the possibility that when properly guided, a proper soul may attain the highest position in a single life. It is not impossible.

Narottama Dāsa Ṭhākura says, *āśraya lañā bhaje tāre kṛṣṇa nahi tyaje:* "If we can get a bonafide guardian, our future in spiritual life is assured." Kṛṣṇa cannot dismiss the guardian very easily, because the guardian has a solid position in the Lord's relationship. If we enter into the domain of our guardian's care, our position will be assured. Our only solace is that we are going through His agent. He's so kind and benevolent that He has sent His agent to recruit us, and that is our hope. We must be thankful for that, and not become traitors to His agent. We must be cautious to see that we do not betray His agent, for thereby we betray ourselves.

Āna saba mare akāraṇa. Others, who have not yet been able to surrender at the holy feet of their guardian or *guru,* are in an uncertain position, and they may be deviated by any agent. Their future is deplorable. They have no shelter, no *āśraya.* If through our *śraddhā* we can have a real ideal in life and acquire a real guardian, then certainly our future is assured practically. Our only duty will be towards our guardian, our Gurudeva, our *āśraya,* and all other duties will be once and for all automatically accomplished and summarily completed.

To traverse the length and breadth of this wide world, where there is nothing but various types of exploitation of various planes, is to sail as a ship without a rudder that can be swept away by sea storms, endlessly and without purpose or objective. It is through *śraddhā* that we can connect with our highest goal of achievement and fulfillment. First, this problem must be solved—then real life can begin.

Measuring the Infinite

Faith is the only instrument for the finite to measure the Infinite. To survey the Infinite, all other methods are futile. Faith is the most spacious substance within us. It can cover a long, long distance. In the Infinite, what faith can we have in faith? We fear blind faith. Yet, in the Infinite, the impossible becomes possible. Everything is possible, but only faith has the possibility of connecting us with the Infinite, while all other methods are useless.

Faith is the only effective link. We must approach the object of our search via a similar plane. We can approach the Infinite only with the help of *śraddhā.* We cannot hope to have any connection with that finest plane of fundamental existence with the help of the eye, nose or ear, or even by intelligence or reason. If we want to have any connection with the finest plane that is underlying this creation, it is possible only through faith *(śraddhā-mayo 'yaṁ puruṣaḥ).*

Śraddhā, faith, can go a long distance. We shall be able to feel and conceive that faith is not merely imaginary; it has its tangible position, a most efficient position within us. When we can disconnect from all phases of perceptual experience, we can live in faith alone. When all the wealth of our experience deceives us and betrays us, our faith will save us.

In the higher type of devotion there is never any desire that Kṛṣṇa or His associates will come to serve and supply us, or that He will show Himself to us. To impose our whim on Him is not actual service. Whatever He likes to do He may do. And whatever may be required of us, we shall consider ourselves fortunate if we are given the chance to supply it. Exhaustively eliminating all our desires, we are to place ourselves fully at the disposal of the Supreme Lord, Who is never to carry out any order or wish of ours.

By nature, Kṛṣṇa is eager to supply everything to His devotees (*yoga-kṣemaṁ vahāmy-aham, Gītā* 9.22). But the higher devotees do not like Him to supply them with anything, or for Him to render service to them. Such is the purity of their devotion. Through their faith, they think, "He is my Lord. I don't want to have His *darśana* merely to satisfy my lower faculty of perceiving that He exists." It is a very low standard of faith to consider that only if we can see Him, then we shall be satisfied that He exists. We have no capacity to see Him. To make Him our object, keeping ourselves the subject, is a low standard of faith. But higher, intense faith fully proves that He is that wonderful cause of everything. He is present.

Earnest Desire Is The Only Price

Mahāprabhu *says nāhaṁ vipro na ca nara-patir nāpi vaiśyo na śūdro... gopī-bhartuḥ pada-kamalayor dāsa-dāsānudāsaḥ.* At the beginning is *varṇāśrama dharma,* regulated life. This is just the beginning, then gradually there is improvement and we are to go up to the absolute service of Kṛṣṇa. Kṛṣṇa is independent of any form of life—without consideration of any law or any form; only service, *kṛṣṇa santus. Yat karosi yad-aśnāsi.* Whatever we do, think, speak, everything should be for the service of Kṛṣṇa. That is the standard of devotion.

And mere formalism may be favorable, but not always. The spirit is all-important, even when crossing every formality. What is required of us is our absolute attraction for service, for beauty. Laws have no status there. In the beginning they have some sort of utility, but when one is a little advanced, one should not care for them, for anything. Only seek *sādhu-saṅga,* adherence to the saints of similar type, a little better than ourselves, our guides in *rāga-bhajana,* those who are in the path of divine love and attraction.

That is the only way. That is the only thing that can guide us. *Laulyaṁ,* the only price is our *laul,* earnest desire, nothing else. *Kṛṣṇa bhakti rasa bhāvitā matiḥ.* Rāmānanda Rāya says to

Mahāprabhu that if one finds it anywhere, one should try to purchase it. What is that? The pure inclination towards the service of Kṛṣṇa. The innermost tendency to want Kṛṣṇa, to get Him, to have Him; the earnest desire to have Him. Anywhere you find that desire, a drop of that divine attraction, try to purchase it for any price. Acquire it! It may be obtained from anywhere or anyone, it does not matter. *Kibā vipra kibā nyāsī śūdra kene naya, yei kṛṣṇa tattva vettā sei guru haya.* A *brāhmaṇa*, a *sannyāsī*, or a *śūdra* who knows Kṛṣṇa, he is *guru.*

Wherever there is a drop of that love divine, only try to get it. And what is the price? Earnest desire for it. *Laulyaṁ api mūlyam ekalaṁ.* The only price is earnest desire. It is not to be purchased with any money, nor is it anything that is acquired by so many formal practices in millions of births. Substance is necessary and not the form. Form is required only as much as it may connect us with that real substance, otherwise it is not necessary. *Sarva dharmān parityajya,* give up all phases of duty which you perceive and perfect. At once try to jump in the ocean of nectar. That is the desired teaching. Earnest desire, that is to be acquired; that is *bhakti* proper.

There are some that want to know about Kṛṣṇa only from the *śāstra,* scripture. In the almanac it is written that this year so much rain is expected, so much rain will come. But if we press the almanac, will a drop of water ooze out of it? The *śāstra* is like that, something like that. The *śāstra* says do this, do that, but the scripture cannot give us Kṛṣṇa. First we get the direction, then we practice; we are to do it. We are helpless when searching with this method or that method.

Vaisnava is Higher than Sastra

Practically, we should come in connection with the service of a Vaiṣṇava. But where, whom to serve? I can't come directly in connection with Him. Who can I serve? The Deity form of the Lord, the *vigraha* is there, the *śāstra* is there—but in a sense these are superficial. The real substance we find in a Vaiṣṇava, in his heart. *Dharmasya tattvam nihitaṁ guhāyāṁ.* The Kṛṣṇa conception, Kṛṣṇa as He is, knowledge and love, we find living in the heart of a Vaiṣṇava who directs all activities towards Him, towards His service.

Faith in the devotees, the Vaiṣṇavas, grants us the most substantial help. Such a position is not flickering, but firm. One who has faith in the Vaiṣṇavas achieves devotion of a tangible character. Otherwise, with only abstract faith in the Lord, without faith in the devotees, we are but beginners in the stage of *kaniṣṭha-adhikārī.* This is an unreliable platform. Our devotion reaches a reliable standard when we can develop faith in the devotees, and recognize their importance. The devotees are above even *śāstra,* the scriptures. The tangible stage when our real faith in them develops is the middle stage, *madhyama-adhikārī.*

In the Vaiṣṇava, the truth is animated more than in the *vigraha* [Deity], the *tīrtha* [holy place of pilgrimage], or the *śāstra* [scripture]. We find a direct connection with Kṛṣṇa in the consciousness of a Vaiṣṇava. We find that which is regulating all his activities and withdrawing him from worldly attraction, guiding him towards some unknown and most desirable direction. He is moving towards that direction. The Lord is making him move in a particular direction that cannot be traced by any loss or gain of this world. What is that thing? "I am there. I am not even in Vaikuṇṭha, nor in the hearts of the *yogīs.* But where my devotees are singing with pleasure about me, I am there." [*Mac cittā mad gata prāṇā bodhayantaḥ parasparam kathayantaś ca māṁ nityaṁ tuṣyanti ca ramanti ca.*] "The thoughts of My pure devotees dwell in Me, their lives are fully devoted to My service, and they derive great satisfaction and bliss from always enlightening one another and conversing about Me." (*Gītā* 10.9)

Pure Spiritual Attraction

In the Rāmānuja *saṁpradāya* there is a story about three devotees who arrived at their temple for some occasion. They did not know one another. In the darkness one is talking, another hearing. Their talk is very sweet. Then the third devotee also joined there and they were talking together, although they did not know one another. They have heard the name of this devotee, that devotee. Then after talking for some time, a question was asked. "We are three here, but do you feel the presence of a fourth person?" "Yes, I feel the presence of a fourth one, and it is that Person about Whom we talk—the Lord has appeared here. In our talk, in our conversation, He has appeared." Develop this attraction, pure spiritual attraction, until nothing can be pleasing to us but Kṛṣṇa, Rādhārāṇī and the *gopīs.* That is what is necessary, for Kṛṣṇa and His group to take possession of the innermost part of our hearts by the thought of His *līlā,* His Name, and His paraphernalia.

manmanā bhāva mad bhakto mad yājī māṁ nāmaskuru
mām evaiṣyasi satyaṁ te pratijāne priyo 'si me

Kṛṣṇa says to Arjuna that he is the most favorite devotee. "I promise you that at the very least I won't deceive you. I say that I am everything and I won't deceive you. *Manmanā bhāva,* always remember Me, *mad bhakto,* be My devotee, serve Me. *Manmanā bhāva mad bhakto, mad yājī,* if you sacrifice anything, do it for Me. *Mad yājī māṁ nāmaskuru,* or at least show respect for Me. You are sure to enter into Me, to come to Me. *Mām evaiṣyasi,* you will come to Me alone; *satyaṁ te,* this is the truth, *pratijāne,* I promise you. *Priyo 'si me,* you are My favorite. The truth is this: do everything for Me, attend Me, always think of Me and you are sure to come to Me. This is the plain truth."

That thinking, the life of engagement, is attraction for Him. How do we develop that attraction for Kṛṣṇa? We get it from the devotee. Superficially we can obtain it from the scripture, but substantially only from the devotee.

Within their heart, within their endeavor, pervading through all their activities, there is a particular attraction and that is a divine thing. We want that. It is the subtlest of the subtle, the nerve structure within. It can move the body. It can help the body to function. We are attracted to the inner energy in the devotee, which makes him do that which we do not find in this world: no attraction for sense pleasure, no attraction for fame, name, or money.

Something else is there: attraction for Kṛṣṇa. We must follow his guidance. "One who comes to serve Me directly, he is not really My devotee. But one who is devoted to My devotee is My real devotee." What is the meaning? *Vaiṣṇava-sevā, guru-sevā, nāma-sevā*; service to the devotees, the spiritual master, and the Holy Name. "His love for Me is so intense that wherever he finds any external connection with Me, he engages himself fully there."

Real Taste for the Truth

Until and unless we find in our hearts a real taste for the truth, we are not safe. First, on the surface, spiritual life begins with *śraddhā*, faith, and underneath with *sukṛti*, or special merit. Next is *sādhu-saṅga*, or company with the saints. Within that is our surrender to *guru*. Then *bhajana* begins, our serving life in various forms, such as *śravaṇa, kīrtana, prasāda-sevā*, or hearing, chanting, and respecting the Lord's remnants. Then *anartha-nivṛtti*, our attraction for objects other than Kṛṣṇa, objects other than God, diminishes. Then *niṣṭha*, continued effort in devotional service, and not for anything else. Then *ruci*, taste, is developed.

Real taste for the truth will be awakened in our heart. We are safe then, but not before that. When spontaneous taste for the truth awakens within us, we are safe. We can make fair progress from that time. Taste will take us. When we have acquired the taste of sweetness, automatically we shall run towards that which is very sweet. Prior to that, we must remain under the guardian. Until and unless we find that the truth is sweet, that Kṛṣṇa is sweet, we are not safe in our approach towards Him. So many distractions may take us hither and thither.

Nama-Seva

In Kali-yuga the service of the Holy Name has especially been recommended in a general way. *Sādhu-saṅga kṛṣṇa nāma ei,* one must climb up to the real plane where he can take the Name proper, up to Vaikuṇṭha, to take *vaikuṇṭha-nāma,* the unlimited Name. It is true that an infinite magnitude of sin may be removed, dispersed, dismissed by one utterance of the Name. But that Name must not be only the physical sound. It must have as its characteristics those of Vaikuṇṭha: unlimited, eternal, from the plane of eternity. *Sādhu-saṅga,* the Name must be taken from Gurudeva, and it should be chanted in the association of the *sādhu.*

Nāma-saṅkīrtana is to preach the Holy Name. But what is the Name? The ten offenses against the Name are to be understood and avoided. The external shallow expression of the Name should be eliminated, and the real Name that is one and the same with the Lord, that Name should be taken. That is *nāma-bhajana,* that is *kīrtana,* illuminating the greatness and magnanimity of the Holy Name. The Name Himself is so charming; the Name is the Lord Himself. In this way we practice *nāma-kīrtana.* Thereby we can be saved from the external contamination of the forces of *karma* and *jñāna,* fruitive work and speculative knowledge.

Nama: More Than Mundane Sound

If we take the Name, then there must be service. *Sat-saṅga. Sādhu-saṅga kṛṣṇa nāma.* Service means to dedicate oneself completely to that which we serve. In that way we shall take the Name. For what purpose are we taking the Name of the Lord? *Kanaka, kāminī, pratiṣṭhā:* not for money, not for sense gratification, not to achieve popularity. We are ready to sacrifice ourselves completely for Him, for His Name. With that attitude we shall take the Name. It is not limited. The whole life within the fist we shall give for His satisfaction. The whole of our energy, we shall risk it for the satisfaction of the Holy Name. We must approach with this attitude. It is guaranteed. The pursuit, the attempt is backed by our whole energy, our whole life, the whole prospect, everything.

With this attitude we shall have to search for a drop of Vaikuṇṭha nectar. Otherwise it is useless. Die to live. Sacrifice, *sevā. Sevā* means death—death of the material ego. *Sevā* means to give one's own self to a particular purpose. The *sevā* of Kṛṣṇa means to give up this mad self, this mundane, concocted self. Try to be saved from our present position. This is not a very laudable thing, our present position; it is a mortal thing, the result of many reactions. So get rid of this shelter. Get out of it, as soon as possible. And enter into the land of confidence and goodness and fairness and sweetness. Try to enter that.

It Is Not So Cheap

We must be sincere and wholesome, without hesitation. Our campaign must be complete, not partial, as if taking one step forward and three steps back. Otherwise we are the finite and we want to get the advantage over the Infinite. We are very small, but we are willing to sacrifice only a part of the small. Our aspiration is to obtain the Whole. Good friend, it is not so easy. *Ataḥ śrī kṛṣṇa nāmādi, na bhaved grāhyam indriyaiḥ.* Only our superficial senses are engaged in Kṛṣṇa's cultivation. For Him it is nothing. Our tongue can produce mundane sound, but that is not Kṛṣṇa. *Sevonmukhe hi jihvādau, svayaṁ eva sphuraty-adaḥ,* that is not the Holy Name, only a mundane sound.

For the Name to be Kṛṣṇa, Kṛṣṇa has to descend there. Don't be self-deceptive; do not think that in taking the Name we have become great *sādhus.* It is not like that. Kṛṣṇa has to come down in the form of the sound to us. He is spiritual; He is transcendental. *Sevonmukhe,* our complete surrender towards Him will attract Him, and He'll graciously come down to grace us in the form of the Name, in our actions, in performing our duties. At every step He will come.

When we give ourselves to Him, He will accept us. He will embrace us. He'll be within and without us. He is everywhere, but only those with clear eyes can see Him, not those who are captured by any prejudice for selfish ends or ordinary things. Don't be captivated by prejudice. When all prejudice is cleared, directly see the highest principle underlying all. Like so much dust, the tendency for exploitation and renunciation has blinded our eyes and we can't see Him.

Those that are lustful look for the beautiful body. Others only think about business because they love wealth the most. They are always engaged with lust or money; the world of their knowledge is revealed to them. There are such strata. They may boast: I have such power, I have beauty, I have wealth. All is false.

The real backing of spirit is Nārāyaṇa, the all-pervading, the all-knowing principle, the all-good. These other thoughts are temporary. Our prejudices of so many types have captured us. Those that are liberated from these influences, they'll find that this is the kingdom of Nārāyaṇa, Who is the support and the guardian of the whole of the world. We see His hand everywhere. Without His direction, nothing can move.

Serve the Name through a Genuine Agent

If we want a guarantee that Kṛṣṇa will be satisfied with whatever process we undertake, the most important tenet of our movement is that we must act under His agent. His satisfaction depends on that. If the agent is a false man, then our whole effort is wasted. But if he is a real agent, then we must gain through him. If through our connection with him we are connected to Vaikuṇṭha, then our actions will be valued. Otherwise we may lose, and commit offenses: *nāma-aparādha, sevā-aparādha, arcana-aparādha,* offenses against the Holy Name, against devotional service, and against the proper worship of the Lord.

It is written in the scriptures. If service is not properly done, then we are sure to commit some offenses against the Deity. Either we give satisfaction to Him, or we give some trouble. That is an intolerable way of conducting that holy process. We must guard against *nāma-aparādha* and *sevā-aparādha.* We must not be over-confident of our previous acquisition. We may have acquired so much, our progress may be such, but we must not be proud. We should not be satisfied with ourselves.

Mahāprabhu Himself said, "I am taking the Name, I am showing so much peace, shedding so many tears, in the Name of Kṛṣṇa. But why? It is all false. My tears are only for show, to convince others that I am such a great devotee." In such a way we must disbelieve that we are devotees. We must be very careful, very, very careful. Kavirāja Gosvāmī and Narottama Ṭhākura have written thus.

"I am neglected, I am left behind, I am excluded. I am so low; I am so contaminated. I am rejected from the Infinite *līlā.* I could not utilize this great fortunate wave." This should be the feeling of a real Vaiṣṇava who has an actual relationship with the Infinite. As much as the finite comes in contact with the Infinite, the disposition cannot but be affected. It is not imitation; it cannot but be the real thing.

"I am empty, I don't get anything," that should be our mood. "I feel emptiness within me. I can't get it, my life is frustrated. My life is going to be frustrated. I don't get a drop of the grace of the Lord, and I have left the world; everything is gone. If you don't accept me, I am undone. Please make me a servant of the servant of the servant of the servant. Give me the remotest connection. Graciously give me some remotest connection to Yourself. I can't tolerate it otherwise." This heartfelt, heart-rending prayer must come from the devotees of the Lord, then we will find our fortune. The charm for the world outside must be fully eliminated from the heart, fully emptied. And the near future will be filled with the nectar of the grace of Kṛṣṇa.

Bhukti and *mukti,* the desires for enjoyment and renunciation are compared with ghosts. These two types of ghosts reside in the heart. So how do we dare to express that *bhakti* lives in our heart? The noble lady of devotion, will she come there, lying on the same bench with these ghosts? How can we expect that? Have we freed ourselves from all these nasty things that we dare to invite the lady of *Kṛṣṇa-bhakti* to come here?

Necessity of True Humility

Our modesty will not be ignorantly accepted as lack of qualification; have no fear of that.

tṛṇād api sunīcena taror api sahiṣṇunā
amāninā mānadena kīrtanīyaḥ sadā hariḥ

"One who is humbler than a blade of grass and more forbearing than a tree, and gives due honor to others without desiring it for himself is qualified to always chant the Holy Name of Kṛṣṇa." (*Śikṣāṣṭaka 3*)

Infinite meaning and prospect, the general direction is given thus. Do we take the process of divine sound, to reach that goal by the divine sound? To come to that level we will have to accept such an attitude of humility. Then we will feel that there is a very fine, fine level through which we can reach there. The finest level is there. But we are to accept such an attitude here, then it will be possible, but not by force. There is no necessity of removing a mountain, or to oppose a river current; big things won't be necessary. Only by cultivation of the spiritual sound will we be able to reach the goal.

But we will have to take such an attitude, and we will feel that we have come to a particular, very subtle level. Only through sound can we go there. Our soul can be attracted, connected with that, only if we can saturate ourselves with this *tṛṇād api sunīcena, taror api sahiṣṇunā.*

That means a great deal, it is not an outward statement. If we adopt this sort of mood, we shall have to cross many oceans. Many oceans we shall have to cross, to experience. From our present position of egoistic boasting, we are to go to the lowest level of a blade of grass. We are to go through country after country, plane after plane. *Taror api sahiṣṇunā,* to reach into that sort of attitude, we will pass on our way so many suns, moons, and earths. Such concrete things we shall have to bid adieu.

Many basic thoughts of the concrete, they have to give way; leave them behind to reach that attitude properly. *Amāninā mānadena.* Our connection with the subtle and higher things necessitates that we ignore the concrete, *amāninā mānadena.* The plane of life will be changed. The plane will change to where the activity should be, where the energy should be invested; not in this plane—that which we see about us as concrete.

Mahāprabhu is saying: don't assert, forget giving resistance, rather if any resistance comes, try to forbear with the best of your energy. Don't try to intrude upon the physical prospects of others. *Mānadena,* don't give any opposition to them. If we can do this, then we are automatically led to a particular plane. We will find harmony beyond our expectation and our conception. A wonderful thing! Only through the Holy Name we find that Kṛṣṇa is over-flowing, all-pervading.

Śrī Caitanya Mahāprabhu instructed Raghunātha Dāsa Gosvāmī to always remain meek and humble and to always chant the Holy Name.

grāmya-kathā nā śunibe, grāmya-vārtā nā kahibe
bhāla nā khaibe āra bhāla nā paribe
amānī mānada hañā kṛṣṇa-nāma sadā la'be
vraje rādhā-kṛṣṇa-sevā mānase karibe

"Do not talk like people in general or hear what they say. You should not eat very palatable food, nor should you dress very nicely. Do not expect honor, but offer all respect to others. Always chant the Holy Name of Kṛṣṇa, and within your mind render service to Rādhā and Kṛṣṇa in Vṛndāvana." (*C.c. Antya-līlā* 6.236-7)

We must not attend to worldly talk, neither should we engage in that. *Bhāla nā khaibe āra bhāla nā paribe,* don't seek after the satisfaction of our tongue and belly, and don't try to wear any good dress to be admired by the people. *Amānī mānada hañā kṛṣṇa-nāma sadā la'be,* give honor to all, but don't seek honor from anyone. In this way we will take the Name of Kṛṣṇa always, continuously.

Vraje rādhā-kṛṣṇa-sevā mānase karibe, internally in our minds we shall try to serve Rādhā and Govinda in Vṛndāvana. As we are in Vṛndāvana, we are serving Rādhā and Govinda. That will be our mental aspiration. Externally we are to go on, living our life simply in this way: no good dress, no good food, no indulgence in worldly topics–neither speaking nor hearing them, always giving honor to all, and not seeking honor from anyone. In this mood we must go on, *kīrtanīyaḥ sadā hariḥ.*

Potency within the Name

The real Name must be *vaikuṇṭha nāma grahaṇam.* That of Infinite characteristic, that is Vaikuṇṭha; it is not in this mundane or measured plane. *Māyā,* illusion, is measured by local or provincial interest, not Absolute interest. *Nāma* must not be rooted there, but it must have its connection with the Absolute plane. Then it will come and transform us and prepare us. It will make us fit for the service of that Absolute plane. Kṛṣṇa is there; it is not a thing of concoction or imagination. It is Reality, and what we think to be real at present is unreal.

The sound must have the divine characteristic. Kṛṣṇa, Hari, these sounds are *nirguṇa,* beyond all material qualities, and divine. *Sabdha brahma nāma-kṛṣṇa: vaikuṇṭha nāma grahaṇam aśeṣāgha haraṁ viduḥ (Bhāg. 6.2.14).* The Name must be of divine characteristic, that which can take away all that is undesirable in us. The Name must have a spiritual conception. It cannot be a mere physical imitation, that which can be produced by lip and tongue alone.

Kṛṣṇa, Hari, Viṣṇu, Nārāyaṇa, all these are Vaikuṇṭha *nāma.* It is necessary that they have spiritual existence, which is all in all. They must have spiritual depth, not imitation. Physical imitation is not the Name proper. It is not *sabdha-brahma*—only the imitation sound may come out, but not real depth. So Name means *Nāma-brahma, Nāma-Kṛṣṇa.*

The Name must have some spiritual background or spiritual truth that is distributed through the physical sound. The sound is not Kṛṣṇa, but Kṛṣṇa is within the sound. The Name must be surcharged with the spirit, and that spirit is not of mundane character. That is not found in the Śaṅkara or Māyāvādī (impersonalist) school. Their belief is that although the Name is not confined within the jurisdiction of the physical, still it is only mental, *sattva-guṇa,* the material quality of purity. That is also a product of this *māyā,* misconception. That is their misunderstanding.

The potency is within. What type of thought or sentiment is imparted through that sound is the important thing. The Māyāvādīs have the same *mantra,* they also chant the Name, but that sort of Name will vanish in Brahmaloka, the highest planetary system in the material universe. They won't be able to cross the Virajā River between the material and spiritual worlds.

Mayavada Nama is like Thunder

When the Māyāvādī impersonalist chants the Name of Kṛṣṇa, our Vṛndāvana Dāsa Ṭhākura says that his praise, his taking the Name, and his devotional characteristics are just like thunder against the holy body of Kṛṣṇa. There is no soothing effect from his chanting. In the Gauḍīya Maṭha [the spiritual society founded by Śrīla Bhaktisiddhānta Sarasvatī Prabhupāda], we are interested in Reality, not in appearances. We want only what is real in the world of realization, the step by step development of spiritual practices, the required adjustment.

We are not enchanted with the outward form; the mere form does not capture us. We are interested in the idea and the step by step gradual development in the conception: what is Virajā, what is Brahmaloka paravyoma? What is Goloka Vṛndāvana? All these things: *karmibhyaḥ parito hareḥ priyatayā vyaktiṁ yayur jñāninas, tebhyo jñāna vimukta bhakti paramāḥ premaika niṣṭhās tataḥ.* It is said in the *śāstra* that of all types of fruitive workers, the Supreme Lord Hari favors one who is advanced in knowledge of the higher values of life. Out of many such people who are advanced in knowledge, one who is practically liberated by virtue of his knowledge may take to devotional service. He is superior to the others. However, one who has actually attained *prema,* pure love of Kṛṣṇa, is superior to him. (*Upadeśāmṛta* 10)

Understanding this gradation is required: what is Virajā proper, what is Brahmaloka, what is the *brahmajyoti* or spiritual effulgence, what is Śivaloka, what is Vaikuṇṭha-loka, and then what is Ayodhyā, what is Dvārakā, what is Mathurā, what is Vṛndāvana—the realistic view of the whole gradation. *Na tathā me priyatama ātma yonir na śaṅkaraḥ:* "O Uddhava! Neither Brahmā, nor Śaṅkara, nor Śaṅkarṣaṇa, nor Lakṣmī, nor even My very Self is as dear to Me as you." (*Bhāg. 11.14.15*) *Naivātmā* [not even Myself], "you are My favorite, Uddhava." How is it possible?

We have to follow the spirit. We are slaves of the truth, beggars of what is flowing down to us from above, the spiritual current, the pure current. The external form does not charm us.

Gradations of the Holy Name

There are those that think that *Hari-nāma, Kṛṣṇa-nāma,* and *Śiva-nāma* are one and the same, like the followers of the Rāmakrishna Mission or the Śaṅkara school. They teach that, but such an idea originates in the plane of misunderstanding. *Śuddha-nāma,* the pure Name, must have its original form in *nirguṇa-bhūmika,* far beyond the misconception of *māyā.* The influence of *māyā* reaches up to Virajā; then there is Brahmaloka, then Paravyoma. The real Name must have its origin in Paravyoma, and *Kṛṣṇa-nāma* originates in Goloka, the most original plane of the whole existence. To be really *Kṛṣṇa-nāma,* it must have its origin in the highest plane of Vṛndāvana.

Nāma-akāra, the mere physical sound, is not the Name proper. The real Name is necessary not only for us to get out of this world of *māyā* or misunderstanding, but for the attainment of the service of Kṛṣṇa in Vṛndāvana. The Name that has its origin in the Vṛndāvana plane, only that can take us there. Otherwise, if the spirit in the Name, the sound, is of any other type, it may take us to that mundane place only.

This is quite scientific; it is not unreasonable. A mere word is not the Name. The meaning and the essence of the meaning, the deep conception of the meaning, that is everything; it is all in all. It is all-important to serve our purpose.

Name Proper from a Bonafide Guru

We shall try to take *upadeśa,* instruction, from a real source, not from just anyone. *Asat saṅgete kṛṣṇa nāma nahi haya*: we cannot find real *Kṛṣṇa-nāma* in the association of those that do not have it. The external sound, the superficial sound may come out, but not the substance. The external cover of the sound, the ordinary sound, that may not be Kṛṣṇa. *Nāma-aparādha, nāma-abhāsa.* It is ordinary sound, not Vaikuṇṭha sound, not spiritual sound.

Where sound is surcharged with spiritual knowledge, with feeling, that is *Kṛṣṇa-nāma,* that is Kṛṣṇa. The superficial imitation of *Kṛṣṇa-nāma* is not Kṛṣṇa; it is mundane sound. That is the difference between mundane sound and spiritual sound. When we have spiritual life within and we speak about Kṛṣṇa, our words are surcharged with spiritual substance.

There is a story about a doctor who had a dispensary where he saw many patients and administered much medicine. One day, the doors of the dispensary were open, and the doctor was absent. One monkey entered there, and monkeys are good imitators. The monkey entered, and taking a seat on the doctor's chair, he imitated the doctor, giving medicine here and there. But the monkey's treatment is not that of the doctor. The external aspect is there, imitation, but the inner aspect is absent.

Similarly, spiritual understanding must be there within the physical actions.

Kṛṣṇa-nāma is not only mundane sound; it is something else. It is necessary that we take the sound from a bonafide *guru* who has spiritual realization, whose words are surcharged with spiritual substance. It is required. Otherwise, it will be all in vain; it is only cultivation of mundane sound. *Vaikuṇṭha nāma grahaṇam aśeṣa.* It is said in the *śāstra* that you should take the Name identified with Infinite *Vaikuṇṭha-nāma*; that sound that has a connection with the Infinite, not the mundane limited sound, connected to the limited world. An ordinary person, a student, must come to a real professor who will be able to offer real education, not to anyone and everyone. This is the norm.

A person of high intelligence can discover something from ordinary events. From ordinary incidents, an expert can find out the higher truth, just like Newton. When the apple fell from the tree, the realization came to him: "Oh, the earth is drawing it, attracting it." Ordinary people see an apple falling, but no such realization comes that the earth is drawing it, attracting it. Newton discovered gravitation. Observation of the ordinary gives new light to an expert, a person with a higher brain. In the same way, the higher spiritualist can obtain deep realizations from the apparently commonplace. But for ordinary persons it is not possible. They should go to a proper source.

It is mentioned in the *Upaniṣads*, in *Bhāgavatam*, *Bhagavad-gītā*, how and with what attitude the disciple should approach the *ācārya*, the spiritual preceptor. If the *ācārya* has practical and scriptural knowledge of the truth, if this qualification is there, he is not bogus, but a real *ācārya*.

We must approach a real doctor to cure disease, not a monkey imitating a doctor. It is common sense. If we have thirst for spiritual knowledge, then we must go to a proper spiritualist, not one that will harm us, *avaiṣṇava mukhod gīrṇaṁ*, an imitation *ācārya*. It is common sense; progress is possible when a real transaction is made. Sometimes that is very difficult. A good professor is necessary, but if the student is not up to standard, then the professor can't do anything. Both must be qualified, student and professor; only then can scholarship be imparted.

Advantage of Kali-yuga

In this Kali-yuga, there is a special dispensation. *Kīrtanād eva kṛṣṇasya mukta-saṅgaḥ paraṁ vrajet.* Mahāprabhu Himself comes to distribute it. It is a better situation than during other ages. It is stated in *śāstra*: *yatra saṅkīrtanenaiva sarva-svārto 'bhilabhyate,* in the Golden Age, those persons that are *āryā guṇa jñāḥ sāra bhāginaḥ,* who can judge things according to quality by clever understanding, they will feel, "I want to dance in the Kali-yuga. There's a special dispensation from the highest." *Yatra saṅkīrtanenaiva.* "Welcome to Kali-yuga, the Iron Age."

Those *sādhus* who have a deeper understanding hanker after chanting in Kali-yuga. "I don't want birth in the Golden Age, but in the Iron Age, *yatra saṅkīrtanenaiva.* Only by the method of chanting the Name of Hari, everything may be attained, *sarva-svārto 'bhilabhyate.* The whole thing is God's special dispensation. So Kali-yuga is special and I want to take birth in that Kali."

Śukadeva Gosvāmī also declares in the assembly of those authentic scholars, *kaler doṣa-nidhe rājan.* This Iron Age is full of defects, but it has one great advantage, *asti hy-eko mahān guṇaḥ:* only by taking to preaching about Kṛṣṇa, one can be freed of all undesirable things and attain the highest goal, *kīrtanād eva kṛṣṇasya mukta-saṅgaḥ paraṁ vrajet.* What is that Kṛṣṇa *saṅkīrtana,* that preaching about Kṛṣṇa? It must be very special, that which can give us so much benefit. What is that thing? We must inquire very attentively. This is not a scheming thing, a deceitful thing. It is a fact, an ontological fact.

Without the help of anything else, only by the chanting of *Kṛṣṇa-nāma,* preaching about Kṛṣṇa, we shall undo all undesirable things and attain the highest end of life. What is that? How do we attempt that? With such deep attention we have to inquire about this. Not to trample it. It is not a trifling thing. It is described that it has so much prospect—dive deeply to understand it. It must be done with that sort of feeling. We must "die to live" with all seriousness. Die to live—with such seriousness we may attain that goal.

What is *kīrtana*? It is distribution to the environment. *Kīrtana* is accepting everything from the higher plane and distributing it to ordinary persons. That should be done in a serious mood. This is *kṛṣṇa-kathā*; this is Kṛṣṇa consciousness, Kṛṣṇa consciousness from the proper source. Derive it from the proper source and distribute it at large.

To preach is not an easy thing in this Kali-yuga, because the environment is very negative. *Kala* means quarrel—there are so many opinions. All are quarreling to establish their own superiority. They are trying hard to establish their different types of thought. In the midst of them all, we have to distribute this, to do it in earnest. We must do something factual. With much energy this dedication must come from our heart with all sincerity. Then we shall get that highest achievement. It is not an ordinary thing, but a reality.

Sraddha is the Minimum Demand

Kṛṣṇa consciousness is causeless; that is, it has no beginning, and *apratihatā,* it has no end. No beginning, no end. It is the central flow or vibration or wave. Any separate interest, separate consciousness, that is *anārtha. Artha* means necessity; whatever is not a necessity, but is posturing as a necessity based on separate interest—that is *anārtha.* What is necessary is to avoid that track of separate interest that misleads us, and to learn to have the Infinite reading, the reading of the Infinite—to identify with the universal flow, the universal wave.

When we are carried away by different waves of separate consciousness, that is *anārtha,* that which is not necessary. The only necessity is to merge in the wave of universal interest. It is for Itself, for Himself. *Ahaṁ hi sarva yajñānāṁ bhoktā ca prabhur eva ca.* "I'm the only enjoyer of all these sacrifices or movements in this world. I'm the only enjoyer and everything belongs to Me, unconditionally." That is God's position. He is paramount, the highest harmonizing center. And we must all submit cent-percent to Him. Any deviation from that is *anārtha.*

Anārtha means meaninglessness, that which has no meaning. Meaning, serving a purpose, is to catch that universal wave, to have connection only with the universal movement. Anything other than that is *anārtha,* undesirable, unnecessary. It will serve no purpose. We are in connection with *anārtha,* the undesirable things that won't serve any real purpose.

Our real cause, the purpose of our lives, our satisfaction, and our existence will be found within the universal wave of the Absolute. That is Kṛṣṇa consciousness, the most universal, fundamental wave. We have to catch that wave. Our goal, our satisfaction, the fulfillment of our life is to be found only there, in that plane, not in this superficial plane of nationality or family interest or social service. All these are provincial interests.

But to stop one's movement altogether, to do away with one's own existence, to attain *samādhi,* cessation of all activity—that is suicidal. We have to give up enjoyment as well as renunciation; give up evil doing and also the abstention from all action. In a nation, so many workers may be failing to follow the proper rules for production, and that is bad, it is disorder. The product will be bad. However, to go on strike won't produce good results either. No work, that is also bad. To work in the interest of the country, only that is good.

From our local, separate interest, we must go to the universal interest, to the interest of the Absolute. Avoid all local interest, however great it may seem, whether self-centered, family-centered, village-centered, province-centered, or human-centered.

Mahāprabhu advised us to purify ourselves with the help of sound divine. But the sound should be genuine, transcendental, Kṛṣṇa conscious, the real wave. There is a minimal demand from us for our purification in this age of controversy. Kali means quarrel, controversy. Everything will create some doubt; everyone wants some proof; everyone has a very suspicious mind.

Take advantage of this sound. A minimal demand is required of us, because the process is very generous. The minimal demand, the minimal admission fee is *śraddhā,* faith. If we do this, if we perform this *saṅkīrtana,* then everything will be done. That basic faith must be there. That attitude will help us. There should be heartfelt cooperation, sincere cooperation with the Kṛṣṇa consciousness agents. That can purify us very easily.

The minimal demand from us is to have the faith that this movement of Kṛṣṇa consciousness will purify us. If we participate in this movement, everything will be done. Such a generous, wide conviction, and sincere cooperation with the agents can help us in a very short time. The cooperation with the divine sound, the sound aspect of the Supreme, is easily approachable for beginners. From that, many other aspects of the Infinite will come to our understanding.

Begin with the sound aspect of the universal consciousness. The sound aspect is easily approachable; others will come gradually. Our approach must be sincere, heartfelt. We are in trouble, and we need this. That will give us real relief from all troubles. It will put an end to all the troubles that we're experiencing now, and also those that we may have to experience in the future.

Qualifications for Chanting the Name

"Oh Govinda. What can I do? There is not a single offender like myself. My Lord, I am ashamed to take my offenses before You and have them forgiven. It is shameful even to point out before You that I am so heinous, that I am such an offender. I feel ashamed to recollect my own bad deeds. I feel ashamed that I shall take them to You and pray for their forgiveness. I am ashamed. Such a class of sinner I am. What more shall I say to You, my Lord? I am such a sinner."

This is the nature of the high devotees; they think themselves unfit for service. What is the way? What is our destination? Progress towards this side, the negative, submissive side. Our place is there, at the farthest end of the negative side, the smallest of the small, the lowest of the low.

Where do we cast our glance, our look? What should we do? Our goal is this, to reach that negative side, sincerely: self-abnegation to the extreme. This is the measurement, to become the lowest of the low. The goal is to realize our proper position there: lowest of the low. Is it possible at all? Is it imaginary, an imaginary quantity? For what purification may we aspire? Self-abnegation.

Analyze, analyze, and discard. Analyze and throw out all egoistic and assertive tendencies: "I am something; I am someone. I have something to be proud of." These have to be eliminated, and eliminated completely. It is not an easy thing. To become big is easy, but it is all false, like racketeering. To say, "I am a big man," is very easy. But to say, "I am nothing," to accept this creed in its true color, its true nature, that is very difficult. "I am no one; I am nothing!" It is very difficult.

Vaiṣṇava haite bara mane jiru sādha, tṛṇād-api śloke tripure gelo bāra. There is a familiar saying in Bengal: "I had a great aspiration to become a Vaiṣṇava, but when I came across the verse describing the qualifications of a Vaiṣṇava, *tṛṇād api sunicena, taror api sahiṣṇunā,* I was disappointed. It is not possible to be humbler than a blade of grass, and more tolerant than a tree."

Amāninā mānadena. Give honor to everyone, but don't aspire after honor. In this attitude we should take the Name of the Lord, of Kṛṣṇa. Then our desire will be fulfilled. We have to take the Name of Kṛṣṇa with such an attitude. We must be humbler than a blade of grass and more tolerant than a tree. When the tree is cut down, it still gives shade to the logger. And it doesn't beg anyone for water. Such forbearance! In this way we have to take the Name of Kṛṣṇa, and we shall find His help at once, in no time. The standard, the qualification for taking the Holy Name, has been recommended thus.

tṛṇād api sunīcena taror api sahiṣṇunā
amāninā mānadena kīrtanīyaḥ sadā hariḥ

"One can chant the Holy Name of the Lord in a humble state of mind, thinking himself lower than the straw in the street. One should be more tolerant than the tree, devoid of all sense of false prestige and ready to offer all respect to others. In such a state of mind one can chant the Holy Name of the Lord constantly." (*Śikṣāṣṭaka* 3)

Śrīla Bhaktivinoda Ṭhākura has explained that we are actually lower than the straw in the street, because in our present existence we are *vikṛta,* or deranged. But the straw is at least passive and maintaining its natural position. We have lost our proper function and become of negative value; we are lacking the positive value of straw because we are adverse to our natural position.

We are going against our own interest with our intelligence. We have intelligence, but it is misguided, opposed to the proper order of things. The straw is poised; it cannot move willfully. But we can move in a wrong way, so we are actually in a more heinous position than the straw. We use our assets willingly to misguide ourselves, but the straw maintains its fixed position without deviation.

In the worldly sense we may hold a position superior to that of a blade of grass or a tree, but what of that? All our credits are being misused for our selfishness. So we are lower than straw. We are armed, but armed for suicide. A madman should not possess a dagger. He is dangerous. He could stab himself at any moment. He is mad.

Krsna is Everywhere

Kṛṣṇa, Kṛṣṇa, Kṛṣṇa. Where is Kṛṣṇa? Come to that level, come to that plane, and we will see that Kṛṣṇa is everywhere. But our eyes and our senses are attracted by the charms of different places, and we have no time to look towards Kṛṣṇa. *Sabathā kṛṣṇe mukti kari janma.* Everywhere there is perception of Kṛṣṇa, but our sight is captured, attracted by so many floating charms, that we cannot see Kṛṣṇa.

Our prejudice for the outside world has covered our eyes, drawing all our attention towards them, and we can't see Kṛṣṇa. We can't see the real well-wisher, the real guardian, the real friend, the real lover. We are so busy with our transactions with external things that we have no time at all to look towards Him. We are ignoring our best friend.

This transaction with the outer environment is continued by our false ego, the false personality. That is the position of a person in bondage, a fallen soul. Our true self is not represented in the transaction that is going on in our name. The senses, the mind and intelligence, are surcharged with other interests, and they are conducting a false transaction. This is a hopeless position. *Sarvopādhi vinir-muktaṁ tat-paratvena nirmalam.*

Anyatā rūpaṁ, that which is just like a disease, undesirable foreign things, have come to cover us. That is *upādhi,* a foreign and undesirable element. So we must disown our foreign covers, all these false identifications with the outer dress. Disown them all; do away with them. They are unnecessary. We thought them to be our friends, but they are our enemies. We must be concerned with the person within, the soul, and that is not illusion, but truth proper. That is *anyatā rūpaṁ.* Successfully eliminating these enemies, we must come to our proper positive position in the world of love and beauty.

Hankering In Surrender Is Our Wealth

When we reach the highest position of disappointment, then sometimes, somehow or other, from the core of our heart we pray, "Oh Lord, I am helpless, save me! I am under the control of so many enemies in the form of friends. Such a hopeless position I hold, my Lord. From time immemorial I am serving all these masters, but they are not satisfied with my service. Now I find myself in this helpless position, my Lord. You should only come on Your own accord, and assert Yourself. Then they will fly away in fear of You. Otherwise I have no hope." This sort of ardent prayer from the core of the heart towards the Savior, that is what is necessary for us.

With our faith and earnestness we can aspire after that mercy. If we increase the quality of our negativity, the feeling that we are so low, the positive will be automatically attracted. We must try to increase the power of our position as a negative unit.

Tṛṇād api sunīcena (feeling lower than the grass), *dainyam* (humility), *ātmanivedana* (surrender). Hankering in surrender is our wealth. We are the *śakti,* the potency, and potency refers to the negative unit of the Positive, the Potent. We should increase our negative side, our hankering. The Positive will be automatically attracted to us.

Whatever beautiful and valuable things we come across, we cannot but surrender ourselves to them. That is the criterion. If we find anything higher in our vicinity, our appreciation means surrendering unto that. According to the degree of our surrender, we have to measure what degree of quality of truth we have found. That can be measured only according to the degree and intensity of surrender, how much we can surrender to what we have found, to the point of no return. And the true devotees know no satisfaction or fulfillment. They feel no trace of satisfaction that they have achieved anything. Never. The inner sweetness of the truth and its infinite characteristic are such. The truth attracts. It can attract to the highest degree and magnitude.

Accept Slavery to Its Perfection

The highest qualification within us is our acceptance of the slave mentality to the Absolute. This is the only way to hanker for the association of the highest existence. We must be ready to accept slavery to its perfection, and then we will be allowed to enter into that domain. Otherwise, we have no hope. It is not very easy to embrace the slave mentality, eternal slavery.

Slavery is our future prospect. Are we ready to think like this? We have to be so broadminded and hopeful that such a higher entity exists. Our hope and faith will have to be of such a magnanimous nature to enter that land. We will sign the bond, the contract to accept eternal slavery! We want to enter that land! We have to search our fortune, and sign the bond of slavery. The company there is so high that even as slaves we want that association. We earnestly hanker for that sweet land where our meager persons can become slaves. Such intense faith is necessary, where all other experience, even knowledge, fails. Only faith can carry us there.

Consciousness of separate interest (*dvitīyābhiniveśataḥ*) has turned us away from Kṛṣṇa. The common interest is solely in Him. Then only our service will be *bhakti*. Without that, everything is lost. *Śaraṇāgati*, surrender, must be present in order to have living devotion, otherwise hearing and chanting are only forms, not life. Therefore *śaraṇāgati* means exclusive connection and identification with the interest of Kṛṣṇa. Since we do not directly see Kṛṣṇa, we serve the *guru* and the Vaiṣṇava who are dear to Him. According to the degree of our self-abnegation in self-surrender, we will be benefited, and the specific characteristics of *śānta, dāsya, sakhya, vātsalya,* or *mādhurya-rasa* will develop.

We must admit our Master's right to make or mar. We are slaves. Mahāprabhu says, *jīvera svarūpa haya—kṛṣṇera nitya-dāsa*: the eternal nature of the soul is servitude to Kṛṣṇa. That is our constitutional position. Have we enough boldness to admit it? Can we admit that our Master has full rights over us? "Yes! My Master has full rights over me. I am ready to go to eternal hell to supply His slightest pleasure." We have heard that the *gopīs* were ready to supply the dust of their feet as 'medicine' to alleviate Kṛṣṇa's 'headache,' even if it meant that they would be condemned to the lowest regions of hell for that transgression. We may find such narrations very sweet, but to accept them is horrifying. *Jīvera svarūpa haya—kṛṣṇera nitya-dāsa*; no risk: no gain. Whole risk, whole gain. Such confidence is necessary. A free, clear, and bold choice; are we ready for that?

Do we want to reside in the land of immortality? Do we want *janma-mṛtyu-jarā-vyādhi* (birth, death, old age and infirmity), or immortality? If we want immortality, we will have to pay for the ticket. We will have to take the visa. We will have to prepare for such a categorical beginning. And the bond we have to sign is slavery to Kṛṣṇa. *Jīvera svarūpa haya—kṛṣṇera nitya-dāsa.* If we want to go to that mystic land, the land of infinite hope, prosperity and prospect, we will have to go as slaves, because that plane is made of a higher stuff than we are.

The Power of the Holy Name

Śrīla Jīva Gosvāmī has written that the ordinary *sādhus,* the *yogīs,* the *brāhmaṇas,* the Śaṅkarites, and those of other schools, have all concluded that by dint of one's knowledge, one's *yoga,* or one's devotion, the results of all previous actions can be destroyed. All, that is, save and except *prārabdha-karma,* those actions that have determined one's present body and are already attached to the body from before this birth.

The *Bhakti* school disagrees. We say that by the power of *Kṛṣṇa-nāma,* even the impurities attached to one's birth, race, creed, caste, or any other thing, can be done away with completely. It is not possible by *yoga, jñāna,* or any other thing, but by *Kṛṣṇa-nāma,* all impurities can be obliterated, even *prārabdha-karma.* When all *prārabdha-karma* is purified, then one comes to the position of the highest birth, that of the *brāhmaṇa.*

Jīva Gosvāmī says that at this point one comes to the status of a *brāhmaṇa* boy. A *brāhmaṇa* boy is not considered eligible to do the work of a *brāhmaṇa,* until and unless he is given the sacred thread and *mantra.* When he is invested with *upanayana-saṁskāra,* only then is he eligible to worship Nārāyaṇa, perform sacrifice, and carry out other duties reserved for *brāhmaṇas.*

By taking the Holy Name we are purified and attain the position of a *brāhmaṇa* boy. But, Śrīla Jīva Gosvāmī points out, because we do not find any system to give the sacred thread to those not born in *brāhmaṇa* families, we may have to wait until our next birth to perform brahminical worship. The Gosvāmī admits that whatever caste one may be, if we take the Name of Kṛṣṇa then we discard any defects of birth, and attain the position of a *brāhmaṇa* lad.

Who Is A Brahmana

Continuing this line of thought, Śrīla Bhaktisiddhānta Sarasvatī Prabhupāda said there is no harm in giving those not born in *brāhmaṇa* families the sacred thread. Our Guru Mahārāja came to introduce that. He said that two things were indulged by not introducing the sacred thread initiation. First, those who receive Vaiṣṇava initiation may think that they are situated lower than the *brāhmaṇas.* On the contrary, they should understand that they are no longer in a lower position and they are fit to perform all the various services. Second, the so-called *brāhmaṇas,* who are proud of their body consciousness, may think that those who have received Vaiṣṇava *dikṣā* are situated lower. Thus, they commit offenses against the Vaiṣṇavas.

Śrīla Bhaktisiddhānta Sarasvatī Gosvāmī boldly came forward to introduce this *upanayana-saṁskāra* system so that *brāhmaṇas* and other so-called higher castes should not have the opportunity to commit *vaiṣṇava-aparādha,* and so that those who have received the Vaiṣṇava *mantra* should not consider themselves lower and unfit for brahminical worship. There is no contradiction with the rules of *śāstra.* According to *siddhānta,* it is not wrong to invest Vaiṣṇavas with the sacred thread, but there was no system previously established. Our Guru Mahārāja established that.

brāhmaṇānāṁ sahasrebhyaḥ satrayājī viśiṣyate
satra-yāji-sahasrebhyaḥ sarva-vedānta-pāragaḥ
sarva-vedānta-vit-koṭyā viṣṇu-bhakto viśiṣyate
vaiṣṇavānāṁ sahasrebhya ekāntyeko viśiṣyate

"The real devotee of Viṣṇu is superior to millions of ordinary *vaidāntika brāhmaṇas.* A practicing *brāhmaṇa* is better than a birth *brāhmaṇa.* Practice means to perform sacrifices and worship Kṛṣṇa. Those who worship Kṛṣṇa with the help of their consciousness are superior to those who worship with material things. Those who are *vedānta-vit* think that their goal is undifferentiated consciousness, but if one can attain differentiated consciousness, one must hold a higher position than millions of *vaidāntika brāhmaṇas.* They suffer from the disease of thinking that spirituality means non-differentiated Brahman. The Viṣṇu *bhaktas,* who can see the personality in consciousness, are far superior. Amongst the devotees, those who regulate themselves according to the scriptures are of the order of Vaikuṇṭha, and those who surrender exclusively to the service of the Absolute Entity with innermost love and faith, are of the highest order." *(Garuḍa-Purāṇa)*

How Sound Enters the Disciple's Heart

Divine realization is not an acquired thing; it comes down by selection from above. It comes down in the continuance of the disciplic line. The Lord supplies it through His agent. It comes down to us because He supplies it. If the Lord wishes to spread His Holy Name—if it is His pleasure to spread His grace below—then out of that necessity it comes down from Him through His agent. The qualification of the agent is his faith. He must especially have faith in his own Gurudeva, the next upper center. He must experience all his activities through the next upper center and prove his faithfulness to him. Only then and in that way will the supply come down.

We are requested not to see *guru* as limited in his ordinary personality, but as the transparent mediator of the highest function in his line. We can see this only if our vision is deep. According to the disciple's depth of *śraddhā,* he will see the Lord present in his Gurudeva. The *guru* principle, *guru-tattva,* is very special, very noble, very broad and very deep.

Strangely, the agent may sometimes not know what things are passing through him by this arrangement.

ahaṁ vedmi śuko vetti vyāso vetti na vetti vā
bhaktyā bhāgavatam grāhyaṁ na buddhyā na ca ṭīkayā

Lord Śiva says, "I know the meaning of the *Bhāgavatam* and Śukadeva also knows it. As for Vyāsadeva, he may or may not know it. The *Bhāgavatam* can only be known through *bhakti,* not by mundane intelligence or by reading many commentaries." *Vyāso vetti na vetti vā*: Vyāsa may or may not know the meaning of the *Bhāgavatam,* but the *Bhāgavatam* is passing through Vyāsa. This is *taṭasthā-vicāra,* an impartial judgement. From the absolute standpoint, it has been said that even Vyāsa may not know the things that come through him to grace others. Although this may sometimes be the case, we should still not admit so easily that Vyāsa does not know.

I once said this to my Guru Mahārāja. We were in Darjeeling and I had composed a Sanskrit *śloka* about Bhaktivinoda Ṭhākura. I had shown him the poem and it greatly pleased him. At that time one disciple was his secretary; Prabhupāda would dictate and that disciple would write letters on his behalf. That day a letter had come from Vana Mahārāja in England that showed knowledge of some confidential information. Prabhupāda asked who had supplied Vana Mahārāja with this information. His secretary answered, "Prabhupāda, you yourself wrote this news to him." Prabhupāda replied, "No, no, no. I did not write this thing to Vana Mahārāja." The secretary humbly replied, "But Prabhupāda, you dictated the letter and I wrote it. I remember. You were giving this news to him." Again Prabhupāda said, "No,

I don't remember." When I heard this, I just remarked, "*vyāso vetti na vetti vā,*" and Prabhupāda laughed.

Paramānanda Brahmacārī, one of Prabhupāda's most intimate disciples, was also there, serving as his personal assistant. He said, "*Śrīdharaḥ sakalaṁ vetti*—but Śrīdhara Mahārāja knows everything." And then I replied, "*Śrī-nṛsiṁha-paramānanda-prasādataḥ*—by the mercy of Paramānanda."

In this way things may come down through the *ācārya* to grace others. Mahāprabhu said to Sanātana Gosvāmī, "I feel the grace of Kṛṣṇa flowing through Me to you. I do not know all these things, they are not Mine." This is why it is said, *vyāso vetti na vetti vā.* The Vyāsa who has written *Bhāgavatam* may or may not know its meaning. It is coming from others through him. This is sometimes possible, but not always. Kṛṣṇa is so independent. All glories to His independence!

We are His servants. What responsibility is with us, His instruments? He may act in whatever way He wills. Everything is going on according to His will; and if He wills otherwise, things will happen in another way. Everything is part of His *līlā,* His play. The Absolute is *līlāmaya. Līlā* is the continuous and irresistible flow of *ānanda,* supreme bliss.

Once the Vyāsa Pūjā, the birth ceremony of our Guru Mahārāja, was celebrated in the Cuttack Maṭha. Many important local citizens were invited, including Janaki Bose, the father of Netaji Subhash Chandra Bose, who was a leading attorney in Cuttack at that time. All these people had taken their seats on a carpet on the floor, whereas Prabhupāda had been given a throne for his seat.

In his address, Prabhupāda said, "I am given so much honor, garments, worship, sandalwood and flowers. Many nice things are being read about me here in my presence. And I am accepting this worship before so many members of the town's elite. Even a beast in the zoo would be ashamed to accept such honors, such respect, in front of so many gentlemen. Should I too not be ashamed? Why then am I accepting them? In fact, I accept them only on behalf of my *guru,* to show that he deserves this honor. This honor is for my *guru* and I accept it only to send it on to him. I am nothing without my *guru.* I am being worshiped because I have received his words, his advice. I am being honored because I have followed his directions, otherwise I would not. Therefore, though it is humiliating and causes me much heartache, I still accept these honors to show his exalted position."

Bhakti Under the Higher Agent Only

When I joined the mission, I wanted to read the books of the mission, including *Bhāgavatam,* but I did not find any encouragement from the authority. The real thing, the real requirement is to use our energy for the service of the Lord. By that process only may we go up, not by satisfying our intellectual necessities. *Jñāna-śūnya-bhakti,* an illiterate man may achieve a higher position in the realm of devotion than a literate man.

By the command of the Lord's agent we may engage in literary culture, even as Mahāprabhu instructed Rūpa and Sanātana Gosvāmīs. Of course, they had acquired their knowledge to utilize it in the service of the *saṁpradāya,* the Gauḍīya disciplic succession. He also asked Raghunātha Bhaṭṭa to hear the *Bhāgavatam* from one who knew its real purport.

Jīva Gosvāmī was the only exception. Mahāprabhu asked him to study independently before he joined the Vṛndāvana party. He left his home and went to Benares, the center of all sorts of learning at that time. He studied different *śāstra* and then joined the others in Vṛndāvana. There, under the direction of Rūpa and Sanātana, he utilized his previously acquired knowledge in the service of the *saṁpradāya.* When we get inspiration from above to study, that study is devotion. Otherwise a whim to study, to acquire scholarship, may not be *bhakti* proper, *śuddha-bhakti.*

The higher agent, the Vaiṣṇava, must utilize my energy. This energy must be spent to satisfy the higher world. Then it will be *bhakti,* it will be devotion. My mental imagination may bring *sukṛti,* but it won't be *śuddha-bhakti* if I have a mind to help the *sampradāya* in a scholarly way. At my own risk I must go on with my study. It is accepted that when one is connected with the higher agent, then it will be considered devotion; otherwise it is not. It is an empirical attempt with some sort of good imagination. But this is not pure *bhakti,* pure devotion. Pure devotion is to carry out the orders descending from above, from the higher agent. The waves are coming; catch them and then act accordingly.

Our Godbrother Nisikant Sanyal said that when we are requested by a Vaiṣṇava to write or read any book, then that constitutes devotion. But when of our own accord we read any devotional book, that won't give us devotion. That will be *karma* or *jñāna.* To surrender unconditionally to the instruction coming down to us, that is *bhakti.* All else is imitation. We find this warning everywhere. This we should understand.

Even reading the scriptures is not devotion unless done on the order of the Vaiṣṇava. Independent reading is only knowledge-seeking. By following the Vaiṣṇava, our bond with the Lord is guaranteed. *Sādhu-saṅge kṛṣṇa-nāma*: in the company of the devotees, chanting the Name or whatever service we render is guaranteed to reach Him. And what is the guarantee of that? The reply will be, "His agent is saying so, and I am therefore engaged. I am not my master; I am his servant." Such consciousness must be genuine, as far as possible. Success depends on this principle.

If we are appointed to preach, to do relief work here, we will execute that duty solely under the appointment of, and in the interest of, that higher plane, without any vanity. We should think, "I must put myself wholly at the disposal of the higher plane, and I shall not be eager to become an *ācārya*, a spiritual master. Otherwise, there is the danger of committing *nāma-aparādha*, offense against the Lord's Name."

Aśraddadhāne vimukhe 'py aśṛṇvati, yaś copadeśaḥ śiva-nāmāparādhaḥ. It is an offense to give the Holy Name to the faithless. It betrays the motivation to gain a position in the higher sphere. This is a type of mundane attachment, a spiritual commerce, as is the habit of caste *gosvāmīs* and other spurious lines. Rather, the healthy attitude should be, "If I am appointed from above, then I shall serve as appointed, and that too, only for the interest of those who have appointed me. I am entering that rank solely for the interest of that higher land." That is the pure and perfect approach.

Śrīla Śrīdhara Svāmī, the renowned commentator of *Śrīmad Bhāgavatam*, has stated, *sa cārpitaiva satī yadi kriyeta, na tu kṛtā satī paścād arpyeta:* "Devotional service must be first offered to the Lord, then performed; not performed and offered afterwards." We should already be committed when we come to serve. We should not collect capital and later try to utilize it in the service of the Lord. The commitment is to Him, to Kṛṣṇa.

We have come to know about Him for Him, not for our sake or for anyone else. We preach only because of the instruction from above. Only if we receive an instruction from that higher quarter, "Go and preach," shall we do so. Only then will our preaching be service, and never if it is done for name and fame. We must have engagement from the higher office, and only on their behalf we shall preach; then it will be genuine preaching. Otherwise, it will be trading. *Na sa bhṛtyaḥ sa vai vaṇik:* Prahlāda Mahārāja has warned us against this trading mentality in the name of spiritual truth.

Devotion is a separate and distinct plane where we live only for the center. We aspire to live and move only as agents of the center, never disconnected from the center. This is Kṛṣṇa consciousness. Reality is for Itself, and we must strictly abide by this rule. He is for Himself, everything is for Him, we are for Him. Whatever we do must also be for Him. We must strictly adhere to this conception, and always examine whether what we are doing is for Him or for any other part, however important we may think it to be.

Connection with Divinity

Bhaktivinoda Ṭhākura says that in the *saṅkīrtana* party, when we are chanting the Name, there must be at least one *śuddha-bhakta,* one pure devotee. At least one *śuddha-bhakta* must be leading the *saṅkīrtana* party. Otherwise the chanting will be *nāma-aparādha,* offensive. Connection with divinity is necessary, descending through the agent, the bonafide agent. He can receive in his heart so many waves of the Lord's wishes; the desires of the Lord strike in his heart.

We must connect with such a center and only then will we attain *bhakti.* Otherwise it may be imitation *bhakti,* not devotion. So many fleeting desires may make it impure: our attraction for knowledge, to satisfy our inner curiosity about *bhakti* before accepting the process; or the desire for fame when delivering a lecture. We must surrender and receive the agent's order. We have to admit that we do not know what is good and bad, that we must have a direct order from above.

When the *guru* is living far away and there is no time to ask him, but we must take some immediate decision, then we should try to think how he would direct us in such a position and act accordingly. We must understand what our Gurudeva would ask us to do in this situation. We should try to get some sort of order from him. He might have said something in a similar situation, and as far as we can understand, we should follow that.

The criterion of *bhakti* is that whatever we do, the starting idea must come from above, irrespective of the action. Whether we are to go to the temple or do anything else, it does not matter. Our action must have the upper connection. That is *bhakti.* It is independent of the three *guṇas: sattva, rajas, and tamas. Ahiṁsā,* non-injury—*sattva-guṇa*; *hiṁsā,* violence—*raja-guṇa*; sleeping and idleness—*tama-guṇa.*

The scriptures and *mahājanas* come to our help. At present we may think that independence will give us proper satisfaction, but really it is incorrect. That thought is our enemy. We want to get out of any circumstantial constraint, and if we become free, we'll be happy. This is wrong. Rather, the opposite is true: we should try to live in a joint family. We must be accommodating; we must correct our nature. Our independence is our enemy.

Subjective Vision

Those in touch with Divinity are all-seeing, all-knowing, subjective. Ignorant people ascribe objective vision to this higher plane. It is difficult to conceive. If we stand before the Deity, we should not indulge our eye or any other sense in order to experience the Deity. When we think of Him as an object of our senses, we are deceived. We should be trained to find the Seer in the seen. *Draṣṭari dṛśyatvam*—try to see the subjective existence.

The Deity is subjective existence. We are the object of His sight. He is all-seeing, all-feeling, all-knowing. The *Bhāgavatam* says that is the proper view. Then we are in a position to view the Reality; we have to come in touch with Reality. It is all super-subjective. Then we come to live in the *dhāma,* the holy abode. That is the *dhāma,* the divine area, where one can feel that the whole environment is superior, made of subjective existence. All should be revered; none are there to serve us, there for our enjoyment. Everything is to be approached with veneration and regard. We are their servants. The Lord and His kingdom are venerable, super-subjective. Then we come into contact with Vaikuṇṭha, the higher entity.

The objective entity is all *māyā*, all *bhoga*. What we see as the object of our enjoyment is illusion and concoction, *māyā*. When everything is revered, worshiped, and treated with respect, then we are in Vaikuṇṭha, in Vṛndāvana. It is mentioned in *Caitanya Caritāmṛta*, *vaikuṇṭhera pṛthivy-ādi sakala cinmaya* (*C.c. Adi-līlā* 5.53): everything is made of spiritual stuff and superior to us. Below there is Māyā and above there is Yogamāyā, the land of the Lord. We want to get out of this entanglement, this separate interest. What is superior, we imagine that to be inferior to ourselves and want to use it for our own purpose and enjoyment. The world of enjoyment is a concocted one.

We should learn to see that everything must be treated with reverence and with serving attitude, everything. Then we can come in contact with the *dhāma*, the land of the Lord, where every particle is to be worshiped. Everything holds a superior position. What is really supernatural, we are treating it as though it is naturally part of the sense experience. No. Just try, *bhidyate hṛdaya-granthiś cidyante sarva-saṁśayāḥ, kṣīyante cāsya karmāṇi mayi dṛṣṭe 'khilātmani* (*Bhāg.* 11.20.30). Disassociate the ego of separate existence totally from enjoyment. Abolish the tendency to enjoy, to utilize whatever we find to satisfy our senses. This angle of vision, this *māyā*, this ego, the center of such experience should be totally abolished. Dissolved. And all doubts will be cleared when we find ourselves in that plane.

When we are free from the clutches of separate interest, then all suspicion and doubt will be cleared. We shall feel this through direct soul experience, the experience of the inner senses that we possess. Then there will be no need for all our attempts and efforts; they'll stop. No special endeavor must be undertaken for our purpose because we have no separate existence. We are particles in the Infinite and that which is feeding the Infinite will feed us also.

We shall find the general interest everywhere. We are not separate, so there is no necessity of acting for our special interest. We shall see the divine arrangement for everyone, including every grain of sand. We are one in the whole and the main current is doing everything, so no *karma*, no action is necessary on our own behalf.

Then it will become very clear that we have our duty in that universal flow, and we are one of them. We are particles there. Automatically the universal force handles us in such a way. That is Yogamāyā, the Lord's internal potency, not Mahāmāyā, the controller of the material universe. That plane is not acted upon by separate interest, but influenced by the general interest of the whole. We have our movement there, and that is service, not enjoyment.

Deep Engagement in Responsible Service

Responsible service can help us avoid falling prey to lust, anger, and other enemies of devotion. Foremost among our protectors is faith, *śraddhā.* Next comes *sādhu-saṅga,* association with pure devotees, and *bhajana-kriyā,* deep engagement in the duties prescribed by the divine master. Deep engagement is necessary, especially for the mind, not merely the body.

Mental engagement can be attained only by responsibility. Some responsible service is given to the disciple. We feel the weight and it occupies our thoughts; we cannot but think about it. The mind is engaged there, surely. Thus, the mind gets no chance to dwell on lower things. This is the beauty of deep engagement in responsible service. In the practical sense, that helps us a great deal. Then association and scriptures will really be of substantial benefit to us: as service (*paripraśna, sevāyā*).

As much as we are able to engage in deep, responsible service, the effect of our impure tendencies will be minimized. They will come and peep, and will step back when they discover that we are deeply engaged. We have no time to give attention to lust and anger; we cannot be enticed. In this way, they will have to retreat. Then if they return once, twice, thrice or more, we may not spare any attention for them. We will be very deeply engaged in *sevā*.

Sevā, service, should not be merely physical; there is mental *sevā*, and only responsibility can capture the mind. In responsibility, the mind is compelled to think on the matter; otherwise, the mind may be free to wander hither and thither even while the body is apparently engaged. So engage the mind in deep service, responsible service.

What is necessary is the dissolution of the separate interest activity. Then one will emerge into the all venerable, all respectful world—no connection with the lower things. We are servants of the servant of the servant. We are the lowest; all others are higher. We shall come into contact with all higher substance, and the lower substance of concoction will vanish for all time. It is *sat-cit-ānandaṁ*. *Sat*, eternal existence; *cit*, all consciousness, all soul, all subjective; and *ānandaṁ*, no anxiety. The general flow is irresistible and automatic, so there is no possibility of any suffering or pain. That is the spontaneous flow of blissfulness, and we shall come to live in that plane. Rather, Yogamāyā, a higher, superior and affectionate power, maintains us. She will capture us and utilize us in the service of the mysterious Lord Kṛṣṇa.

Under Our Affectionate Guardian's Hand

Yogamāyā comes and influences us, and by the magic touch of that affectionate hand we are taken into the land of our dreams. It is a land where we self-forgetfully engage ourselves, *jñāna-*

śūnya-bhakti—all affection. We are under the affectionate guardians' hand. We do not know anything, but we are handled by our affectionate guardians in such a way that we live in the land of mystery, of dreams. We think that we are holding a very low position, but in the *taṭasthā-vicāra* (impartial judgement) this sort of life is the happiest position of a *jīva* soul. We are playing under the affectionate hand of the guardians and have some natural innate faith and consciousness to work according to their direction.

Jñāna-śūnya-bhakti. There is no calculation, no self-interest, but we are so given to the central cause that it is as in a dream. Automatically we are working like an instrument, and we are happy. We are manipulated and handled by faith, by affection, by goodness, by love, by mercy. There is no necessity of any individual selfish calculation. The very soil is thinking of our interest. Everyone there, at the cost of their own interest, is seeking the interest of others.

There is no dearth of *ānandaṁ, rasaṁ,* that for which we are searching. No dearth of that there. Profusely, everything is there. Affection, sympathy, mercy, and love are overflowing in the land of opulence. In any way we can, we must enter that plane; they will take care of us. The soil will take care of us! The soil is so high, so elevated, so good, *bhūmiś cintāmaṇi, vṛksa kalpa taru, gamanam nātyaṁ kathā gānaṁ.* Sweet, sweet, sweet, sweet, sweet, sweet, everything is sweet in the land of sweetness.

Distributing Their Inner Wealth

It is described in *Bhāgavatam* and *Caitanya Caritāmṛta,* and it is found scattered in other *Purāṇas,* that Mahāprabhu—Rādhā-Govinda combined—came to distribute Their own inner wealth to the public. It is possible for us to approach and gain admittance into that flow. It is not static, but is a dynamic flow.

It is necessary that we should become free from those that are subservient to us. Our tendency in the *baddha-jīva* conditioned position, is that all should serve us and please us, but we must become free of that attitude. Not only must we be indifferent to them, but also we must have some positive service engagement. All that is around us is higher—every particle is of a higher, superior substance. That is what is necessary, *cid-vilāsa.* On the whole our progress means that we shall not come in contact with any lower substances. We are the smallest of the small, the lowest of the low. We are encouraged to accept the mentality of a servant, the servant of the servant of the servant. It is not hyperbolic; it is reality. We have to understand real life, in service. All is good around us, superior to us. Necessarily we shall always invite some improvement in ourselves through association with the higher agents. Every second we can imbibe something positive.

Cast Ourselves to the Infinite's Whim

Turning away from limitation we are jumping into the infinite ocean. From the tangible finite position, we jump towards the Infinite. He will see us. The apparently stable things cannot give us shelter. We are willingly leaving the company of the tangible association and casting ourselves toward the Infinite. Jumping into the ocean—it is not an easy matter—neglecting the tangible thing on which we are standing, the matter under our control. It is somewhat tangible, but flickering. For the present, where we take our stand, it is apparently tangible. But because it is transient we need to disassociate ourselves from it and cast ourselves towards the Infinite.

We are taking a very courageous step now. Throwing ourselves at the whim of the Infinite, from the tangible to the Infinite, we are going to take a very courageous step. How will the

Infinite deal with us? Will He adore us, or will He ignore us totally, or will He make some negligent arrangement for us? There is no surety.

Āśliṣya vā pāda-ratāṁ pinaṣṭu mām. We may be lost in the wave of the infinite power, *vā pāda-ratāṁ pinaṣṭu mām adarśanām marma hatāṁ karotu vā.* We may not even have any chance of coming into contact with Him, *yathā tathā vā vidadhātu lampaṭo.* He's whimsical in our understanding. He's the adoring One and He is ignoring us. No explanation can be called for, *mat prāṇa-nāthas tu sa eva nāparaḥ.* But we have no other alternative than to surrender to His whimsical activity. This attitude we must adopt.

To cast ourselves into the Infinite whim, this is a very, very uncertain and extremely courageous act, and we are going to do it willingly. We do not know what will be our fate. Still we want that promotion to a connection with the superior power. It seems to be a risk, but still it may be a substantial gain. We have come to the right place for shelter. We are being connected with the real plane. It is not a sham; that will be our consolation.

The favor of so many lower agents, that is flickering, and there is no stability. We may be ignored by the central power, but if at any moment we can draw their notice, our position will be very safe and high. So we are taking a great risk for our greatest prospect in life, though it may not be easily obtained. It is a risky act, *sarva-dharmān-parityajya.*

Otherwise, to remain in our own present position and progress in a slow way, that is also recommended, *sva-dharme nidhanaṁ śreyaḥ, para-dharmo bhayāvahaḥ.* "Do not be too ambitious. Keep your position firm and try to advance slowly." That is the ordinary recommendation.

But for those who have courage, there is *sarva-dharmān-parityajya.* "Give up everything and try to come to Me. I am there and I shall save you." From His side this kind of consolation is there. "I am not blind, I can see anything and everything. If you really come to My shelter, I am ready. I shall embrace you." From His side the statement is such.

From the perspective of the devotees who are swimming in the ocean, and pressed by the current, undercurrent and overflow, it is very difficult! Still they cannot leave that campaign, that revolutionary effort. The constitutional path and the revolutionary way, both are there. But the constitutional way makes for very slow progress. It is not certain when we shall reach the goal, and sometimes there are setbacks.

Better to Serve in Heaven

It is better on the whole to leave the world of deception, *māyā*, misunderstanding, as soon as possible, even taking all possible risk. Jump with great speed in the hope of meeting the non-treacherous and loving plane. This *māyā* is treacherous. So many units fighting with one another, this is the position here. To get free of this and jump into the Absolute area is considered to be of very, very high and great value. The very slightest position there is far, far greater than the highest position in this world of misunderstanding.

We are laboring under so much suspicion; so engrossed in and oppressed by *māyā*, the misrepresented part of the world, that we cannot even think of the conception of truth and goodness. We are so far from the standard of goodness and truth; we cannot understand what should be the real symptom of higher existence. We are so fallen.

Satan says, "It is better to reign in hell than to serve in heaven." That is generally the outcome of our life experience here. We want to reign in hell rather than serve in heaven. But just the opposite will be really helpful to us. Die to live. Leaving this realm, we want to pass through to the highest. Crossing beyond the association of the all-accommodating Brahman, beyond the Paramātma conception, beyond even the source of all sources and Master of all energy, Nārāyaṇa, there is Kṛṣṇa in Vṛndāvana, satisfying the whole existence with the fulfillment of love. There it is apparent that Infinity's approach to the finite is in its fullest sense, as if He is one of us. He is so close to us, and His love and affection are so much extended there.

Power of Affection

Śrī Kṛṣṇa-kārṣini. The peculiar power in love is this: that the high is controlled by the low through some tendency, and that is called love. When a little boy catches the finger of his father and draws him to some quarter, the father goes there. The father is more powerful and the boy's power is insignificant, but the father is defeated by the power of affection. Affection and love are there, where we find that the small controls the big.

Submission to the master is so intense that the master becomes subservient to the servant through affection: "At My beck and call he can give his life. So how should I deal with him?" Automatically, the master's heart goes to the servant. That is love, *prema.* Such wonderful potency is in that love and affection. The Absolute is controlled by His potency.

Generally the owner of the potency guides the potency, but sometimes the potency guides the owner. That is love. It is not the physical capacity but the fine capacity of the very subtlest force, *ahaṁ bhakta parādhīno.* "I feel as if I am interdependent, not Absolute. I feel that I am controlled by them only by devotion; I am not master of My own Self." The Absolute says like that. What wonderful thing is *bhāgavata-prema*? It is present in the highest sense in the case of Kṛṣṇa in Vṛndāvana. *Aham iha nandaṁ vande yasyālinde paraṁ brahma,* "I have no attraction for *Mahābhārata, Veda, Upaniṣad* and all these things," *nandaḥ kim akarod brahman, śreya evaṁ mahodayam,* "but my only attraction is for Nanda, because I found that the Supreme Powerful Absolute is crawling in his compound as a baby boy." In the *Bhāgavatam* this is a very valuable situation. What is this? The Parabrahman is in such an ordinary position. Is He Parabrahman, or is He something else?

Yaśodā, Kṛṣṇa's Mother, is punishing Him, but when trying to bind Him, at every attempt the rope is two fingers short. The rope is only two fingers shorter than necessary to bind Him around the waist, but whenever one more foot is added, it is the same two fingers short. She is punishing Him and He is crying, but still the difference is there. Against His will she is trying to bind Him around the belly, but the rope is two fingers short. More rope is added, but it is always two fingers short, again and again. He is sucking her breast and when she is punishing Him, He cries, "Oh, don't beat Me, My mother, I won't do any more of these things." At another time, when He was yawning, Yaśodā found the whole *brahmāṇḍa,* the entire creation, within the boy's mouth. Then she was afraid, but the next moment a cat meowed and the boy climbed on her lap, out of fear. "Oh, He is my child, my son. He is not all-accommodating Brahman, no! He is my child!" He is playing in this way, like hide and seek.

Infinite Touches the Finite

When the Infinite comes to the finite in its closest touch, then sometimes it shows that Infinite character and sometimes its most finite character. Playfully, He does so many big things. When Tṛṇāvarta came to kill Him, He was on the lap of Yaśodā. Immediately His Mother felt that the boy was very, very heavy, so she could not keep Him on her lap. She had to put Him down, and Tṛṇāvarta took the boy away in a storm. Then some minutes later they found that the great demon's body had fallen on the earth, and the boy, grasping the throat of the demon, was on top. Then Yaśodā swiftly went and collected the boy, 'Oh, fortunately the boy landed over the demon's dead body. Otherwise, He would have been crushed.' Tṛṇāvarta, that great demon, was finished by the boy, but playfully.

The most miraculous things are coming to a simple level. Most playfully and in a simple way He is doing great deeds, which take so much time, so much power, so much valor, and all is finished in only a second in a very peculiar way. Great things are done with a very small attempt. The Infinite's approach to the finite in the closest form is controlled by a special tendency, and that is love, *prema*.

Bhakti is such a thing. We shall try to understand what is this devotion that can control the Absolute. Mahāprabhu has come to suggest that we follow this path only, and it is in Vṛndāvana. Try to have a position, a place in Vṛndāvana, in that level, in that plane of life. With this general conception we shall have to approach Vṛndāvana. And what is Vṛndāvana? It is not the sum total of some appearance. A mere imitation of a particular group of appearances cannot give such a result. The very life is such, so valuable—the life transaction must be there.

Die to live. Sacrifice. We must invite that sort of death that will kill death itself. If we want to live in that high plane, we shall have to give ourselves completely—this is the price of that valuable goal. What is that subtle power? How do we acquire it? What should be the price? How deep should be the transaction?

Easy Grant to Your Appeal

From the throne, Pratāparudra Mahārāja came to do the service of a sweeper before Jagannātha. This melted Mahāprabhu's heart. Before then, so many proposals came to Mahāprabhu, "The king wants to see You; if You allow him, he may come and have Your *darśana*." "No, no, that is undesirable. People may say that this *sannyāsī* has some greed for money and power, so He wants to have a connection to the king. That gives a bad reputation to a *sannyāsī sādhu,* so I do not want him to come see Me. That will show indirectly that I have a desire for money. I don't like this." But when Mahāprabhu saw that he took the position of a sweeper for Lord Jagannātha, naturally His heart melted and He embraced the devotee.

When we are going to have a touch of the Super-subjective, we must know that He is all-seeing, all-feeling, all-hearing. The very basis of spiritual life is like this. Then we shall come in contact with the higher reality; otherwise we shall go on plodding in the mud of imagination. The attitude should be to want to be utilized by Him, and try for any chance of serving Him: "I have come here to serve, and not to enjoy the scenery."

He is Infinite and He likes the finite. The finite is His friend. But when the finite wants to show a sham tendency to become big, He dislikes it. When one takes the minutest position, then He comes to embrace him, *tṛṇad api sunīcena, taror api sahiṣṇunā, amāninā mānadena, kīrtanīyaḥ sadā hariḥ.* Do not aspire after anything, and whatever comes to attack us, try to know the futility of the attempt. All is under one hand. The Supreme hand is behind everything, so resolve to tolerate all. We must exhibit tolerance, until the upper hand comes to control. We don't have to hinder or oppose anything—*tṛṇad api sunīcena.*

Do not disturb the environment, and if the environment comes to oppress us, then take the course of tolerance. Do not return tit for tat. Try to find the Supreme will there. We should feel, "I have done something wrong, so this is coming to control me and to exact the reaction for my offenses. *Tat te 'nukampāṁ susamīkṣamāṇo.* In the perfect vision, we are not to quarrel with the environment. Not even a straw can move without the Supreme will, without the order of the Supreme will.

So, whatever is coming to attack me is my necessity. It is necessary for me, to correct me."

When the mother is punishing the child, she does so only with the good intention to correct the child. Similarly, the Absolute has no vindictive nature to punish us, but His dealings are only for our correction. We shall have to see and approach in that way.

Tat te 'nukampāṁ susamīkṣamāṇo bhuñjāna evātma-kṛtaṁ vipākam: "Whatever undesirable things we find here are the result of our previous *karma,* and by the good will of the Supreme, that previous *karma* is going to be finished. We will be relieved. We will be made fit for higher service to Him, so this has come." That is the advice in *Bhāgavatam.* Don't quarrel with the environment. Try to be adjusted with it, correct ourselves. Everything is all right.

Then *amāninā,* do not hanker after any position, *mānadena,* but give respect to one and all. With this attitude take the Name, and our appeal to the Supreme will very easily be granted. We will have an easy and quick grant for our application if we approach Him with this attitude. This is the key to our success, our way to be happy. Do not waste energy in every direction, but command the whole thing in one direction, drawing it in from all sides. Do not waste energy to fight with the environment for anything, but the whole effort should be directed towards the Absolute. Then in no time, success will come to crown our attempt.

Highest Criterion of Lila

Whatever pleases Kṛṣṇa, that is good. *Kṛṣṇa-līlā* accommodates everything, even mistakes. A mistake may set something right. Kṛṣṇa wanted Yudhiṣṭhira to tell a lie, but Yudhiṣṭhira hesitated and finally he uttered *aśvatthāmā hata iti gajaḥ* (Aśvatthāmā, the elephant, is dead). Kṛṣṇa asked him to tell a lie, but Yudhiṣṭhira hesitated.

Submission to Kṛṣṇa's request, whatever satisfies Him, that is truth. The satisfaction of Kṛṣṇa is the final test, not whether it is good or bad, measured by the standards of this world. Only the satisfaction of Kṛṣṇa; the highest criterion of *līlā* is there.

In the pastimes of Rāmacandra we don't find all these things. There *nīti,* or respect for the rules and regulations, has the upper hand. But with *Kṛṣṇa-līlā* we find the inner importance, eliminating the external rigidity of morality.

Karṇa insulted Yudhiṣṭhira on the battlefield. Yudhiṣṭhira left the battle and Arjuna followed. Kṛṣṇa also came for a rest in the midst of the war, for some refreshment. At that time Yudhiṣṭhira rebuked Arjuna, "You have taken me and entangled me in this war. I was not in favor of war. I depended on you and you do not care to fight sincerely for me. You were there and Karṇa insulted me. I curse your Gāṇḍīva!"

Arjuna had made an oath that he would behead whoever would offend his Gāṇḍīva bow, or he would die himself. Yudhiṣṭhira cursed the Gāṇḍīva, and Arjuna was about to take out his sword. Kṛṣṇa said, "What are you doing, you fool? Are you going to behead your elder brother, to fulfill your promise? What is the value of that promise? Did you not promise thousands of times that you would make Yudhiṣṭhira, your elder brother, the king, the Emperor? But what are those promises, when you are ready to carry out one bogus promise to behead your elder brother? So many promises are made on the battlefield. The war is continuing in full rage, and you are going to behead your elder brother?

"Do you think that this is the purport of the law? Do you think that moral law has been created for such a triviality? Eliminating the substance, you are taking only a part of the form and making much of a mole-hill. Yes, there are eight kinds of death. To praise one's own self, that is also a kind of death. So you praise yourself, you're so big, so big, so big. And that is a kind of death." Then Arjuna put away his sword.

The purpose is the satisfaction of Kṛṣṇa—the Center, the Absolute good Who is all-conscious and all-knowing, omniscient. His satisfaction, that is the highest criterion of every action, and all other laws are subsidiary to that law. There are so many laws, and so many grades, but the highest point is that all are leading to the satisfaction of Kṛṣṇa. That should be the highest criterion of everything. *Kṛṣṇa sukhataḥ.* He is an autocrat, Absolute, but He is Absolute good. That is the justification. Absolute good is autocratic, and we all are like members of a military camp in relation to the general. There is no other consideration. All law is concentrated in the order of the general, for He knows better than all the soldiers.

We must have our aim fixed towards the higher realm. All must come from there. We cannot waste our energy in any engagement that is considered good or bad from our perspective. This judgement will spring up only from the relativity of this *māyic* world. We must be very careful that when we catch a wave, the wave is coming from the finest plane, not the gross plane. The thought that motivates us, that excites us to act, from which plane does it come? Is it from the higher, finest plane? Can we catch the news of that wave? If we can read the waves of that higher plane, it is all right.

We should always catch the wave coming from that higher plane. That helps us to begin our activity from there and our services will return there, to be recorded in that plane. That will help us qualitatively in a very extraordinary manner. For qualitative improvement we shall disown our present environment, even including the mental sphere. Try to get information from the highest possible plane and then bow down to that, and not to the external environment in consideration of any good or bad.

Guru Is Servant of His Disciples

On one occasion, Prabhupāda Bhaktisiddhānta Sarasvatī delivered a speech to his disciples and friends in which he began by saying, "Oh my friends who are delivering me from great danger." He was addressing his disciples, "You have come to deliver me from great danger. You have come to save me. You are so many extensions of my *guru.* The position of those who come to hear about Kṛṣṇa is not lower than that of the speaker. Your presence is a sign that you have received grace, *sukṛti,* and that you possess love for Kṛṣṇa. You have all come to help me in my way of realizing Kṛṣṇa. You are all my friends and helpers. You have come to rescue me from a dangerous position."

This is how Prabhupāda began his address. How very beautifully, skillfully and harmoniously he presented the philosophy, the ontological aspect, the conclusion. What is the position of *guru*? The *guru* is a servant of the disciple. Externally, the disciples are seen to be servants, but internally we consider the *guru* to be the servant of all his disciples. He tries to make them fit for the service of Kṛṣṇa. The *guru* is serving so many persons so that they may become fit to serve Kṛṣṇa, just as when we go to the temple to clean and arrange things so that it will be acceptable to Kṛṣṇa.

The *guru* goes even further. He says, "I am in danger. You have all come to give me some engagement. You are forcing me to engage in His service by talking about Him. You are helping me engage in the culture of the soul. You are coming to save me.

The knowledge of Kṛṣṇa has no limits; it is infinite. The search for Kṛṣṇa can never be finished, so you cannot rest. You cannot say that you have come so far and now only a few more miles are left before you will finally get Kṛṣṇa once and for all. No, it is not like that! Our search for Kṛṣṇa is like swimming in an unlimited ocean, and you have come to encourage me in my movement toward Kṛṣṇa. You are so many friends who have come to rescue me in this ocean of Kṛṣṇa-love and Kṛṣṇa-knowledge. We are joined together in our search for Him."

Approach Guru through Sraddha

The position of *guru* should not be considered mundane, identified with his mundane appearance. We can get benefit from our relationship with *guru* only through *śraddhā*. Only through *śraddhā* are we able to approach him, no matter what the distance, near or far. Of course, through physical vicinity we can get the chance of hearing from him and witnessing many practical dealings that may help us on our path. Proximity can give us knowledge of Vaiṣṇava *sadācāra*, the proper conduct of a Vaiṣṇava. In this way we can have some sort of conception about these things, but *śraddhā* must be there.

Śraddhā, reverential faith, must be there in either case—physical closeness or distance is not the question. In the lower stage, physical nearness has more efficacy. By the *gurus'* movements, his talks, and from his instructions we learn spiritual etiquette. And many spiritual ideals may also become clear in his company. So physical vicinity will be useful in the lower stage, but *śraddhā* must be there, otherwise we may commit offenses.

Physical nearness devoid of faith may be the cause of offenses against Gurudeva. Sometimes the senior godbrothers may be very helpful in our dealings with Gurudeva when we are beginners. Śrī Gurudeva's conduct may not always be very clear or helpful for us, so in that case some senior godbrother may come to help us and explain his movements and do away with any difference we may see in him.

īśvarāṇāṁ vacaḥ satyaṁ tathaivācaritaṁ kvacit
teṣāṁ yat svavaco yuktaṁ buddhimāṁs tat samācaret

"The instructions of the great personages are always true, but their conduct and their practices may not always be useful to the beginners. So the sober person will accept those practices that are backed by his words, understanding that in his higher stage he may do something which may not be useful to those of a lower stage. He has such spiritual power that what may be seen as a defect in the beginner, cannot harm him in any way. Therefore the fair minded beginners will accept those practices which are in consonance with his instructions, as being useful to their progress." *(Bhāg:* 10.33.31)

We should not imitate but rather we should follow. Not *anukaraṇa* (imitation) but *anusaraṇa* (to follow in the footsteps). We must understand the difference. Faith or *śraddhā* is the first thing that is necessary for us; then we can have our spiritual guide's connection, whether we are near or far from him. It is vital that the connection be in the proper line, independent of gross or subtle influence. The energizing plane that stimulates our enquiry about our own inner welfare, that is part and parcel of the quest.

Brahma-jijñāsā is the quest for the plane of understanding. This has been given in *Vedānta,* and when it comes to Śrīman Mahāprabhu in the line of *Śrīmad Bhāgavatam,* it is developed to *kṛṣṇānusandhāna,* the search for Śrī Kṛṣṇa. *Vedānta* is the flower, and *Śrīmad Bhāgavatam* is the ripe fruit of spiritual knowledge. That which is somewhat mixed with activity, ritual, and knowledge in this plane, is found in the *Veda.* When that flowers in *Vedānta* it becomes purely "Where am I, what am I?" When the fruit is ripe it develops into utility; that is *kṛṣṇānusandhāna.*

Search for Our Heart's Fulfillment

In *Vedānta* the enquiry is about the Infinite environment, where we are particles only, and in *Śrīmad Bhāgavatam,* the nature of inquiry is more developed. *kṛṣṇānusandhāna:* "Who is my Master, who is my Guide, for Whom do I exist?" This is the plane of *Śrīmad Bhāgavatam,* which is madly seeking, "With Whom may I have the fulfillment of life? Where is that Master of my heart? I cannot continue without my Lord." Mahāprabhu came with that: *kṛṣṇānusandhāna,* the ripe fruit of the *Veda* tree, the plane of *Śrīmad Bhāgavatam.*

We are searching everywhere for *rasa,* for satisfaction. We may undertake many different works, but the common factor in all is the quest for satisfaction. Śrīman Mahāprabhu has given us the plane of *Bhāgavatam,* which asks, "Who can satisfy all the thirst within me? Where is my Lord, the fulfillment of my heart?" Real enquiry must be for this only; otherwise inquiry will never stop. When inquiry comes to this stage and we have proper guidance, then gradually we will be taken to Him, our Master.

Who are we searching for, that *rasa,* that happiness, that pleasure? That is our Master, our Guardian, and not our servant. We must not think He has come to satisfy us, with us as masters. He is everything to us, everything for which we are moving this way and that, the goal of our inquiry, or whatever we are doing; He is the center. We are searching for fulfillment, and fulfillment in the highest stage means this: Kṛṣṇa.

Our real search begins only when we come across the *sat-guru,* the *Kṛṣṇa-bhakta.* Earnest enquiry begins there. *Praṇipāt, paripraśna, sevāyā*—we must be conscious that we are to be utilized by Him for Whom we are searching. Only by *sevā,* service, can we be admitted into that higher world. From the very beginning stage onwards, it is *śraddhā* that can lead us to the great plane, the noble plain.

Acquired Taste

jāta-śraddho mat-kathāsu nirviṇṇaḥ sarva-karmasu
veda duḥkhātmakān kāmān parityāge 'py anīśvaraḥ
tato bhajeta māṁ prītaḥ śraddhālur dṛḍha-niścayaḥ
juṣamāṇaś ca tān kāmān duḥkhodarkāṁś ca garhayan

"Developing *śraddhā* in the narrations of My glories, disgusted with all material activities, knowing that all sense enjoyment leads to misery, but still unable to renounce it, My devotees should remain happy and worship Me with great faith and conviction. Even though they sometimes engage in sense enjoyment, My devotees know that all sense gratification leads to unpleasant reactions, and they sincerely repent all such activities. (*Bhāg.* 11.20.27-28)

We become indifferent to all other pursuits, because we can understand that all other activities bear some unpleasant reaction. Yet, although we can conceive that they all produce pain, we cannot free ourselves immediately from their clutches. The debt is already incurred, and our debtors won't allow us to escape. We are in the midst of so many acquisitions. It is not very easy to leave them at once by our own sweet will. Previously, we consciously incurred some obligations, and we cannot abruptly cut off their connection; they won't set us free.

By enduring the trials of all these tribulations, we will stand. We will endure and grow beyond the jurisdiction of these mundane forces. The more pressure comes from the outside, the more firmness we should feel in the necessity of the Lord's help. At that time, we turn our backs to all the pains of this world, and we keep Him in front. We begin to move forward. Whatever happens, we cannot complain. It is in our Master's jurisdiction whether He sees fit for us to undergo these trials or not. But we won't leave our ideal—we cannot. Whatever may come, let it happen, never mind.

Descending Humility

Still, we should reproach ourselves: "What have I done? What have I done? It is rather justice that I should be tormented and troubled in such a way. It is not wrong. Really, just dealings have come to be exercised over me. Why should I have committed this wrong? I entered this wrong alliance, entered into the tribe of the *guṇḍās,* the criminals, for exploitation. The reaction that is coming to me is well deserved and good." We blame ourselves. We do not blame the environment for troubling us, but we see a concentration camp within. We blame our own selves, our own free will and fate.

That becomes the nature of our temperament at that time. We should not look to place the fault on the shoulders of others, but take the whole burden: "Yes, the environment is doing justice to me, the traitor, the ambitious, the oppressor of the environment." When we are in such a state of consciousness, our *bhakti-yoga* or devotional engagement becomes more and more intense. The intensity of our progress accelerates!

proktena bhaktiyogena bhajato māsakṛn muneḥ
kāmā hṛdayyā naśyanti sarve mayi hṛdi sthite

"When intelligent persons engage constantly in worshiping Me through loving devotional service, their hearts become firmly situated in Me. Thus all material desires within the heart are destroyed." (*Bhāg.* 11.20.29)

The Lord says, "With accelerated motion, his intensity towards Me grows. Then, by My appearance, all his internal and external discrepancies are gradually destroyed and evaporated.

When, by such an approach, he reaches My domain, or rather, I come down—extending My existence to his heart—then, at once, everything else disappears".

The Knot of Material Existence is Slashed

bhidyate hṛdaya-granthiś cidyante sarva-saṁśayāḥ
kṣīyante cāsya karmāṇi mayi dṛṣṭe 'khilātmani
(*Bhāg.* 11.20.30)

Then *bhidyate hṛdaya-granthiś*—all the ties and entanglements, corners and angles—they vanish. Crookedness vanishes! We find ourselves in the midst of a straight, plain, graphic, spacious and all-embracing environment. Our atmosphere changes. All the ties of so many attractions to various achievements are at once dissolved. They have no necessity in this land. In a word, they have no value. In this land, our past achievements are meaningless. The emphasis is on who we are and not what we are or were. Where does our identity lie? Today! We have gained entrance here because we longed for service, because we longed for that spiritual identity. Ahead of us may lay certain spiritual achievements; behind us is merely a wasteland. Leave that. Forever.

Hṛdayenābhyanujñāto—(*Manu Saṁhitā* 2.1): internal approval comes to assure us that we have arrived in our own land. *Cidyante sarva-saṁśayāḥ*: there is no room for any doubt. We find that all our hankerings are more than fulfilled here: "I was searching, my whole body was searching."

In the *Vaiṣṇava-padavali*, the Anthology of Vaiṣṇava Songs, there is an expression*: prati aṅga lāge kānde prati aṅga mora.* In the acme of divinity, *mādhurya-rasa,* where Śrīmatī Rādhārāṇī is *Śakti* (the divine potency of the Lord), She says, "My every limb is crying out for the respective limb of My Lord. Not only My self, but every part of My body earnestly aspires for the corresponding part of My Master's body."

Cidyante sarva-saṁśayāḥ, every part bears witness: "Yes, we have reached the destination we were striving for, this is our full-fledged satisfaction. This is our soil, this is our home." Every atom of the body will say it. No trace of any doubt will be found, for there is no longer any room for that. But every atom will find its fulfillment: "This is my home, this is my land. I find the comfort of home."

Kṣīyante cāsya karmāṇi: (The Lord says about his devotees), "And the force of reaction won't come to trouble them, to drag them down or attract them backwards. That too, is severed. *Mayi dṛṣṭe 'khilātmani:* I am the fullest of the full perfection. They can depend on My friendship."

This should be the course of our life, our cherished goal. *Śrīmad Bhāgavatam* tells us this. Home, sweet, sweet home. We are children of that soil. In one word, that is the goal.

Sraddha is More than Calculation

Bhaktisiddhānta Sarasvatī Ṭhākura, an expert astrologer, would calculate certain plans and then go to Śrīla Bhaktivinoda Ṭhākura for advice. Bhaktivinoda Ṭhākura would say something that might be contrary to or not corroborating his calculations. But Bhaktisiddhānta Sarasvatī Ṭhākura would always follow the instructions of Bhaktivinoda Ṭhākura.

He had proper respect. *Śraddhā* is more than calculative truth. Bhaktisiddhānta Sarasvatī Ṭhākura helped to establish that the *viśuddha siddhānta* type of astronomical calculation might be correct in the material sense. But still he did not utilize it. Because Bhaktivinoda Ṭhākura followed the calculation of P. N. Bachi for Ekādaśī, Janmāṣṭamī, and all other things, our Guru Mahārāja has accepted that. But *śraddhā* is truer; the words of the *mahājanas*, the practice of the *mahājanas* are more valuable than human calculation.

The physical truth, the material truth does not have much value. After all it is the very strong, yet false, attitude of the mind. So this truth should not be given greater respect than *ācaran*, the intuitive practices of pure devotees. The intuition of a pure devotee should be given preference over this materially truthful calculation of the ordinary persons.

Faith does not have any connection with the factual 'reality' of this world. It is completely independent, *śraddhāmayoyam loka.* There is a world that is guided only by faith. Faith is everything there and it is of infinite nature, all-accommodating. Everything may be true in the world of faith by the sweet will of the Lord.

Calculation does not have any value there. It is inconclusive and destructive in its ultimate aspect, so it should be rejected. Material knowledge, the materialists that accept it, the fallible calculation of the exploiting souls, these have no value whatsoever. But in the world of the Infinite, faith is the standard, the only standard to move hither and thither, just as the compass is the only guide in the Infinite ocean.

Truth Is Hidden in the Hearts of Great Souls

When sailors cannot see anything, the compass is their only guide. Similarly, we find this statement regarding the world of the Infinite, *svayaṁ samuttīrya suduṣṭaraṁ dyuman bhavārṇavaṁ bhīmam adabhra sauhṛdāḥ.* In the *Bhāgavatam* 10.2.31, it is stated that our only guides, like a compass, are the footsteps of those great personages that have traveled on the way. That should be our only guidance. The way is marked by the holy footsteps of those that have gone to the highest quarter. That is our only guidance, *mahājano yena gataḥ sa panthāḥ.*

Yudiṣṭhira Mahārāja also said, *veda śrutayo vibhinnā nāsau.* The real secret is concealed in the mysterious cave, the hearts of these great souls, *dharmasya tattvaṁ nihitam guhāyāṁ, mahājano yena gataḥ sa panthāḥ.* The footprints of those that are going to the divine world chalk out the broad path. That is our surest guidance. Only they may be reliable guides.

All else may be eliminated because calculation is fallible. All reliable instruction comes from the Absolute Infinite. But any mode of instruction can come from anywhere, at anytime. With this broad view, Vaikuṇṭha means no limitation. We are in a boat, floating on the Infinite ocean. Anything may come to help or hinder.

Good faith, only our optimistic good faith may be our leader, our Gurudeva. *Māyānukulyena navasyate nāmaḥ guru karṇa dhāram. Guru karṇa dhāram*: the *guru* is the guide. In the infinite ocean we have boarded a small boat and the destination is uncertain, inconceivable. But it is conceivable to our Gurudeva. *Guru karṇa dhāram*—we are going with that faith, with sincere faith within. *Mahājana yena gataḥ sa panthāḥ, svayaṁ samuttīrya suduṣṭaraṁ,* it is a horrible ocean with so many waves and so many dangers. Whales, *timiṅgila* monsters, and other things are there; it is full of danger.

Bhāvat padāmbhoruha nāvam atra te nidhāya yātāḥ sad anugraho bhavān. Their footsteps are our only hope. We are to depend on that. Our only relief is that there are so many lighthouses, their footprints, so many lighthouses in the infinite ocean to guide us to that place. We need faith, *śraddhā māyām loka,* hope in the Infinite, Vaikuṇṭha. *Śraddhā* is surcharged with good hope in the Infinite.

Vaikuṇṭha is Infinite, and if we wish to draw the attention of the Infinite to ourselves, the only way is *śraddhā.* By *śraddhā* we can attract the Infinite and nothing else. And when faith gets a definite form through *bhāva,* it comes to be *prema,* love divine. After crossing Vaikuṇṭha we may find the cosmos, the spiritual cosmos and *śraddhā,* the light in the darkness. Only *śraddhā* can guide us when we are traveling in the Infinite. I have heard that this is the way to that place. *Śraddhā* will keep our heart enlivened, hopeful. *Śraddhā śabde—kṛṣṇe bhakti kaile sarva karma*: no risk, no gain; more risk, more gain. *Sarva dharmān parityajya mām ekaṁ śaraṇaṁ vrāja.* "I am everywhere, no room to be afraid at all. Only come to that plane. I am your friend; I am everywhere; I am the all in all, and you are My own." This is our only fare for the journey.

Duty of a Vaisnava

It is the duty of a Vaiṣṇava citizen to work under the guidance of a higher Vaiṣṇava. That should be the duty. The guidance must come from such a high level; such aspiration, the highest plane. This is the conception of Vaiṣṇavism proper. If we can understand, then we shall try to be guided under such a high conception. The dictation should come from above, and then we may hope that we will reach that plane one day.

We shall take up that thread if we have real eagerness for such life, if we consider that this is the highest form of life, the noblest form of life. It is what is found in Vraja. This aspiration will gradually take us there—the earnestness, the taste. That will give us real birth, and gradually take us there.

Laulyaṁ and śraddhā. When *śraddhā* grows, it is considered *laulyaṁ,* spiritual greed. We must want that sincerely. That is the price, our intense desire. Sincere earnest desire, that is the price. By no other price can it be purchased. Yes, we want that. We can't live without it. We cannot live in this plane. If it is possible that there is a nobler plane of life, we must go there. We cannot tolerate this atmosphere where everyone is exploiting each other and the environment. We want to be rid of this plane.

Under the guidance of the *guru* who is in connection with Kṛṣṇa, we should just throw ourselves into His service and carry out His order. The order is coming from Him through *guru* and *sādhu.* We must place ourselves at the disposal of that *śuddha guru,* a *sādhu* who is already in direct connection with Him, who is His agent. We place ourselves at his disposal: whatever he will ask, we will do it—that will be real service.

Therefore, it is said in the *śāstra* that the service of the Vaiṣṇava is better than the direct service of the Lord. If we approach the Lord directly, then we have to imagine or suppose what may be His instruction. Thinking that this must be His order may or may not be correct; it may likely be contaminated, adulterated by our conception. But when service is coming through the real *sādhu,* His agent, then if we can do that, it has a direct connection with Him, a real connection. This brings more improvement than any direct approach.

At present we are in the midst of a particular experience of a world that is unreal, that will soon evaporate. But what we are searching for through the *śāstra* and the *sādhus* is all truth—that plane where Kṛṣṇa lives—our personalities there are in direct connection.

yā niśā sarva-bhūtānāṁ tasyāṁ jāgarti saṁyamī
yasyāṁ jāgrati bhūtāni sā niśā paśyato muneḥ

It is stated in the *Gītā* (2.69) that what is night to one is day to another, and what is day to one is night to another. We are now wakeful only in the calculation of the local and provincial interest of the world. The human conception thrown on the Infinite has different stages. Different types of thinkers thrust their own color upon the environment and live accordingly, thinking that it is all sanctioned. But that is all misconception.

The Absolute has His own conception according to His perception, and we must be converted to that viewpoint. Only our soul can have experience and get membership there, not this material body. The eye and the mind cannot grasp that concept. It is only through our ear that this conception may come to our soul. The soul will be awakened and all the rulings of the mind and senses will evaporate. Then we will get our real spiritual body. It will emerge from our present conscious body and mind.

Everything must be of spiritual order, not an imitation. The *sahajiyā* school tries to find what they have heard about Kṛṣṇa in this mundane plane. In this plane they want to find it, but it is not possible. We have to go there through *sādhana* under the direction of the real *sādhu*.

Revolutionary Preaching

Bhaktivinoda Ṭhākura's writings were mainly very sober, inspiring slow and steady progress. We find in his books that he has not taken many bold steps. That is not recommended there. He recommended mostly the *gṛhastha āśrama*. The *āśrama* of the *tyāgi*, the renounced order, is risky. Bhaktivinoda Ṭhākura shows this throughout all his books; his mood is like that.

But our Guru Mahārāja's movement was revolutionary, not defensive in character. He would accept anyone who had the least attraction for Kṛṣṇa or Mahāprabhu and give them help. So in this mission of his, *sādhu-saṅga*, saintly association, was provided in so many centers. *Sādhu-saṅga* is the most valuable thing that can help us in our progress. He arranged for *sādhu-saṅga* by opening many different centers, where devotees could live and cooperate among themselves and march on. *Sarva dharmān parityajya mām ekaṁ śaraṇaṁ vrāja.* And Svāmī Mahārāja's (Śrīla A. C. Bhaktivedānta Svāmī Prabhupāda) campaign also was risky and revolutionary.

I am of a more conservative nature. It is only the grace, the lofty ideal of Mahāprabhu that has taken me away from my conservative nature. He has taken me away from the strict rules of a *smārta brāhmaṇa* family. I had to absorb many new things. Still, I think that I have joined the vanguard of the rebels.

Śāstra-cakṣusā darśitaḥ—one must have the eye of scripture. It is mentioned in *Manu Saṁhitā* that the animals perceive by their nose, by the scent. The Vedic scholars, spiritual scholars, perceive through the eye of scripture. The king perceives through his ears, which means he relies on agents or informers. And ordinary people perceive things through their eyes.

Those who derive their understanding from scriptural knowledge, they are known as *paṇḍita*. The understanding influenced by the scripture, that is *paṇḍa*. And whoever possesses that understanding, he is *paṇḍita*. The *paṇḍita* should perceive through scripture, through the lens of scripture. A devotee also tries to see things and to deal with them according to the rules and regulations of scripture, not relying merely on prior sentiment or old *saṁskāra*. Mahāprabhu's ideal impressed me very much. By His grace, although born in a very strict *smārta brāhmaṇa* family, I was able to shake off all these things, because my attraction for Mahāprabhu was very intense.

When I first came in contact with the Gauḍīya Maṭha devotees, they said that their conclusions were absolute and that all the advice coming from so many other missions and so many instructors should be rejected. "*Sarva dharmān parityajya*, abandon all else; this is the Absolute Truth, you must accept."

Oh, I thought, how is this possible? They are very proud, puffed-up with pride; these people are all false. But I already knew something, and this *śloka* came to my mind, *chidyante sarva-saṁśayāḥ:* all misgivings are cut to pieces. (*Bhāg.* 1.2.21). Yes, I thought, it is already there, in *Bhāgavatam*. And in the *Upaniṣads* also: *yasmin vijñāte sarvam etaṁ vigñātaṁ bhavanti.*

That is something wonderful. If we understand that, we get everything simultaneously. If we know Kṛṣṇa, we know everything. It is in the *Upaniṣads,* it is in *Śrīmad Bhāgavatam,* and these Gauḍīya Maṭha people were saying this from the same plane. If it is possible for me to come to such a universal plane of knowledge, then this is a wonderful thing. First I came with this objection and then progressed by this process. Gradually I found that it is real, it is possible. What these people said is true, *chidyante sarva samśayāḥ.*

Bhidyate hṛdaya granthiś, the entanglement within us, that will be untied. The universal necessity of our own lives, that will disclose itself. The inner tendency of our hearts is sealed, and it will be broken. It will come out with golden spirit: we are such and such. All doubts will be cleared. *Kṣīyante cāsya karmāṇi.* All necessity for effort to acquire things, that will also be given up. Everything is there. Nothing is to be acquired. Such a plane will be open to us and we shall find that we are residents of that plane of opulence, of the Infinite. It is revolutionary, most revolutionary!

The German scholar Max Mueller wrote about the treasury of India's *Upaniṣads.* He said, "If the whole treasury is distributed to the world, then the whole world will be enriched. But nothing will be lost in the storehouse of India. The whole world will be enriched, but India will still remain as the richest." The whole world may be offered this treasure of the *Upaniṣads* and not a part will be lost. God is also like that, the fulfillment is such. Searching for Him means all these things. It is the fullest aspect.

We cannot imagine what degree of satisfaction there is. How much can we know, how much can we calculate? What degree of satisfaction can we calculate? It is very meager. Our Guru Mahārāja used to give the example of a boy born in a dark prison house. From outside, one gentleman invites him, "Please come, I shall show you the sun." Then that boy who is born in the prison will take one candle to light the way, even though no candle is required to see the sun. That boy from the prison will think, "Am I a fool? Nothing can be seen without the help of a light." But that gentleman will drag him out to see the sun.

By the sun's light we can see everything. Guru Mahārāja used to explain it in this way. Such wonder will come to every soul in bondage that establishes a connection with Brahman, Kṛṣṇa, the proper God conception. All wonderful. *Ātmā parijñānāmayo,* self-effulgent. Kṛṣṇa does not depend on any other thing to make Himself known.

Still there is always a section of people that cannot have any conception of that plane. This is the defect in them. The sun is self-effulgent, but the owls cannot see. So many animals cannot see the light. They must be cured. The sun does not exist for them because they have no suitable eye. To a particular section the question is whether God exists or not. That small section is there and it will always remain blind. But that does not mean that another section cannot see, or that the sun does not exist. It is not like that.

Kṛṣṇa is self-effulgent. He has the power to show Himself to all. *Oṁ ajñāna timirāndhasya jñānāñjana śalākayā cakṣur unmīlitaṁ yena,* the duty of the *guru* is to remove the cataract of ignorance from the eyes. When the cataract is removed, then the eyes can see.

Scientific Progress is Not Progress

It is only deviation from the truth that brings us to the mundane world, cent-percent deviation from the truth. How and where that deviation begins, we do not know. But deviation from the truth has taken us into this false area. Science is only increasing the circumference of the mortal world. It is a world of exploitation and according to Newton, for every action there is an equal and opposite reaction. We must be conscious of this fact. All acquisition here is nothing, like a boomerang it will return to nothing.

Scientific progress is no progress. It is movement in the wrong direction. It is only borrowing. It is not earning real profit at all, but rather it is like taking a loan from nature, and payment will be exacted from us to the last cent. So there is no gain, no profit, just exploitation. Science measures the circumference of the world of exploitation. Everything is objectified. We are wresting power from nature, taking a loan, but the loan must be settled, rest assured. This is not progress.

The first principle of any living entity is to remain alive; that is the first principle, that should be the starting point. In *Bṛhad Āraṇyaka Upaniṣad* 1.3.28, we will find *asato mā sad gamaya, tamaso mā jyotir gamaya, mṛtyor mā amṛtaṁ gamaya.* This should be the primary tendency of our quest. What are these three phases? *Asato mā sad gamaya:* I am transient and I am impermanent; make me eternal. *Tamaso mā jyotir gamaya*: I am ignorant, in nescience; take me from ignorance to knowledge, from darkness unto light. *Mṛtyor ma amṛtaṁ gamaya:* I am in this mortal world, I am unhappy, unsatisfied; take me to the plane of *ānandaṁ,* enjoyment. From sorrow, misery, guide me to a fit life there.

These should be the real principles of life, and any research must begin here only, with these three phases: to save oneself, to save the world, and to remove the darkness. Our research must remove the misery and give the nectar, the sweet, sweet life. *Sac-cid-ānanda: satyaṁ, śivaṁ, sundaraṁ.* This should be the subject matter of our search, the line of our search. All others are false, a wild goose chase.

We are suicidal; this so-called science is suicidal. Atomic researchers will prove very soon that science devours itself. It sucks its own blood. This civilization sucks its own blood and it will feed on its own flesh or the flesh of its friends. Material science means this; it is not knowledge. Real knowledge, vital acquaintance of pure, real knowledge, must absolve us and others, remove darkness, bring light, remove misery, and bring eternal peace. That should be the direction of our attempt, of any attempt.

Strong Preaching

Śrīla Bhaktisiddhānta Sarasvatī Ṭhākura Prabhupāda requested, "Go and speak to the world the message of Śrī Caitanya Mahāprabhu and hear this message yourself also. You yourself hear and speak to the world." That was his plane of thinking; with great earnestness he came to push the divine news into the world. "Don't come back. Go and speak to the world and listen yourself." With so much earnestness he came to preach, not only by speaking, but pushing on with Kṛṣṇa consciousness in any way, by giving an explanation, a lecture, even by quarreling, or going to court.

All possible means should be used and engaged in Kṛṣṇa consciousness. Even the court and the judge must be engaged in talking about Kṛṣṇa. They should be forced to do that if necessary. Approach everywhere with Kṛṣṇa consciousness. Stop all worldly activity. Everywhere the talk of Kṛṣṇa must go on in some form or other.

In his last days in Purī, I told Prabhupāda when I was alone with him, "What you have done for the propaganda of Mahāprabhu, of *Kṛṣṇa-kīrtana*, so far, no *ācārya* has ever done." He asked me, "Do you think like that?" "Yes," I said, "I see the exhibitions, the chanting of the scriptures, lecturing, even going to the court, anywhere and everywhere you try to press on with Kṛṣṇa consciousness at every point. Complete opposition to *māyā*. The *māyic* movement, the flow of *māyā* must be stopped, and Kṛṣṇa consciousness will flow everywhere. With the activity of *māyā* stopped, this will bring Kṛṣṇa consciousness everywhere. That is life."

No importance should be given to the *māyic* world. Even if there is a fire burning, we should not say, "Oh! I shall first put out the fire and then I shall come to join the *Kṛṣṇa-kīrtana*." No! No! No! If the whole world is burnt to ashes, there is no loss. Rather if we are saved by fire from the conception of this material world, we shall be fortunate.

The whole world may be burnt to ashes, but we are not affected in any way. All our necessity is in the holy feet of Kṛṣṇa. With such revolutionary instructions Prabhupāda came out to preach. "Don't lose any time."

"If there is fire I must extinguish it and then I will come to join you in *Kṛṣṇa-kīrtana*." No, no, that is our enemy! The material conception is our enemy! We are souls. And this is our enemy, the *māyic* conception that drags us down to this material conception of life, disease, infirmity, and death. Misconception means death, miscalculation means death. That was Prabhupāda's spirit. Go on with Kṛṣṇa consciousness.

Preaching Requires Organization

Organization is necessary only to spread truth to the people for their benefit. Mere organization has no value in and of itself. When the organization is distributing something healthy to the atmosphere, that organization is to be welcomed. Otherwise, if any organization fails to distribute truth, it goes amiss, it commits suicide, and it fails to do its proper duty. There may be so many political, social, and other organizations—there are many.

We are in a mission, in an organization, under the guidance of the higher realized soul. We can face many dangers. When we preach, we shall have to face so many difficulties. But with the help of the higher guidance, we can fight, we can subdue them, or we can invite them to the higher result. In this way we can give opposition to the opposition.

Preaching means offensive effort; we must attack *māyā*, misconception. At this time we shall not think that we shall give no opposition to the adversary—*sahiṣṇu*, that we shall be very patient. When we are engaged in preaching, we must approach and face opposition and try to overcome it. But if we can't do it by ourselves, we shall invite them to hear from our Gurudeva and be disarmed. In this way we shall go on carrying the orders of the Vaiṣṇava. The local environment may wound us, but our spiritual stamina will increase by following the order of the higher agent. We shall be more benefited through *Vaiṣṇava-sevā*.

Vaiṣṇave pratiṣṭhā, we should not want any popularity among the ordinary public, as they are mostly insane. We want a position in the eye of the masters of my Gurudeva: "Yes, he is an enthusiastic servant; he will prosper." When they look upon us with some affection and encouragement, that will be our capital. Their affection for us, their goodwill, that will be our capital as we pass on our way towards the higher realm.

When we are in a solitary place and are chanting the Name, then of course *tṛṇād api sunīcena*, extreme humility must be strictly observed. But when engaged under an *ācārya* in a preaching campaign, our attitude should be a little different, more like carrying out the order of the higher spiritual general. That will draw more affection and benefit for us from the higher plane, than our solitary *bhajana*.

Real Progress is Soul Progress

We have to give up the undesirable, the body cover. That is not the soul proper. Die to live. Die means give up the ego, and an inner golden self will come out. "Die to live" means to die as we are now. As we are at present, we must die. The old conception of our selves is completely false. We must have a new birth. And then we will find that our real self is in that plane of immortality. Die first. But on the other side is birth, true life. We must first eliminate the lower portion; eliminate all misconceptions of life.

In 1934 or so, during the time of Prabhupāda, I spoke with one gentleman in Kutan. He was a follower of a large mission. They had big, big signboards there for the "Sevā Āśrama," and other things of grand size. But if an auditor went there, they would prove themselves to be bankrupt. They had no capital, only false capital. There was a big signboard, but their capital was a false thing, a hoax. It was neither real wealth nor welfare. They did not have a reality to distribute to the people. They were bogus, *māyāvāda*. They were giving a foul diet to the patients, an unhealthy diet; that was their business.

Where is the patient? The patient is within. The soul is the patient. And they were helping the body, independent of the interest of the soul. Without caring for the interest of the soul, they were serving the body. And with that arbitrary help, the body is going more and more against the interest of the soul.

We generally do not organize help for the *guṇḍās* (robbers). For the students, for the social workers, we organize help, but never for the *guṇḍās* who are misguided. Generally all souls are misguided; they are living the life of the impudent. Giving them indiscriminate help without changing their direction, that is pushing them towards hell. That is not the proper goal, to push towards that side, towards danger. Indiscriminate help in this plane is no help at all.

First one must have *sambandha jñāna*, a good direction, the correct conception of the proper destination. And then help will be of some use. Otherwise, without a proper destination, it is only whimsical. A whimsical push will not help anyone in the way of progress. It is not real progress.

In Madras, one gentleman said to me, "First help the patients and keep the soul and body together. Then you may talk with him about the truth, about Hari, about Kṛṣṇa consciousness. If he dies, to whom will you speak?" I replied, "Suppose there is a famine and I am distributing some food. So many are surrounding me, obtaining this food I am distributing. Someone runs away from that place. Should we stop the food distribution and run after him? Or shall I continue distributing the food to the many? Stopping that distribution, should we run after him? There are so many living souls, and some are dying. So I must not run after the dying to bring them back into the body, stopping my distribution of the nectar to the many. It is like that."

That which they conceive to be truth is actually untruth. And furthermore, the process that they have accepted as the means to help others is also wrong. It is completely wrong. They have no true diagnosis, but they are very busy giving treatment and diet. Diagnosis is the most important thing. What is amiss with us, what should be our best interest, the summum bonum of life—that should be settled first. The question of help will come next. Whether help is available or not, where is the guarantee? How are we to settle what is helpful and what is not helpful?

Progress must proceed in the right direction. And what is that right direction? Maximum exploitation, skillful exploitation, irregular exploitation and regular exploitation, that is *karma*. And renunciation, *jñāna*, is the opposite thing. Exploitation and renunciation—two opposites. But a third direction must be found to conciliate all contradictions.

Reality is something else. *Tad viddhi praṇipātena paripraśnena sevāyā upadekṣyanti te jñānaṁ jñāninas tattva-darśinaḥ* (*Gītā* 4.34).

"Just try to learn the truth by approaching a spiritual master. Inquire from him submissively and render service unto him. The self-realized souls can impart knowledge unto you because they have seen the truth."

Real Dedication

The most important thing is the standard, and that must come from a real plane, not a vitiated plane, an ordinary plane, a vulnerable plane. *Tad viddhi praṇipātena, paripraśnena sevāyā, jñānam, jñāninas tattva-darśinaḥ.* It must come from a plane where these two qualifications exist: *jñāni* and *tattva-darśi,* the conception and also the practical application. Both qualifications must be there to derive the standard of what is right and what is wrong.

Our attitude also should be of such type: *praṇipātena, paripraśnena, sevāyā. Praṇipāt* means to surrender to such knowledge. That is not an ordinary class of knowledge that we can objectify; it is super-subjective. *Praṇipāt,* we must surrender. We want something that is superior to us. We want Him, the Absolute Subject, not an objective thing.

Praṇipāt also means that we are finished with the experience of the world outside. We have no more interest for anything in the plane where we have traveled already. *Praṇipāt,* we offer ourselves exclusively at His altar, and we want to have His grace. In this mood we approach the higher knowledge.

Paripraśna, honest inquiry, is always allowed. But inquire sincerely, not with the inclination to discuss in the mood of *tarka,* argument. All our efforts should be concentrated on understanding in a positive direction, leaving behind the state of doubt or suspicion. With all attention we shall try to understand, because it is coming from a higher plane.

Sevāyā, this is the most important thing. We will not receive that knowledge simply to utilize the experience for our benefit.

That plane won't come to serve this lower plane. We must pledge to serve that plane. With this attitude we approach that plane, that sort of knowledge. We shall serve Him, that higher knowledge, and we won't try to make Him serve our lower plane. That selfish desire won't allow us to enter His domain, the knowledge won't descend. It won't come to serve this lower plane. Rather we shall have the fullest conviction that we must offer ourselves to be utilized by Him, and not that we shall try to utilize the received knowledge in our own way to satisfy any lower purpose. If we receive that knowledge, we must serve.

Praṇipātena, paripraśnena sevāyā: with the *sevātti-vṛtti,* we shall dedicate ourselves to Him, not that He will dedicate Himself to satisfy our lower animal purpose. With this attitude we shall seek the plane of real knowledge, a proper estimation of our environment. *Praṇipāt, paripraśna sevāyā.* This is Vedic culture. It is always imparted only in this process and never by intellectual approach.

Our Prabhupāda used this analogy: the honey is in a bottle, the bottle is sealed, and the bee is trying to lick the honey through the glass. Foolish people may think the bee is licking the honey. Similarly, the intellect cannot approach *ātma,* spirit. It may think that it is capable, but it is not possible. The barrier is there, like a glass. Intellectual achievement is not real achievement of higher knowledge of the higher plane.

Only through faith, through sincerity, through dedication to His agents, can we approach that higher plane. If they admit us, then we can enter that land, that plane of higher living, divine living. *Praṇipāt, paripraśna* and *sevā,* the candidate must have these three qualifications before approaching the Truth. We must approach with humility, sincerity and dedication.

This is mentioned in the *Gītā* many times, and also in the *Bhāgavatam* there is a particular passage, *śābde pare ca niṣṇātaṁ brahmaṇy-upaśamāśrayam.* In the *Veda,* in the *Upaniṣad* also, *guru śrotriyam brahma-niṣṭham. Guruṁ evābhigacchet. Guruṁ eva*: we must approach the spiritual master. *Abhigacchet* means to approach without hesitation. We should go with a clear heart, an honest heart. *Guruṁ evābhigacchet,* with a full heart we must approach him.

In our Prabhupāda's language, we should not purchase a round-trip ticket when approaching the *guru.* He used to say always, "You have come here with your return ticket? Do not come like that. Come for all time." *Sa guruṁ evābhigacchet.* We must say in our hearts, "I have seen; I have full experience of this mortal world. I have nothing to aspire for here. With this clear consciousness, I must go. This is all mortal, no one can live here. No means to live here, no possibility, so I only want to live, and to save myself, my life. I am running to the shelter, the real shelter, with this earnestness." *Abhigacchet, samitpāṇiḥ,* the disciple should bring the necessary materials, we should not trouble the *guru.* With our own resources we should go, *abhigacchet samit-pāṇiḥ śrotriyam brahma-niṣṭham.*

Praṇipāt means to bid adieu to all the experience of the material world. That is the meaning of *praṇipāt.* "I am finished with this place. I have no attraction for any material aspiration. All my hopes may be granted from above; I am finished here. I have taken leave from any sort of prospect from this mundane world. I don't want it. This is finished. I have come with an expectant attitude."

Janma-mṛtyu-jarā-vyādhi-duḥkha doṣānudarśanam. The whole kingdom, the whole material realm may be offered, but we should reject it. We should despise bad association, mortal association, the association with mortality, disease, and all these things. With full attention we have to come to investigate whether it is possible for us to have this hope. *Praṇipāt,* then *paripraśna.* Honest inquiry is allowed; it is not that blind faith will take us anywhere. But our inquiry must be sincere.

Enter the Land of Dedication

The all-important factor is *sevā*—we must want everything for His satisfaction, not our satisfaction. *Sevā* means dedication, the land of dedication; we want to enter into the land of dedication and the land of exploitation takes leave of us. No one can thrive in the land of exploitation. That is a loan. Exploitation means that we are incurring a loan, and we have to repay it. We are bound—for every action there is an equal and opposite reaction. We will devour ourselves; it is suicidal.

Exploiting civilization is suicidal; it must devour itself. It is living on a loan from nature. How proudly they show their heads raised high, but their welfare is all on loan from nature. It is extorted from nature, and the debt must be satisfied to the last cent. Pride and boasting are all negative. No positive contribution comes from this civilization of exploitation. Exploitation must stop. Exploitation means to extort things from others, and that must be repaid. It is a natural law. This civilization is worth nothing.

We must enter into the land of dedication and everything will be preserved. Whatever contribution we shall make will be kept safe. However, we won't draw any benefit, we only shall deposit our contribution. It is there, in the land of dedication, a new land, a land of wonder. We want to enter, to have admission there. Exploitation is hateful in itself, and dedication is the purest of the pure. We want to be residents of that other land. We won't take anything from there, so pure it is. And there the land is gradated.

The gradation of purity is according to its intensity, quality and quantity. In this way, *vicitra,* nature is variegated. And on the highest gradation is spontaneous love and beauty in the kingdom of Kṛṣṇa. The dedication of the *gopīs* is of the highest grade. They are willing to remain eternally in hell in order to remove a little pain, a fictitious pain, Kṛṣṇa's pretended headache. This type of dedication is the highest.

Āśliṣya vā pāda-ratāṁ pinaṣṭu mām adarśanām marma-hatāṁ karotu vā. That kind of love, that sort of attitude—such intense dedication, the acme of dedication—can never make us separate from Kṛṣṇa. What does dedication mean? Dedication manifested in its highest state, that is union in separation. Ostentatiously we may be driven away from Him. But in the heart, our faithfulness is increasing in degree.

If we are punished, still we shall adhere to His service. The connection, the link will become invulnerable. Even by separation, by any sort of punishment, we cannot be detached. This is the highest form of unity seen in the deepest plane. No one can take this thing away from us, if we have a connection of such quality.

Āśliṣya vā pāda-ratāṁ pinaṣṭu mām adarśanām marma-hatāṁ karotu vā. Stage by stage it is going deeper and higher. *Adarśanām marma-hatāṁ karotu vā, yathā tathā vā vidadhātu lampaṭo.* Even what is our right, our rightful claim, may be given to others in front of our eyes. That also cannot detract from our high ideal. When we acquire such a dedicated nature, then we are relieved to that extent. We come within the jurisdiction of Kṛṣṇa's confidence. By dealing in this way, we cannot be separated; we enter the area of highest confidentiality of the Absolute.

When we are free from exploitation and posted in the plane of service, dedication, then hate is eliminated and we embrace everything. Only the spirit of dedication can make it possible to embrace everything. Exploitation has no possibility, and hatred comes from exploitation. Dedication makes everything and everyone our friend. We don't want anything in return, so everything will come to us. We don't want to extort our selfish desires from anything, not even from the environment. *Viśvaṁ pūrṇa-sukhāyate.*

The Māyāvādīs and the renunciants indulge in hatred. But the devotee is just the opposite. *Karmis* exploit, and the *jñānis* hate. The devotee embraces everything, but with reference to the center, to Kṛṣṇa. In the Kṛṣṇa connection, *Kṛṣṇa-sambandha*, everything is embraced. "Oh, he is my friend. I can utilize him in the service of Kṛṣṇa." Sometimes even the flower will remind us, "Oh, take me to Kṛṣṇa."

When we are fully established in the plane of dedication, everything will help us and remind us, "Oh, go to Kṛṣṇa." In an all-friendly atmosphere, all can be acquired. It is full of devotional spirit, the spirit of dedication. Hatred can have no room there. Hatred is in the temperament of the renunciant, *tyāgī-mukti-kāmī*, and not the *bhakta*. *Nirbandhaḥ kṛṣṇa-sambandhe yuktaṁ vairāgyam ucyate.* Since everything is in connection with Kṛṣṇa, how can I hate it?

In the acme of dedication there is only love, Vraja Vṛndāvana *bhāva*. And preaching—preaching is *saṅkīrtana*. Preaching is real service to Kṛṣṇa, and not just counting beads. Service. Because Mahāprabhu and Gurudeva order it, I have to chant the Name, counting the beads. I must do my duty to the *mällika*, the string of beads. "The *mällika* should not fast." That was the word of Prabhupāda.

Active Dedication

The devotional school wants service by dedication, crossing the plane of exploitation and renunciation or indifference; active dedication and service. In the beginning there is the help of scripture and also there is much excitement—that is all grandeur, all power. That is found in the worship of Nārāyaṇa. And later we can understand that love is the real essence of life. Without that love we should not exist. Love is such a precious wealth that we should deny our very life if we do not have that inner wealth, love for Kṛṣṇa, for the Absolute. And His love comes, His beauty comes. Affection, beauty, love, harmony—this is the highest conception ever to come to this world.

Dedication is the foundation of love, the structure of love. Without dedication, no love can stand. The greatest Autocrat and the greatest dedicating agent is Rādhārāṇī, *mahā-bhāva svarūpa.* Rādhikā. Why *Rādhā-dāsyaṁ,* service to Rādhikā? We want to dedicate ourselves, and the highest ideal of dedication is Rādhārāṇī. She is the greatest devotee of the Autocrat Kṛṣṇa. Dedication is seen in its zenith there. Those who achieve Her association in any way, even a slight connection with Her purifies them all. That is the highest wealth.

Mahāprabhu came only to prove to the world the highest dignity of Rādhārāṇī. It is the statement of those who are closely connected with Rādhārāṇī that Mahāprabhu has distributed Her hearts' nectar. He is our greatest benefactor; our canvasser is the most intimate companion of Kṛṣṇa. Gaurāṅga has come to establish in the market that our hearts' wealth is of the highest nature. If He did not come to express this to the world, then how could we live? Our life would have been impossible. If the greatness of our Mistress were not displayed, accorded the highest regard, how could we bear to live?

Beauty, Charm and Sweetness

To attract the ordinary public in our Bombay preaching, we would state that the purpose of our movement was to harmonize *karma, jñāna* and *bhakti.* This was spoken outwardly, announced only to canvass the general public. How is it possible that we want to harmonize *karma, jñāna* and *bhakti*? I said, "Of course the outward appearance may be kept, but in spirit what we are doing is quite a different thing."

Karma means applying effort, not for our sake, but for the

Supreme Lord. *Jñāna* means searching, but searching for what? Not for collective exploitation of nature; nor for Paramātma, nor for Brahman; not even for the Nārāyaṇa conception of the truth. We are not searching for Absolute power, but for Absolute beauty, Absolute love.

Ultimately, by our sacrifice, our surrender, our devotion, we attain *vimucyeta, vimukti, viśeṣa mukti,* the highest type of salvation or emancipation. It is a positive attainment, not just the end of the negative conception. Only to get out of the negative side is not real emancipation or liberation. To enter into the positive safest position, that is our real interest.

Designations (*upādhis*) have been thrust on us, *sarvopādhi vinir muktaṁ tat-paratvena nirmalam. Anyathā rūpaṁ,* that which is just like a disease—an undesirable foreign thing has come to cover me. That is *upādhi.* That is *anyathā rūpaṁ* . Successfully eliminating that, we must come to our positive and proper position in the world of love and beauty. It is a very important thing that power is not the ultimate controller; beauty is. The control of beauty is very sweet, normal and natural.

Power, awe, reverence, grandeur, these all become stale in light of the *Bhāgavatam*'s Kṛṣṇa conception of Godhead. The Nārāyaṇa conception has become stale, so to say. Beauty, love and harmony are the highest goal ever discovered. Śrī Caitanyadeva gave us that, Vṛndāvana has given us that, and this is Kṛṣṇa consciousness. Our Guru Mahārāja and Svāmī Mahārāja have given to the wide world this Kṛṣṇa conception, the conception of beauty, harmony, love. It is original, the universal cause, this conception of the Absolute, not anything else.

With this fundamental conception we may find relief. We may feel that we are out of danger; we are no longer the victims of power. The power in Vaikuṇṭha, the grandeur, awe, reverence, that may not be an inner hankering of any substance. Beauty is a hopeful assurance of our highest position; it is charming.

Bhaktivinoda Ṭhākura predicted that when the world's scholars understand the worth of that which has been given by Śrī Caitanyadeva, then all religion must vanish. It cannot stand. When the conception of the Absolute is identified with beauty and love, all sorts of different conceptions cannot stand in competition. All will embrace it: "I want beauty, Ultimate beauty, Ultimate harmony, Ultimate love, loving each other. If that is possible, then I don't want any other proposal." We must run in that direction; the general indication will take us.

All other religious conceptions are compelled to vanish. When viewed with the divine eye, the eye of divine knowledge, all other conceptions cannot appeal to the highest class of thinkers. *Pṛthivīte āche yata nagarādi grāma, sarvatra pracāra haibe mora nāma,* "In every town and village on this earth the glories of My name will be chanted." This is not a mere declaration by Mahāprabhu. There is an intellectual as well as an intuitive foundation to this prediction.

Part Two

Follow the Angels

Follow the Angels

What is the substance of my inner search, my innermost search? At last I have come to that. Gaurāṅga has given the fulfillment of my innermost demand. He is mine. Without Him, no one should have any conception of life. The greatest thing is here, and if I cannot have it, what is my life worth? I would be better to die; I should have died long ago. If I cannot come in contact with such a valuable thing in this life, I would rather die. *Janmiyā se kene nāhi maila,* I should have died at birth, if I cannot come to my eternal prospect, my inner fulfillment.

pāiyā mānuṣa janma, ye nā śune gaura-guṇa,
hena janma tāra vyartha haila
pāiyā amṛtadhunī, piye viṣa-garta-pāni
janmiyā se kene nāhi maila

"Anyone who attains a human body but does not take to the cult of Śrī Caitanya Mahāprabhu is baffled in his opportunity. *Amṛtadhunī* is a flowing river of the sweet nectar of devotional service. If after getting a human body one drinks the water in a poison pit of material happiness instead of the water of such a river, it would be better for him to have not lived, but to have died long ago." (*C.c. Adi-līlā* 13.123)

kṛṣṇa-līlā amṛta-sāra, tāra śata śata dhāra
daśa-dike vahe yāhā haite
se caitanya-līlā haya, sarovara akṣaya
mano-haṁsa carāha tāhāte

"The pastimes of Kṛṣṇa are the quintessence of all divine nectar, and *Caitanya-līlā* is an inexhaustible lake of that nectar which, flowing in hundreds of streams, floods the hearts of the devotees in all directions. Therefore, O nectar-seeking friend, please let your mind swim in that lake like a regal swan." (*C.c. Madhya-līlā* 25.271)

These two scriptural references reveal the extraordinarily wonderful characteristic of our goal in Kṛṣṇa. Our goal in Kṛṣṇa is of such extraordinary nature. The devotees give descriptions in different ways, but without that goal one should not live.

The wholesale dealer selects the choicest commodities for promotion when approaching new customers. The proprietor is astonished by the choice. He says, "You have presented well these most valuable things of Mine. I was not even conscious that such things were Mine! You have taken so many refined things from My storehouse. Were they in My store? Your choice makes Me more valuable, infinitely more valuable. You have found such beautiful things of Mine. I cannot but feel proud. By your touch, by your connection, these beautiful things have been discovered in Me."

Kṛṣṇa's obligation towards Rādhārāṇī, the wholesale dealer, is such. Partial dealers come from different groups, but Rādhārāṇī is the wholesale dealer of all commodities available in Kṛṣṇa's store. *Na pāraye 'haṁ niravadya-saṁyujāṁ (Bhāg. 10.32.22)*. Even Kṛṣṇa Himself cannot measure the greatness of Rādhārāṇī.

In Kṛṣṇa's pastimes, the potencies are *sandhinī, saṁvit,* and *hlādinī. Hlādinī* holds the highest position, because of complete self-surrender. Next is *saṁvit,* and then third is the position of *sandhinī.* Thinking, feeling, and willing; willing is *sandhinī,* thinking is *saṁvit,* and feeling is *hlādinī.* Ordinarily we may think that feeling is the last of all, but no, it is the first.

Feeling is first. Feeling, real feeling, has been given such a high position. Feeling controls us all. We are all searching, and feeling commands us. We think feeling is the result. No, feeling commands everything. First feeling, then thinking, then willing. Generally the *karmis,* the fruitive workers, give the upper hand to willing, to willpower, and the *jñānis* concentrate on thinking. "We command the will, so we hold the high position." But feeling is the basis of everything—controlling everything. That is so; we have to understand the position of feeling.

Do Not Approach Directly

Our Guru Mahārāja, Śrīla Bhaktisiddhānta Sarasvatī Gosvāmī Prabhupāda, asked that we keep Rādhārāṇī in great reverence, "On your head, over your head—don't be bold enough to approach directly: *Pūjala rāga-pātha gaurava-bhaṅge.* Try to keep Her and Her group at a respectful distance, above your head. Don't rush towards that position. It is not that cheap." How valuable They are for those situated in *rāga-mārga,* who worship Kṛṣṇa in this way, the way of love!

In His deep trance, Mahāprabhu experienced *Vraja-līlā* and expressed His ecstatic feelings. The *sahajiyās* try to imitate these things by their mundane mind; they attempt to experience that *līlā* through their imagination. But that is not possible. If there is any imitation, only offenses will be created. Those offenses will be recorded in the circle of the examiners of the upper quarter, and they will give a stamp of disqualification: the imitators are criminal and unfit.

Imitation will be held against us and hamper our future progress. We must be very careful not to commit offenses, *aparādha.* It is better to be a newcomer with a fresh introduction than to have a criminal record. We must be very, very careful in our quest for the highest objective of our eternal life. Our Guru Mahārāja, Śrīla Bhaktisiddhānta Sarasvatī Ṭhākura, has especially given this caution, and he attracted us to the line of exclusive devotion.

Mahāprabhu has distributed what He experienced in His deep trance. But we must be ready to pay for it, and our Guru Mahārāja came for that purpose. *Pūjala rāga-pātha*—don't go hurriedly. Fools rush in where angels fear to tread. That experience is for the highest minded. It is the highest. One must go step by step. If we omit any step, we will be nowhere.

We should be mindful of every step, and automatically that will take us in the right direction. Don't ever try to run very hurriedly. Try to remain a little down and back. That will forcibly take you to the goal, naturally. The higher Vaiṣṇavas will take you there. You can't go there on your own, *yam evaiṣa vṛṇute tena labhyas.* That is true all the way, *yam evaiṣa vṛṇute tena labhyas.* Your acceptance will come from the higher quarter. You should go, but don't try to trespass. Otherwise you are gone, finished.

Prema-sevā, loving service, is not an ordinary thing, a mechanical thing. Don't try to finish it, to limit it; it is of an unlimited nature. Don't rush to enter there, to trespass. Don't commit offenses. This is the highest prospect of your life after many lifetimes. The center of the Infinite is everywhere; the circumference is nowhere. Don't create a circumference around the center of your highest prospect.

My Ideal Is Always to Serve Him

Raghunātha Dāsa Gosvāmī, who holds the highest position of *mādhurya-rasa prayojana ācārya,* says *dāsyāya me raso'stu raso'stu satyam, sakhyāya me mama namo'stu namo'stu nityaṁ.* What does it mean? Fools rush in where angels fear to tread. Is that plane an intellectual field about which we can reflect or remark in any way we like, in our own fashion? Dāsa Gosvāmī, who is situated in the highest position of the *prayojana-tattva,* the preceptor of *prayojana* in *mādhurya-rasa rādhā-dāsya,* says: "I'll try to show my reverence to the *sakhya,* but I crave in real earnestness for *dāsya-rasa.* Rādhārāṇī Herself wants me to serve always. Because Kṛṣṇa wishes to enjoy me, He enjoys. But my mark, my ideal is always to serve Him."

In *mādhurya-rasa,* the highest conjugal relationship, even Rādhārāṇī's own tendency is always to serve Kṛṣṇa. Her inclination is towards *dāsya-rasa,* service. Is *sakhya-rasa,* intimate friendship with Kṛṣṇa, a very small thing? No, it is too high for me. *Pūjala rāga-pātha gaurava-bhaṅge.* From a distance I want to show my respect to *sakhya-rasa,* but I really crave *dāsya-rasa.* That should be the inclination of a real devotee. If we disregard all these things, we are playing like children.

Do Not Discuss Higher Lilas

We are not to enter into the discussion of the higher and subtle aspects of the *līlā* of Rādhā-Kṛṣṇa. That is not to be discussed in public. That is the distinction between the Gauḍīya Maṭha and the *sahajiyā* section. The *sahajiyās* are trying to imitate all these things, but we have no faith in imitation. The higher *līlā* will come personally, and it will awaken in an irresistible way. When the program of the *sādhana* stage is finished, it will come automatically, spontaneously. It is not that we will know the form first and then we will reach there. That is not the policy accepted by Guru Mahārāja, Prabhupāda.

Pūjala rāga-pātha gaurava-bhaṅge, that is always upon our head. The prospect of our life's future, life after life, cannot be finished so easily. We shall rather foster the hope, the pure hope that we may be taken one day into that service camp with this idea: *Pūjala rāga-pātha gaurava-bhaṅge.* It is very sweet. The *rāga-pātha,* the path of spontaneous devotion, is above our heads. We are servants of the *rāga-pātha.* We are in *viddhi-mārga,* the path of regulated practice, under *śāstric* rule. We must live and move under *śāstric* rule, and always keep the *rāga-pātha* above our head. *Pūjala rāga-pātha gaurava-bhaṅge.*

The whole tenor of Guru Mahārāja's life was such: "That is high, very high, and from below we are to honor that." We must establish this conception, the proper regard for that higher *līlā,* throughout the entire world: "That is too high."

Preach the Basics

There are many attractive things below that highest *līlā.* The charm and reasonableness of the higher plane are enough to convince a person to come to this side. These *līlās* should be left high above our heads. We are to handle all this *līlā,* especially *mādhurya-līlā,* very cautiously.

Once Prabhupāda arranged to preach in Vṛndāvana for the full month of Kārttika. He asked Bhāratī Mahārāja at that time to explain the Seventh Canto of *Śrīmad Bhāgavatam,* the story of Prahlāda. He did not ask for narrations about Kṛṣṇa, Rādhā, Yaśodā or anything of Vṛndāvana. "Preach *śuddha-bhakti* of Prahlāda first. People are ripe in *sahajiyā,* imitation of devotion. Just try to make them understand, to enter the plane of *bhakti.* That is great; what to speak of *Kṛṣṇa-līlā*—that is far, far above." There in Vṛndāvana the people wondered, "What is this? They are explaining *Bhāgavatam,* but leaving aside the Tenth Canto. They are explaining the Seventh Canto, the *Prahlāda-līlā,* the lower portion of *bhakti*. That is wonderful and strange."

I found later on that Śrīla Prabhupāda himself spoke for several days on the boundary line between Rādhā Kuṇḍa and Śyāma Kuṇḍa. He read and explained the *Upadeśāmṛta* of Śrīla Rūpa Gosvāmī. He did not speak about Śrīmatī Rādhārāṇī or about Kṛṣṇa, but about *Upadeśāmṛta*—the basic teachings. His attention was always focused on the basics, because the fruit will come naturally. "Pour water onto the root and the fruit will come up by itself."

Sitting between Rādhā Kuṇḍa and Śyāma Kuṇḍa he explained not *Bhāgavatam*, but *Upadeśāmṛta*. *Upadeśāmṛta* contains the substance of Mahāprabhu's teaching in the language of Rūpa Gosvāmī. Śrīla Prabhupāda explained these topics and not anything of *Govinda-līlāmṛtaṁ* or Viśvanātha Cakravarti's *Śrī Kṛṣṇa Bhāvanāmṛta*. The higher topics of *mādhurya līlā*, Rādhā Kṛṣṇa's amorous pastimes, were left aside.

Intimate Connection is Rejected

Once a certain gentleman wanted to discuss these intimate *līlās* with Prabhupāda. Previously he did a great deal of service to the mission, but he laid much stress on those higher topics, and ultimately he left the association of Prabhupāda and lived a secluded life. He was a man, but superficially assuming the identity of a *gopī* he wanted to enjoy an intimate connection with Kṛṣṇa. He wanted this intensely, but Prabhupāda remarked disapprovingly, "Oh, he has turned into a lady, a *gopī*, and after coming in contact with Kṛṣṇa she produced a child!"

Not To Live at Radha Kunda

Pūjala rāga-pātha gaurava-bhaṅge. Prabhupāda instructed that we must not go to live in Rādhā Kuṇḍa, the most sacred place of pilgrimage. One day near Lalitā Kuṇḍa, where there was a single-story building at Svānanda Sukhaṇḍa Kuñja, he said, "A second story is necessary, but I will not be able to live there." I asked, "If you will not live on the first floor, who will live there? What is the necessity of further construction?"

"No. You don't know. Better persons will live there: Bhaktivinoda Ṭhākura, Gaura Kiśora Bābāji Mahārāja. They will live there, and we shall stay on the ground floor and we shall serve them." Again he said, "I shall live in Govardhana. Rādhā Kuṇḍa is the highest place, the place of our Guru Mahārāja, our Gurudevas. They will live here in closer connection with *līlā*, but we are not fit to live there. We shall live in Govardhana, just a little far away. Because we shall have to come and serve our Gurudevas, we must be near, but we must not live in closer connection with them. We are not fit."

Not to Interfere with the Higher Lilas

Our master did not allow us to read the books where the higher *līlās* are described: *Govinda-līlāmrtaṁ, Stava-kusumañjali, Ujjvala-nilamaṇi*. He did not allow us to study and to discuss them. Rather, he would be very much disturbed if he heard that someone was interfering with the higher *līlās* in those books. He did not like it.

There are three chapters of *Śrī Caitanya Caritāmṛta* that we were generally not allowed to discuss fully, including the conversations with Rāmānanda Rāya. Where the *līlā* portion of Rādhā-Govinda is mentioned, we were not to delve. Of course when *pārāyaṇa* (consecutive chanting of the whole book) was taking place, we were to go on reading those sections, but without giving any particular attention to the *līlā* of the highest order of *rāga*. That was barred: "Don't try to come into details there. That will come automatically when it is time. Do not make it a public discussion. Do not place it in the public eye."

Duṣṭa phala karibe arjjana—Śrīla Bhaktivinoda Ṭhākura warns that we will get only a bad result if we venture to cross that line. It is *aparādha*. From the lower position, the steps are shown: *śraddhā, sādhu-saṅga, śravana, kīrtana,* then *anartha-nivṛtti,* when the undesirable things vanish. Then comes *ruci,* then *āsakti,* then *bhāva-bhakti,* the sprout of real devotion. Then *prema-bhakti,* and *sneha, māna, praṇāya, rāga, anurāga, bhāva, mahābhāva*—by such steps we are to approach the highest plane.

Not to Listen to Rasa-Lila Katha

The following incident in Vṛndāvana indicates how strongly he felt in this way. Prabhupāda had a friend there from his childhood, an attorney, who came to see him, so Prabhupāda went to return the visit to this friend from his boyhood. Śrīpāda Paramahaṁsa Mahārāja was with Prabhupāda and they went together. They were told, "He is upstairs." They went there and saw that a *Gosvāmī* was explaining the *Rasa-līlā* section of *Śrīmad Bhāgavatam*. Prabhupāda just bowed down his head and came away. Immediately he came away.

His friend also came down, leaving that *Rasa-līlā* discussion, and said, "The *Rasa-līlā* explanation is going on, but you did not take your seat at all. You just bowed your head and came down. What is the matter?" Śrīla Prabhupāda replied, "Our *guru's* order is that it will be offensive to attend the *Rasa-līlā* discussion, so I had to come down. This is my *guru's* order: to attend *Rasa-līlā* explanation is *aparādha*."

We have no right to attempt to hear. We are not qualified. We shall commit offense thinking that Kṛṣṇa is a man like us, and these *gopīs* are so many women, and they are performing this debauchery. This idea will appear in the mind. It will replicate in our heart and we will have to go down. Therefore, we must not attend those discussions.

Rasa-līlā should not be used to capture people by their lust. It is tempting to distribute that *līlā*—we like it so much—but it is misguided. For canvassing we should not use the highest and most valuable gem. We must not show it in the market to capture attraction. An ordinary gem may be taken to exhibit in public. Anyone and everyone are not qualified to discuss *Rasa-līlā.*

Follow the Will of Our Gurudeva

Prabhupāda has ordered such strict behavior, and we also follow that. At so many other places they show the *Rasa-līlā* with dolls, but I never do that. Following what is true to my understanding of my Gurudeva's will and his words, I do not make any show of *Jhulana-līlā* or *Rasa-līlā* or anything of that nature. I find in my heart that this is not pleasing to my Guru Mahārāja. But in so many Maṭhas I see at present, I hear also, that they are doing that, but I strictly abstain from showing *Jhulana-līlā* and *Rasa-līlā.* That is too high for us.

I must be true to the words of my Gurudeva if I want my realization and not just some sort of popularity. Some may discuss the higher *līlās* to attract people, to make money, or even to develop a favorable field for preaching, but I do not do this. I do not want popularity or any recognition as a higher *ācārya.* I am a student.

Still I am a student. I consider myself to be a student, a faithful student. What I heard from my Gurudeva, I try my best to stick to that, to keep my position there as I heard from him. I do not want to mutilate that in any way to suit my purpose. I try not to do that. Of course for big propaganda some may adopt different ways, as they see fit. They are now free. But I am not one to do so, to go on in such a way. I try to follow my Guru Mahārāja, Śrīla Prabhupāda.

Guru Mahārāja, Śrīla Bhaktisiddhānta Sarasvatī Ṭhākura,

preached exclusively this *mādhurya-rasa,* but with great precaution. He used perhaps 90% of his energy to point out the negative side, the imitation—"This is not *mādhurya-rasa*"—and clear away these *sahajiyā* misconceptions. He had to spare, in his words, 'gallons of blood' to establish what is not that *mādhurya-rasa.*

Smarana Subservient to Kirtana

Some *ācāryas* are of the opinion that *smaraṇa,* internal remembrance, is more important than *kīrtana* (chanting), because *smaraṇa* is exclusively connected with consciousness, or is more concerned with the subtle part of our existence. They feel that *smaraṇa* is the most effective form of *sādhana,* or means to the end. But our Guru Mahārāja and Śrīla Jīva Gosvāmī, and also Kavirāja Gosvāmī Prabhu, laid stress on *kīrtana*—especially for beginners. Guru Mahārāja says in his song *Vaiṣṇava ke* (Who is a Vaiṣṇava?):

kīrtana prabhāve, smaraṇa haibe,
se kāle bhajana nirjana sambhāva

"Internal remembrance can occur by the power of *kīrtana,* and only then is solitary service possible." *Nirjana-bhajana* or *smaraṇa,* exclusive solitary devotion unconscious of the environment is not at all possible for beginners. Śrīla Jīva Gosvāmī says:

yadyapy-anyā bhaktiḥ kalau kartavyā
tadā kīrtanākhya-bhakti-saṁyogenaiva.

"In this Kali-yuga, of the nine basic forms of devotional practice, the forms other than *kīrtana* certainly should be practiced, but they must be conducted subserviently to *kīrtana.*" (*Bhakti-sandarbha, saṅkhya* 273) This is the principle of Mahāprabhu's preaching. *Kīrtana* has its own special characteristic, particularly in Kali-yuga.

kaler doṣa-nidhe rājan asti hy-eko mahān guṇaḥ
kīrtanād eva kṛṣṇasya mukta-saṅgaḥ paraṁ vrajet

[Śrī Śukadeva Gosvāmī said] "O King, the age of Kali, the repository of all evils, has but one glorious characteristic. In this age, those who simply chant the Holy Name of Kṛṣṇa are liberated and reach the Supreme Lord." (*Bhāg.* 12.3.51)

Also, Śrīla Madhvācārya has written in his commentary on *Muṇḍakopaniṣad*:

dvāparīyair janair viṣṇuḥ pañcarātraiś ca kevalam
kalau tu nāma-mātreṇa pūjyate bhagavān hariḥ

"In Dvāpara-yuga, Lord Viṣṇu is exclusively worshiped by the people according to the principles of Deity worship delineated in the *Pañcarātra* scripture, but in Kali-yuga, the Supreme Lord Hari is worshiped only by the chanting of His Holy Name."

In the *Śrīmad Bhāgavatam,* when the incarnation of Śrī Caitanya Mahāprabhu is mentioned (*Bhāg.* 11.5.32), the method by which the people will worship Him is also given: *yajñaiḥ saṅkīrtana-prāyair yajanti hi sumedhasaḥ.* Here, *yajñaḥ* means sacrifice, dedication, which is *saṅkīrtana-prāya,* or *saṅkīrtana-pradhāna,* which means 'predominated by *saṅkīrtana,* the congregational chanting of the Holy Name.' Those endowed with sufficient piety perform this *kīrtana.* So, in this age of iron, *kīrtana* has its own special privilege, granted by the Supreme Lord—Mahāprabhu's specialty is preaching, *kīrtana.* He inaugurated and conducted *Hari-kīrtana.*

Our Guru Mahārāja, Śrīla Jīva Gosvāmī, and others have accepted *kīrtana.* To write about the Lord is also within the jurisdiction of *kīrtana.* To preach is to assert, to take the message to others. To engage in answering the questions of the environment automatically demands concentration, which is very rare in this age. When doing *kīrtana*, one automatically cannot but give all concentration and attention. One cannot speak independently; intuitively, one must be completely attentive. For this reason, *kīrtana* is recommended as the highest form of *bhajana*, especially in the age of Kali.

bhajanera madhye śreṣṭha nava-vidhā bhakti
'kṛṣṇa-prema,' 'kṛṣṇa' dite dhare mahā-śakti
tāra madhye sarva-śreṣṭha nāma-saṅkīrtana
niraparādhe nāma laile pāya prema-dhana

"Of all forms of Divine Service, nine forms are superior, for with great potency they bestow upon the devotees love for Kṛṣṇa, and their personal relationship with Him. Of the nine, the best is *Nāma-saṅkīrtana*. By offenselessly taking the Holy Name, the treasure of love for the Lord is attained." (*C.c. Antya-līlā* 4.70,71)

Mahāprabhu accepted five principal limbs from the nine that are mentioned in the *Bhāgavatam*:

sādhu-saṅga, nāma-kīrtana, bhāgavata-śravaṇa
mathurā-vāsa, śrī-mūrtira śraddhāya sevāna

"Association with the pure devotee, chanting the Holy Name, hearing the *Śrīmad Bhāgavatam*, residing in Mathurā-dhāma, and faithfully worshiping the Deity." (*C.c. Madhya-līlā* 22.128)

Of these five, Mahāprabhu has given *Nāma-saṅkīrtana* the highest position. *Nāma-saṅkīrtana* is considered best of all—designated as such by the *ācāryas*. Our Guru Mahārāja especially promoted *kīrtana*, as indicated by *śāstra*, the scriptures. But if other *ācāryas* have shown preference for *smaraṇa* in any instance, it is in the sense that *kīrtana* may be performed within the material environment, whereas *smaraṇa* is independent of any material consideration. From this point of view, *smaraṇa* may be deemed "higher," but that is not accepted in a general way. It is a special opinion.

In *Caitanya-śikṣāmṛta*, Śrīla Bhaktivinoda Ṭhākura clarified that there are two types of devotees in the stage just prior to attaining the highest plane of *Paramahaṁsa* or *uttama-adhikārī*. The devotees who cross the middle stage (*madhyama-adhikārī*) and reach towards the highest position are called devotees in the stage of *premaruruksu*. They are classified in two divisions: *goṣṭhyānandi* and *viviktānandi* (or *bhajanānandi*). The first are always engaged in preaching, and the latter take to *smaraṇa* or *nirjana-bhajana*, a solitary life of worship, without mixing with the environment.

One is not superior to the other. The *viviktānandis* generally like secluded life and practice *smaraṇa*. Those who are of the *goṣṭhyānandi* type perform *kīrtana*, preaching, and attain the highest position without the need to practice exclusive *smaraṇa*. Those who have attained the highest plane are known as *premārūḍha*.

Imaginary Perfection is Self-deception

Guru Mahārāja clearly said that when we are in a lower position, *smaraṇa* is injurious. Rather, we should take to *kīrtana*. *Kīrtana prabhave, smaraṇa haibe, se kale bhajana nirjjana sambhāva*. *Sahajiyās* (members of the imitationist school) are fonder of *smaraṇa* than *kīrtana*. They are 'followers' of *smaraṇa*. They lead a secluded life, and mentally they attempt to identify themselves with a particular *sakhī* of their own age. They pretend to perform her duties, to occupy her place of service in a particular place of Vṛndāvana, in a particular *līlā*, under the guidance of a particular *sakhī*, and so on. They are required to meditate on all these things by their so-called *guru*.

That is the process amongst the *Sahajiyā* school, but we do not accept that. We consider it all false and imaginary. They are not fit for the plane. They do not have real *sambandha-jñāna*, knowledge of Reality. They only practice the habitual repetition of a particular mental speculation, but *anartha-nivṛtti* (removal of contamination) or any other process based on it cannot be effected thereby. Their imagined achievement is sheer concoction. They are not aware of the facts—the ontological gradation from Virajā to Brahmaloka, Vaikuṇṭha and Goloka. They are *pukūra-curiwāle:* pond thieves—imagining their residence at Rādhā Kuṇḍa. To think one can steal a pond is self-deception. We consider that kind of '*smaraṇa*' to be self-deception.

The Death Blow to the Sahajiyas

The *Sahajiyās* propagate that without directly receiving *siddha-prāṇālī* (revelation of one's internal identity as a *gopī*) spiritual perfection is incomplete. Let them do so. Our Guru Mahārāja wrote several poems, one of which is *Prākṛta-rasa Śata-dūṣanī*, 'A Hundred Defects in the *Sahajiyā* Conception.' The defects are innumerable, but our Guru Mahārāja put forward a hundred of the defects in their process of 'advancement.' Mainly they take spiritual advancement very cheaply; they are not prepared to pay the real price. But the death blow to them is this:

upajiyā bāḍe latā 'brahmāṇḍa' bhedi' yāya
'virajā,' brahmaloka, ' bhedi' 'paravyoma' pāya
tabe yāya tad upari 'goloka-vṛndāvana'
'kṛṣṇa-caraṇa'-kalpa-vṛkṣe kare ārohaṇa

"As one waters the devotional creeper, the seed sprouts, and it gradually grows until it penetrates the walls of this material universe and goes beyond the Virajā River, which divides the spiritual world and the material world. It attains *brahma-loka,* and then reaches the *paravyoma,* the spiritual sky, and then reaches the foremost spiritual planet Goloka Vṛndāvana. Rooted in the heart and watered by *śravaṇa-kīrtana,* the *bhakti* creeper grows until it attains the shelter of the desire tree of the lotus feet of Kṛṣṇa in the topmost region of the spiritual sky." (*C.c. Madhya-līlā* 19.153-4)

One must first cross the different gross and subtle layers of the *brahmāṇḍa* (mundane universe); then Virajā, the extremity of the jurisdiction of Māyā, or misconception; then the Brahman conception, the halo of the real or transcendental world; then, Vaikuṇṭha, which is *Paravyoma,* a sphere of consciousness.

The *jīva* comes from *taṭasthāloka,* the marginal position or the abscissa, and must go through higher planes where even the soil is more valuable than the infinitesimal spirit soul. *Vaikuṇṭhera pṛthivy-ādi sakala cinmaya.* What is Vaikuṇṭha? There the soil, earth, water, everything is of purer consciousness than the person who is going to enter there.

Entering the Land of Gurus

It is a land of *gurus*. There, they are all *guru,* they are all of superior value by nature; yet, we have to pass over them. As an example, consider that it may be necessary for our service to momentarily place a foot on the throne of the Lord (perhaps to place His crown on His head, etc.). But afterwards we come back down, offer our obeisances, and then come out from the Deity room.

In the same manner we must enter and remain in a soil that is made of a stuff more valuable than our own selves. When serving the emperor, a slave may come near his bed, where even his near and dear cannot go, or hesitate to go. The slave can approach, but only for service. So it is only for the divine service, for the necessity of the Highest, that we can pass through that soil. It is not an easy thing; it is inconceivable. Fools rush in where angels fear to tread.

Vaikuṇṭhera pṛthivy-ādi sakala cinmaya. We must understand the conception properly. The *jīva* has emerged from the *taṭasthā-śakti* or marginal potency. He is a part of the marginal potency, and he must enter the higher plane. This gross world is of gross potency, *apara-śakti;* the *jīva,* although marginal, is of a potency superior to this gross world, or *para-śakti.* Above both is the Internal Potency, or *antaraṅga-śakti.* We have to enter the plane of *antaraṅga-śakti.* This marginal potency is to enter the plane of *antaraṅga-śakti*—Paravyoma, and the highest quarter, Vṛndāvana, Goloka. It is not a trivial matter.

Cheap Imitators and Pseudo Devotees

Śrīla Gaura Kiśora Bābāji Mahārāja practiced *smaraṇa* in a hut near the Ganges. Another Bābāji constructed a *kuṭīra* nearby, a small hut, and went on imitating Gaura Kiśora Bābāji, performing *madhukāri* (subsisting on alms), sitting and meditating, and wearing similar cloth. Bābāji remarked, "If a lady enters into a maternity ward, she cannot produce a child only by imitating the sounds and symptoms of labor. Many things are necessary before that!" Only by imitating the *paramahaṁsa bābāji, bhajana* cannot be practiced. One must have a connection with *śuddha-sattva,* the real plane, and then all the higher symptoms may appear. Otherwise, only speculative antics will manifest.

nā uṭhiyā vṛkṣopari, ṭānāṭāni phala dhari'
duṣṭa-phala karile arjana

Śrīla Bhaktivinoda Ṭhākura asks in *Kalyāṇa-kalpataru, Upadeśa* 18: "If one wants fruits without taking the trouble to climb the tree, what sort of fruits can one expect?" The fruits will be ruined, or rotten. Without proper progression, it is all imagination, a madman's feat. One must gradually reach the plane of truth, *śuddha-sattva*. There are so many planes to cross: Bhūr, Bhuvar, Svar, Mahar, Janar, Tapar, Satya-loka, Virajā, Brahmaloka. Mahāprabhu says that the creeper of *bhakti* grows and rises up to Goloka, and our devotion must cross all these planes (*C.c. Madhya-līlā* 19.153-4).

But the pseudo-devotees do not care to know what is Paravyoma, what is Brahmaloka, what is Virajā, what is the *brahmāṇḍa*. Without caring to know about these things, they approach any *guru*, receive some *mantra*, and go on meditating. But if one meditates upon Rādhā-Govinda-*līlā* in such an ignorant state, instead of entering Rādhā-Govinda-*līlā* one will become entangled with the ladies and gentlemen of this world. One will become entangled in the domain of lust and will have to go to hell instead of going up to Goloka.

Love and Lust

Carma-māṁsamāyā—kāma, prema—cidānanda-dhāma. Carnal appetite is lust, whereas love is the abode of divine ecstasy. Imitation is not success; on the contrary, it degrades. Imitation degrades and imagination is only a mental exercise. The mind is separate from the soul. *Śraddhā*, divine faith, is connected with the soul, *ātma*; but the mind is matter. Mind is material, a part of the material potency. This is also clarified in *Gītā* 7.4:

bhūmir āpo 'nalo vāyuḥ khaṁ mano buddhir eva ca
ahaṅkāra itīyaṁ me bhinnā prakṛtir aṣṭadhā

The mind is a product of the material potency, and the *jīva is* a product of *para-śakti*, the superior potency. *Svarūpa-śakti*, the Lord's personal internal potency, is higher than the *jīva*. The function of the mind is speculation *(manodharma)*; that is its nature. It has nothing to do with truth. Mental speculation is drawn from the material world, the world of misconception. The mind is full of misconception *(avāṅ-manaso gocaraḥ)*. It cannot reach the stage of feeling or perceiving the truth proper. It is only related to mundane things in the plane of exploitation.

The mind cannot be pure, just as a fossil cannot produce life. Similarly, the mind cannot produce *śraddhā*, divine faith. *Śraddhā* is original and fundamental. When the Supreme Lord appears in the heart, the mind vanishes. Reality is just the opposite of speculation. Darkness cannot produce light; light comes and darkness vanishes. Truth appears when pure consciousness emerges and mental speculation vanishes. The mind is concerned with misconception. It is an element of the *apara-śakti*, the inferior potency. That potency is both subtle and gross. Earth, water, fire, air and ether are gross manifestations; mind, intelligence and ego are subtle. But they're all material.

The soul is transcendental. *Svarūpa-śakti*, or the Lord's personal potency, *bhajana*, or divine service, and Goloka-Vaikuṇṭha are all supra-mundane and transcendental. They are beyond the soul, not on the denser realm where the mind is located. Properly speaking, purity or impurity cannot be attributed to the mind. If we do, everything will be misunderstood. The mind emerges from the false ego and it is imbued with the tendency to exploit.

Mahāprabhu says, *mora mana—vṛndāvana*: "My attention is elsewhere, in Vṛndāvana." Vṛndāvana is not an element of this mundane plane. The residents of Goloka also possess senses, but the affairs of the mundane world are never represented in that plane.

The mundane mentality is a product of exploitation, sense exploitation. We need relief from this mind. We are surrounded by poisonous thought. In the narration of the *Tridaṇḍi-sannyāsī* in *Śrīmad Bhāgavatam* (*Bhāg.* 11.23.45), all the disciplines agree that the mind should be checked.

dānaṁ svadharmo niyamo yamaś ca śrutaṁ ca karmāṇi ca sad-vratāni
sarve mano-nigraha-lakṣaṇāntaḥ paro hi yogo manasaḥ samādhiḥ

"Charity, constant and conditional prescribed duties, mental and sensual control, hearing the scriptures, holy vows and duties—all these are observed to gain subjugation of the mind. Mental control is known as the supreme *yoga*."

Exploitation, Renunciation and Dedication

We must serve. In this world there are exploitation and renunciation; beyond them is dedication. Dedication is the proper and normal situation. There are gradations according to our inner tendency for serving, our particular calling. We may be allowed to enter that plane where all around is reverential soil. We must go there. Through effort it is impossible, but it is possible by grace, *kṛpā*. That impossible grace is called *kṛpā*, His grace, His free will. He is the Supreme Autocrat.

Affection *(rāga, anurāga)* does not differentiate between great and small; it is very generous. Only through affection and love is it possible to expect to attain that plane one day. But it is not so easy. Once, when a young devotee began to manifest various apparently devotional sentiments, others came to me, saying: "He is showing many signs of higher *bhāva* (sentiments), are they real?" I said, "Never!"

I Have No Love For Krsna

Mahāprabhu says *na prema-gandho 'sti darāpi me harau,* "I am hankering for a drop of real *prema*; and I have not attained it yet. I am weeping, shedding so many tears, crying 'Kṛṣṇa, Kṛṣṇa.' It is all hypocrisy, because the positive proof is here: I am alive without Him. I have not disappeared; I did not dissolve. I am living, I am eating, and I am sleeping. This is positive proof that I have no genuine love for Kṛṣṇa." Mahāprabhu Himself says that.

Bhāva is such a valuable attainment, and we think ourselves masters of it overnight! Fools, deceivers, self-deceivers! In the positive, assertive way it can never be attained. Only in the negative, submissive way can we have some conception. Śrīla Bhaktivinoda Ṭhākura says, *vicakṣaṇa kari', dekhite cāhile haya, haya ākhi-agocara*: "Suddenly a flash came, but when I tried to look, it disappeared. It was withdrawn." In this way, in a submissive way, we can have some idea. Whimsically He may come, and suddenly I may feel, "Oh, here is some experience of the higher knowledge and love, but if I try to capture it, there is nothing, vanished."

Sacrifice Our Mundane Experience

Do you want to live? Then come to die. We shall have to invite wholesale dissolution of everything in our experience. Hegel's words help us: "die to live." What is generally considered a concrete, valuable thing must be cast into the fire, in exchange for some hope that is unknown and unknowable. That is sacrifice. In Vedic ritual, we pour clarified butter into the fire as a sacrifice to please the Lord. *Ghee*, a valuable foodstuff, is burnt in the fire to create a healthier atmosphere. Of course, to say such a thing is improper and ridiculous according to material understanding, yet the benefit from the unknown quarter is there.

Be disgusted with your known world of knowledge, of pleasure—everything. Die to live. Now it appears to be all risk, no gain. Then, when the destination is reached to a certain extent, it will be all gain, no risk. Actually, what we risk is all concoction, misunderstanding. We only need to throw our misconception into the fire to gain a proper conception of reality. When the unreal is put into the fire, we gain the real. This is what "die to live" means.

Here, in this world, we are habituated to think, "I am monarch of all I survey." We want to become a ruler. Whether we are sovereign or not, our tendency is to want to be a monarch. All of us want to be a monarch. There is also another reactionary group that says, "I do not want anything. I want nothing but dreamless sleep. Cessation is the most valuable thing in our experience, complete cessation of this life."

Both these aspects of enjoyment, exploitation and renunciation, must be eliminated, and we should find a third plane in which to live. That third plane is the noble life, the life of dedication; a life of duty to and for the whole, not any part: "I live for the whole, and that whole is a part of Lord Kṛṣṇa." This is the meaning of becoming a lover of the beautiful. In that way we have to understand, and march onward.

Tangible Dedication

Dedication with a spirit of service should be always kept in mind. Sacrifice is necessary. The entire higher plane is that of dedication; not exploitation or renunciation. Exploitation, self-aggrandizement, that is exploitation, *pratiṣtha*. It must be avoided, because it is dangerous in the plane of dedication. If I have the tendency to exploit, to pose as a big personality, that will be very detrimental. The faithfulness of a servant must always be maintained and protected very scrupulously. None can deceive me; none can check my progress, except myself.

I must scrutinize and analyze my own inner temple and brush aside any undesirable things. *Guṇḍicā mārjana*: cleanse the temple just as Mahāprabhu showed us. *Guṇḍicā mārjana*. There are many types of undesirable things that should be brushed aside. We should make progress, and come closer to our Lord for service. He will take me closer for the quality of my service. Service must be the pivot of everything, whether studying, collecting resources, or recruiting devotees. The serving spirit should be kept intact always.

Śaraṇāgati means self-dedication. The manner of activity of the dedicated self will become *bhakti.* Whatever one may do, one will do on behalf of Kṛṣṇa. One must cite Kṛṣṇa's interest as the sole motivation, not some separate interest, *bhayaṁ dvitīyābhiniveśataḥ syād.* Consciousness of separate interest has separated us from Kṛṣṇa. And the common interest, the realization that all interests are harmonized in Him, that is *bhakti.* When the common interest is gone, everything is gone.

Śravaṇa, kīrtana, they are only mere forms, not life. In order to have a life of devotion, there must be *śaraṇāgati. Śaraṇāgati* means exclusive connection with Kṛṣṇa, exclusive identification with the interest of Kṛṣṇa. Because Kṛṣṇa is not seen in this plane, the *guru* and the Vaiṣṇava are to be served. In this way one will be benefited through extreme self-abnegation and surrender, according to one's disposition.

That surrender will have peculiar characteristics. *Śānta, dāsya, sakhya,* there are different *rasas,* or devotional dispositions. There are also subdivisions in the different *rasas.* In this way, each soul will be located in the plane of dedication. Without *śaraṇāgati,* all devotional practice is mere formality. One will lose the very life thereof, and it will be something other than *bhakti.* According to the nature and intensity of our sacrifice, in proportion to our dedication, we'll be allowed to enter the internal nectarine movement. When we disregard this principle, we become imitationists, *sahajiyā.* We must be very careful, because the mundane is a perverted reflection.

On the other hand, the Māyāvadī impersonalists may not

have any aspiration for worldly enjoyment, and when they take the name of Hare, Kṛṣṇa, and Rāma, they may manifest some sentiment, shivering, and tears. They may manifest these apparent devotional symptoms, but that is also a type of perverted reflection. It is not real devotion because Māyāvadīs are committed to the creed that Nārāyaṇa, Viṣṇu, Vaikuṇṭha, and everything other than the Brahman effulgence are within the jurisdiction of the mundane idea.

In *Harināma-cintāmaṇi* we find that Māyāvadīs may show some devotional symptoms in body and mind, but their impersonal creed bars their entrance into Vaikuṇṭha proper. They erroneously believe that Vaikuṇṭha is part of the material universe, lower than Brahmaloka. That is their creed. So *sahajiyā* imitation may not be there, but their devotion is not pure. It may be in the jurisdiction of *sattva-guṇa,* material purity, at most. They do not have real substantial faith beyond the conception of Brahma: the higher, deeper vision of Vaikuṇṭha, Goloka, and Vṛndāvana. They can't understand the real nature of self-dedication.

By dedication we enter a perfectly different world. Dedication is better than renunciation. Renunciation of the negative is good, but it is destructive. It will lead to the zero conception of everything. However, by accepting, searching and attaining our inner selves as units of the world of dedication we find a new world before us, a new land. The Māyāvadīs can't believe this. They cannot believe that if we are transformed, then our innermost selves become members of the plane of dedication.

Tangible Depth in Divinity

When backed by the *sādhu,* the *guru* of very high stature, we can do anything. By the grace of his support, whatever *kīrtana* is practiced will be effective. Meditating silently may be praised as more efficient in a particular context, but if we venture superficially to chant the Holy Name in that way, there will be great opposition, and we may become atheists. It can happen if we do not have sufficient support to fight against the odds. We must not venture to attack the enemy when our position is weak. But when backed by the great generals and sufficient munitions, we must march on. That will help us to engage in real *kīrtana.*

The real factor is *sādhu-saṅga,* which has a connection with the higher power. Otherwise, nothing has any value. The stand must be taken on the real plane of *sādhu* and *śāstra.* We must cultivate the real thing, protect the reality of the *bhajana.* For the weaker devotee, the *sādhaka* or aspirant, the greatest necessity is *sādhu-saṅga,* even as the scriptures are necessary for knowledge. *Sādhu-śāstra-kṛpa.* If we have the mercy of the saints and the sanction of the scriptures, then our *kīrtana* will be best.

Our attention should always be towards the negative, submissive side. If we can practice in submission, our promotion cannot be checked. Without qualification, if we are very eager to go upward, there will be a tendency to fall down. *Dāsyāya te mama raso 'stu raso 'stu satyam:* "May I have the aspiration for servitude." For *bhajana* or internal service, such a temperament should always be followed. *Tad dāsa-dāsa-dāsānāṁ dāsatvaṁ dehi me prabho.* "May I always be the servant of the servant of the servant."

Promotion is inevitable if we always try to adhere to the lower duty. Eagerness for promotion is the enemy; that is for *pratiṣṭhā* (renown), and that will undermine everything. Śrīla Prabhupāda Bhaktisiddhānta Ṭhākura said that imitation arises from the attraction for *pratiṣṭhā,* the desire to hold the superior position and acquire a name for oneself. That is the great enemy. Don't fall prey to *pratiṣṭhā,* the eagerness to hold the higher position. Rather, *dainyam,* humility, is the healthy sign of a devotee.

Vṛndāvana Dāsa Ṭhākura says that one who feeds thousands while obtaining his own nourishment is greater than he who only feeds himself. *Kīrtana* means to cultivate oneself while helping many others at the same time. But when we have no capital of our own, if we go to preach we will meet much opposition, *asat-saṅga,* and the *aṅkura,* the bud, will be nipped. If we are *kaniṣṭha-adhikāri,* neophytes, we should not preach to others without vigorous backing. *Kīrtana* means to preach, to approach others. We should not venture to do that as *kaniṣṭha-adhikāri,* because we may be converted to atheism. Only after passing through the proper stages—*śravaṇa-daśā, varaṇa-daśā, sādhana-daśā* and *prāpana-daśā* (the phases of hearing, acceptance, practice, and attainment)—can one preach independently (*āpana-daśā*). Otherwise, we can only preach with the help of someone in *prāpana-daśā.*

We should have an immovable connection with Reality, an absolute conception of Reality. Such a stable position is necessary. Become invulnerable; develop certainty, *sambandha-jñāna.* Then we shall be able to understand and harmonize the differences that we find in the writings of the *ācāryas.* We will know then what instruction to apply in each situation, and under what circumstances one or another particular process has been advised. This is practical knowledge.

Effective Bhajana

Anything in connection with God, including all types of *bhajana,* is good. We are not against anything of that nature. However, we must consider what will be most effective according to our capacity. At the same time, we must not commit any offense of omission. How can we be so audacious as to say that *smaraṇa* is superior and that other types of *bhajana* are of a lower order? We may distinguish very cautiously, but not merely to satisfy our curiosity. We must not venture to make light of such matters. These are all serious points.

To consider one Vaiṣṇava over another is not a game; the distinctions are very subtle. They are devotees, and we must not venture to place one above the other according to our crude necessity. It is not an academic exercise; we should not amass some theoretical knowledge to impress our students. It should not be accepted in that line. We shall always be conscious of the practical side: "They are so great, and where am I? Who am I passing judgment over?" There should be some limit to our adventurous audacity. Only if the real necessity arises shall we venture to establish the superiority of Lakṣmī over Śukadeva or Ambarīṣa.

Approach Nityananda Prabhu

We pray to Nityānanda Prabhu. We want to come to an adjusted position: "If I have committed any offense, *aparādha,* when dealing with so many subtle things about the great personages, please, Nityānanda Prabhu, absolve me of that offense and restore me to my normal humble position." Vṛndāvana Dāsa Ṭhākura says, "I bow at the feet of the Vaiṣṇavas; may there be no offense in my attempt to serve them."

sarva-vaiṣṇavera pā'ye kari nāmaskāra,
ithe aparādha kichu nahuka āmāra

When we deal with so many great things, such as trying to speak about great personalities of the highest order, we should beg Nityānanda Prabhu to pardon us for our audacity. He is *patīta-pāvana,* savior of the fallen souls. He is *adoṣa-darśī*—generally He does not take any offense.

Real Humility

Humility means not to encroach on the rights of others. However, it should not be self-destructive; it must be natural. Humility is accepting no position, because a servant has no independent position. Because he is always at the command of the master, he is always situated within infinite possibility. The servant is humble to his master, not to the *guṇḍās*. His humility must be directed chiefly towards the master. Be humble towards the Lord's own, the Vaiṣṇava. Be humble there. When it is necessary for Hanumān to burn the golden city of Laṅkā, his humility is not disturbed. He is as humble as anyone can be in carrying out the order of Lord Rāmacandra. He is fully given, wholly surrendered to his Master.

Humility, in other words, is surrender. Humility means to present no opposition to the command of the master from Vaikuṇṭha, the upper section. Humility does not drag one into subordination to the serpent, tiger or jackal. Our real relationship is with the Vaiṣṇava. That is the plane where devotees take their stand. We are concerned with the Vaiṣṇava. And humility means that we do not resist our master's instruction. Without opposition, we carry out whatever order comes to us. We possess humility, *sunīcatā*; we are not prejudiced.

Generally we think of humility as pertaining to the outside world, but this is not correct. To the right-thinking person, the members of the external world are deluded; they are mad. Humility lies not in the standard of madness, or in catering to mad people. A madman has no standard of his own. Therefore, humility means to have a standard apart from the outside world.

Prabhupāda has defined humility as 'that which is absent where there is a spirit of enjoyment.' The enjoying spirit, the spirit of exploitation, means aggression. There cannot be humility in aggression. Humility is cent-percent service. There is no humility in exploitation, or in renunciation either. These two are opposed to the normal nature of the world. They are totally misconceived; they are our enemies. They challenge the normal reality of the spirit.

The spirit of exploitation and the spirit of renunciation, both are a revolt against the proper working of the truth. They are totally misconceived. Real humility must be in relation to the fullest aspect of the truth, not to the misconceived world. The standard is not that of the madman.

In real devotional service whose objective is to please the center, a competitive spirit between two persons will not negate humility. The devotees feel inspiration and direction from the center, and cooperate accordingly. They are connected with the Absolute center, so Yogamāyā may arrange competition. They are not responsible, because their necessity is only to please the center.

The Absolute is that way, but not out of necessity. *Aher iva gatiḥ premṇaḥ, svabhāva-kuṭilā bhavet.* It seems to be crooked, but it is not; it is the very nature of Absolute dealings. It is necessary only for the variety and diversity of our service to Kṛṣṇa. It is designed from the upper-quarter. The devotees are not responsible for that. There may be competition, but we should not infringe on the property of others.

Our Duty

Our duty will always be to dedicate ourselves more and more intensely, and we shall do that according to how we may be commanded by the higher agency. We must always keep ourselves ready for that intervention. Cent percent we shall obey the instruction from the upper quarter, without any hesitation. That is our duty. Whatever will be asked of us, we shall do.

On the battlefield, if the general asks a particular battalion to fight in the first battle, they may not say: "Why shouldn't the second battalion be commanded to go? Why should we go first? We shall die, and they will rejoice in the victory after the last battle. Why should we go first?" The military will shoot them then and there! It is the generals' prerogative; it is not left to the soldiers to determine which battalion will engage first. Only the highest authorities command. Complaining against that high command invites immediate death.

Angels Fear To Tread

Fools rush in where angels fear to tread. Like fools, we rush into the subtlest realm of sentiments of the highest order, so we must beg to be excused by the high personalities. *Apasiddhānta* or philosophical adulteration strikes very harshly. It was Svarūpa Dāmodara's service to examine any poems or writings for purity before they were taken to Mahāprabhu. If writings with *apasiddhānta* were offered to Mahāprabhu, He would be very severely disturbed. *Apasiddhānta* cruelly attacks the ideal of the higher-thinking persons.

They may be offended. We shall try to enter into that garden without disturbing any plant or person roaming in that sphere. We shall enter not with curiosity, but with all humility and respects for them. Otherwise our talks will be pure intellectualism, and not *Hari-kathā.*

Do Your Duty in Your Plane

First go to Nityānanda Prabhu, and by His grace you will go to Mahāprabhu. Strictly stick to *Gaura-līlā,* Mahāprabhu, and you will automatically find within your heart that *rādhā-rasa-sudhānidhi* is flowing. Don't attempt directly to have it. It will come automatically, spontaneously.

yathā yathā gaura-padāravinde
vindeta bhaktiṁ kṛta-puṇya-rāśiḥ
tathā tathotsarpati hṛdy-akasmād
rādhā-padāmbhoja-sudhāmbu-rāśiḥ

"As devotion unto the lotus feet of Śrī Gaurasundara is attained by a greatly pious person, inevitably the ocean of nectar which is the service of the lotus feet of Śrī Rādhā is accordingly born within his heart." *(Śrī Caitanya-candrāmṛta 88)*

Percolated by the mercy of Śrī Gaurāṅga, try to approach Śrīmatī Rādhārāṇī. Then there will be no possibility of any contamination entering our heart and disturbing us in that plane. Śrī Gaurāṅga will impede that contamination. If we have the shelter of Śrī Gaurāṅga we can be sure that we will very safely, smoothly, and intimately attain the service of Śrīmatī Rādhārāṇī. Otherwise it is very dangerous, and sometimes suicidal. If we do not approach through Śrī Gaurāṅga, the attempt will be reactionary.

It is very dangerous to approach Śrī Vṛndāvana and Śrīmatī Rādhārāṇī directly. We must approach as commanded by Śrī Gaurāṅga. In other words, if we can appreciate the life of Śrī Gaurāṅga, the ideal of Śrī Gaurāṅga, then *kāma* (mundane desire) will be exhaustively eliminated. We will be purified so that we can be accepted in that domain of the highest *līlā*. We shall not approach intellectually, for that will fill us with misconceptions. We will have to expend much energy to do away with that layer of misunderstanding. Therefore, our Śrīla Prabhupāda did not allow these things.

We must do our duty in our plane, according to what we deserve, and the result will come naturally. That is his instruction for all time, not only temporarily, but for all time. Don't approach directly, for then we will get *māyā* instead of *yogamāyā*.

Kṛṣṇa knows it perfectly well; Rādhārāṇī knows perfectly well when we are to be taken into the confidential area. That cannot be acquired other than by Their sweet will, the flow of Her sweet will, or His sweet will. Try to have the real thing, not any imitation or reflection. Reflection and shadow, these two kinds of misconception may appear. Of the two, reflection is more dangerous.

We are cautioned often: "Don't try; it will come automatically. Go on with the program given by the *śāstra* and the *guru* and it will happen. If you have such a possibility of fortune then it will come to you. It is not a material experience that can be given to one and all. It is not to be tackled in such a way."

Yathā yathā gaura-padāravinde. Engage your full attention in *Gaura-līlā* and your realization will come automatically. Indirectly it will come to you from the higher domain. When the higher realm is pleased, it will come down for some time to give you the experience, and you will simply be astonished. Then, even when it departs or is withdrawn, you will have nothing to lament. Realization is a living thing. We cannot make it our object. It is such a higher reality, such a higher thing!

It is difficult to participate in the intimacy between an ordinary man and his closest friends, and so it is with the *līlā* of the Supreme Lord. How can we dare enter into those pastimes, and publicly it is more so! It is not possible. Externally we can try to give some description of the outer possibilities, but not the actual thing. We won't venture to enter there.

Not an Academic Endeavor

When Śrī Caitanya Mahāprabhu talked about the higher *līlās,* He was in a trance. He gave a description of His wonderful, direct experience of *Kṛṣṇa-līlā.* Several times we find that sort of deep *līlā,* the higher *Kṛṣṇa-līlā* related by Mahāprabhu Himself: the *Govardhana-līlā;* the *jalakeli-līlā* (when He jumped unconscious into the ocean and for hours was carried by the waves of the sea to Cakra-tīrtha from Svārgadvāra); the *jalakeli* of Kṛṣṇa; the *līlā* at Caṭaka Pārvata. The nature of those descriptions was not an academic endeavor, learned from a book. Such experience cannot be written in black and white; it cannot be read and narrated as a bookish thing. It is real.

Defect of the Intellect

In *Harināma-cintāmaṇi,* it is stated that the temptation may come, but we must not think that everything can be encompassed by our limited intellect—*acintyaḥ khalu ye bhāvā na tāṁs tarkeṇa yojayet.* That which is inconceivable, we may not place under the jurisdiction of reason. When the inconceivable is extended to us, we will be astounded with a mere glance. *Na tāṁs tarkeṇa yojayet:* don't attempt to drag the inconceivable into the zone of reason. The higher quarter is autocratic in its nature. It may come in one shape to one, and it may go in another shape to another. It is so expansive and free in its nature. It is infinite. The Infinite is the origin of those pastimes. We should always be prepared to accept whatever experience of the Infinite may be granted to us, but we should not attempt to make the Infinite an object of our experience.

Fools rush in where angels fear to tread. With this spirit, and not out of curiosity, we must approach the process. By the same token, by God's grace, we should not disbelieve everything unless and until we have the full experience and know every last detail.

The Finite Cannot Know the Infinite

The finite cannot expect that the whole Infinity (Kṛṣṇa) will enter within a tiny cell of awareness. But by our earnestness, Kṛṣṇa comes down to touch the finite by His partial representation, when He is satisfied with our serving attitude. We should be always conscious of the fact that we are infinitesimal and cannot hope that the whole Infinite will come within our fist. That is nonsense.

Only follow the recommended path of *śraddhā,* faith; that is our serving attitude, surrender. Then whenever and whatever little experience He'll kindly make us taste, we shall taste. We should understand that as the proper characteristic of a finite inquirer; otherwise we will be over-endeavoring. If we cannot understand the plain truth that we are finite, then it is impossible to understand the Infinite. We want to know the Infinite, but we cannot make Him the prisoner of our finite box. Only by our humble temperament can we attract Him. As much as He kindly wills us to taste Him, that should be enough for us.

One drop will inundate the whole of the world; this is His nature. Can we be so audacious as to draw the Infinite and force Him to enter into our fist? That is suicidal. We must always be conscious of our own position. With a sober consideration we shall try to understand the ways and means that are extended to us by the gracious, great personalities. Very patiently and very modestly, and only when He wants to make it known to us, can we know anything. And only as much as He wants, we will know; that much, and not more. That is our position. To know the whole thing is ludicrous; it is suicidal. That is the most foolish, reactionary conception.

Reject Your Knowledge

Jñāne prayāsam udapāsya (*Bhāg:* 10.14.3): Relentlessly we must discard (*ud-apa-asya*) all proposals that our intellect may offer us. Whatever the intellect can judge and accept or reject must necessarily be of a lower nature. We are to summarily reject that, and understand that we must bow down our heads (*namanta eva*).

Knowledge is our enemy, because knowledge in this world is all misleading. Its very basis is misleading. However ample it may be, it is a negligible part of the Infinite. We have collected, gathered and pushed into our brain all misleading falsification. Our brains are full of deceptive *māyā*, misunderstanding. That is our enemy. We have to clear these things out and put in fresh things that are received from the other world by pure sources.

Theoretical knowledge is one thing, the practical another.

Relentlessly we must cast aside the old knowledge, *udapāsam. Namanta eva,* we must learn submission, and in that way He will be propitiated and come to make something about Himself known to us. Whatever small thing we will come to know, that will inundate our entire being. One drop of the Infinite is sufficient to cover the whole universe; such is His character. The Infinite is not a small thing that we can tackle easily. With one drop of the Infinite the whole finite can be inundated, flooded.

The Infinite has full control over knowledge, science, happiness, everything. If we are to approach such a great, great, great thing, what should be the proper attitude? We must be conscious of our position. We are not masters, but servants of the servant of the servant of the servant of the servant. This is the proper way to approach.

In the same manner, we are to approach the scriptures with a submissive heart and attitude. "Please reveal within our heart what is contained herein." *Śāstra* should be approached with a submissive attitude, not in a challenging mood. By dint of our power we cannot conquer what is described there. We cannot conquer all thoughts. That is not the proper attitude. Scriptural truth is a higher thing; it is *cetana,* independent. It has free will, this *śāstra* in the form of so many letters. The Lord's associates also exercise His free will in the matter of our approach to the *śāstra.* They can reveal the meaning to us or they can withhold it.

Approach the Guru

It is good if disciples develop a consciousness of being personally unfit. Although we are unqualified, we should have some understanding within, that Gurudeva is taking us towards the higher quarter. We will see things as we look about the environment. We may be fools, but others are not. We can see how they accept Kṛṣṇa. The experts in the scriptures have also given their opinion. According to our capacity we should consult *sādhu* and *śāstra*. With the help of these two (*sādhu* and *śāstra*) and the approval of our innermost heart we can approach the *guru*. With their help we can accept *guru*.

But there are those who are deceiving themselves, "O, my *guru* can cure so many diseases," and "O, my *guru* can make me prosper in the material life." That is self-deception. In the world there are many different types of *gurus:* there are those who give material prosperity and some *tyāgī gurus* give us eternal sleep, saying that this is the real place of taking rest and achieving peace. There are so many classes of *gurus*.

Generally our *sukṛti* guides us from underground. *Śraddhā* is the real merit that can take us to a proper *guru*, and *śraddhā* comes from our past acquired *sukṛti*, or auspicious activities. That *sukṛti* comes unconsciously from the agents of Kṛṣṇa. In this way, the real progress of a *jīva* is traced, ultimately.

Become an Angel

dāsyāya me raso'stu raso'stu satyam
sakhyāya me mama namo'stu namo'stu nityaṁ

The essence of verse 16 of *Vilāpa-kusamāñjali* is to let our respect flow towards the friendly devotional disposition, *sākhya*. We respect that friendly disposition, but pray to obtain the disposition of a servant, *dāsya*. We should always move expressly towards the goal of having the temperament of a servant, while giving respect to the friendly disposition. We should not venture to tread on that plane. Fools rush in where angels fear to tread. Don't be a fool; become an angel. Try to follow the angels. We should always respect the higher plane and try to remain connected with the lower service.

When Mahārāja Pratāparudra began his service, which is that of a sweeper, Mahāprabhu came to embrace him. We should not forget that: it is the very backbone of devotion, to tend always towards the lower services. Then automatically from the other side the choice comes for us, from the higher plane. We should not try to impose on Him, but show our modest tendency to go to the lower level. And it is the duty of the higher to take us to the proper place.

Dāsyāya me raso'stu, our sincere attraction should be towards lower service, toward cultivating the temperament of a servant. We must have the knowledge that we are not fit for anything higher. We will respect that. This should be our attitude: we are not fit for that high plane. Many Vaiṣṇavas of higher character are there. We must engage in service at a lower level, then automatically from the higher level it will come to us. Yogamāyā is not sitting idle there. Whomever will be fit for any particular plane, Yogamāyā is there to adjust everything for them. Automatically, she will take us from a particular plane and put us in some higher plane. The residents of the higher plane are not inanimate objects; they are all conscious.

Die To Live

Sevonmukhe hi jihvādau. All attempts must be made with the understanding that we are meant for Him, for His pleasure. That is the main principle of our advancement: *sevonmukhe hi jihvādau.* Then it will be possible for us to reach that plane. We are meant for Him, to die for Him. Die to live. The whole process is die to live, always. Dissolve this ego. To leave this ego means to embrace death; subtle death is to leave a particular ego. One layer of ego may require many births to reach its death. The entire ego should be dissolved. We are meant for Him, for His pleasure. Die to live. We want our wonderful dream satisfied.

We should engage ourselves in the lowest form of service. *Tad dāsa-dāsa-dāsānaṁ dāsatvaṁ dehi prabho.* Our faith should be so firm and of such quality that the least prospect of His service, of divine service, will satisfy us. We may not get the chance there in the higher class, but with our lowest connection with divinity we may go on satisfied with our lives. Mahāprabhu says, "Just consider me a speck of dust at Your feet, Kṛṣṇa."

ayi nanda tanuja kiṅkaraṁ patitaṁ māṁ viṣame bhavāmbudhau
kṛpayā tava pāda-paṅkaja-sthita-dhūlī-sadṛsaṁ vicintaya

"O Nanda-nandana, son of King Nanda, although I am Your eternal servitor, I have fallen into the terrible ocean of material existence due to the fructification of my own deeds (*karma*). Please graciously consider me to be a particle of dust at Your lotus feet." (*Śikṣāṣṭaka* 5)

That should be our aspiration: "Consider me to be one of the specks of dust at Your feet." That is too much! Our faith should come to such a grade in quality that we will be satisfied to become a speck of dust at His feet. Then by His sweet will, anything may happen. But our humble aim should be to have even the least connection with the real divinity instead of a concocted relation with Kṛṣṇa.

Not an Ornamental Thing

Pūjala rāga-pātha gaurava-bhaṅge—this is enough. *Tad dāsa-dāsa-dāsānāṁ dāsatvaṁ dehi prabho.* This is not a figurative thing; it is not mere poetry. Mahāprabhu says:

nāhaṁ vipro na ca nara-patir nāpi vaiśyo na śūdro
nāhaṁ varṇī na ca gṛha-patir no vana-stho yatir vā
kintu prodyan-nikhila-paramānanda-pūrṇāmṛtābdher
gopī-bhartuḥ pada-kamalayor dāsa-dāsānudāsaḥ

"I am not a priest, a king, a merchant, or a laborer (*brāhmaṇa, kṣatriya, vaiśya, śūdra*); nor am I a student, a householder, a retired householder, or a mendicant (*brahmacārī, gṛhastha, vanaprastha, sannyāsī*). I identify myself only as the servant of the servant of the servant of the lotus feet of Śrī Kṛṣṇa, the Lord of the *gopīs,* who is the personification of the fully expanded (eternally self-revealing) nectarine ocean that brims with the totality of divine ecstasy." (*C.c. Madhya-līlā* 13.80)

This is not merely an ornamental thing; it is reality. To feel our own actual inferiority is to become eligible for the higher service. This is reality. So much selflessness, so much self-abnegation is necessary for a servant of the lowest order to enter into that domain. So much self-abnegation is necessary to come into that plane. There is an undercurrent, and if we really want contact with that plane, we shall have to reach the finest of the fine within ourselves, without demands. In this meek way we are to transform ourselves, and then we can contact that plane.

If there is the least tinge of exploiting tendency, any speck of the ambitious life, we will not be taken there. That is another thing, *pratiṣṭhā. Pratiṣṭhā* is self-assertion: to be stable, to be immortal, to be invincible. It is not self-giving, but rather self-asserting: "I must stay, I must live." No, we must die for the interest of Kṛṣṇa if necessary. *Mārobi rākhobi—yo icchā tohārā, nitya-dāsa prati tuwā adhikārā.* "Slay me or protect me as You wish, for You are the Master of Your eternal servant."

A suicidal soldier! For the cause of the country, we must die if necessary. We must efface ourselves, or we may be effaced. If it is necessary, our very existence may be annihilated for the satisfaction of Kṛṣṇa. To find that plane, such temperament, such selflessness in high degree is necessary, so much subtlety is required.

Systematic Knowledge is Knowledge Proper

Once a senior Mahārāja repeated to me something that Prabhupāda had said. It was a circumstantial remark that this Mahārāja wanted to utilize in a universal way. But I objected, "Prabhupāda made this statement, therefore it is correct. But you are not placing it in context; it is not the whole thing. He also said other things, so we have to harmonize everything he said. We cannot ignore the other aspects of his teaching. We have to come to an adjustment that is a systematic understanding of his words."

This Mahārāja had laid stress on only one particular point, one partial aspect of Prabhupāda's teaching. He wanted to take that particular point and nothing beyond it. We must seek a systematic understanding of the goal. Systematic knowledge is knowledge proper.

There are many different types of disciples under the guidance of every *guru*, but not all are necessarily of equal character. Their natures may be quite different. One person will be able to understand some points, another will grasp something else, and yet another will understand even more. In this way there may be a gradation among the disciples. The main thing is faithfulness.

Simplicity means to be free from prejudice. That is what it means to be simple: to be empty, to be dispossessed, to be in the null position, to be clear. To be free of all possessions, that is simplicity.

Relative and Absolute Considerations

There are two things that must be understood: what is form and what is substance. Ignorance of these is the main obstacle to our progress. *Sva-dharme nidhanaṁ śreyaḥ, para-dharmo bhayāvahaḥ.* Progress means to deal with the difficulties presented by form and substance. It is sometimes necessary to make progress by adhering to one's formal position. If advancement is not sure, if there is any doubt of progress, then it is judicious to take the formal position. But in fact there is no progress by holding back. Progress means leaving the former position and going on to something else. Only one who is hopeful of a brighter future should leave his formal position and advance. Those who are of a doubtful or suspicious mentality would be better off holding fast to their already consolidated foundation and taking a stand there.

It is a difficult thing to adjust properly the relative and absolute positions, the absolute and relative considerations. Generally we accept the relative position, keeping in the background the consciousness of the absolute consideration. Absolute consideration is always superior, but that is risky. The relative position generally helps us not to go down. *Sva-dharme nidhanaṁ śreyaḥ, para-dharmo bhayāvahaḥ*, this is the type of relative position.

Wait and see. Don't go forward; don't go backward. Maintain your position. Keep your own position. But when you get the chance to make any progress you should not lose it. However, you must be sure. Otherwise, leaving the former position you are going to take a risk. Progress is necessary; it is indispensable that you must make progress. So you must take a risk, but you must take it in such a way that you don't lose your former position.

śreyān sva-dharmo viguṇaḥ para-dharmāt svanuṣṭhitāt
sva-dharme nidhanaṁ śreyaḥ para-dharmo bhayāvahaḥ

"It is better to perform one's prescribed duties, even though imperfectly, than another's duties perfectly. To face defeat in the course of performing one's own duty is better than engaging in another's duties, for to follow another's path is dangerous." (*Gītā* 3.35)

To maintain the former position for defensive necessity, that is helpful. But still we must have our tendency to make progress. *Sarva dharmān parityajya mām ekaṁ śaraṇaṁ vraja, ahaṁ tvāṁ sarva pāpebhyo*; that is our goal. The absolute consideration is our goal. The relative position, that is for our safety. Progress is necessary, but very carefully we must go ahead, so that we may not lose our former position.

Try To Go Ahead

We must obey authority. Instructions from the authorities are important, and are always given in every community. However, we seek the truth. Those who do not care for that which is presented by the authorities, they will come out to seek the real, the complete truth, not the stereotyped thing. Everyone is more or less under a particular social binding. And it is told repeatedly in the *Bhagavad-gītā*: *sva-dharme nidhanaṁ śreyaḥ para-dharmo bhayāvahaḥ.* Strongly here it is spoken, "Don't leave your own religion, the conception of your particular duty. Don't leave your present position. Rather you should die, and after death, some change may come. Don't leave your position."

"Maintain your present position, it is recommended strongly so that we may not fall down." Then, *sarva dharmān parityajya mām ekaṁ śaraṇaṁ vrāja* is also there. If we get the chance to advance towards Him, with a risk, we must try to go ahead, to attain perfection. But we must be sure that we are advancing, that we are in the realm of progress, not going down. That sort of faith is crucial. With a clear conscience we must try to forge ahead; it is not that in the name of advancement we are going back.

Generally we are justified here in our present situation, *para-dharmo bhayāvahaḥ*. We have taken our stand at present and accepted this duty, the consciousness of this duty. However, it is also stated, *sarva dharmān parityajya*: "Abandon all other duties, and just come to Me." The real cause of advancement will come. One cannot but take the risk of going away.

Risk Means Progress

During the time of my Guru Mahārāja, there were many who did not take *sannyāsa*, the renounced order. Later on, however, they found they could go more swiftly towards the goal by taking *sannyāsa*. To take *sannyāsa* means to take a risk. To take a risk means to make further progress. One who takes risks is prepared for further progress. So, should we remain in the same position we held in the time of Guru Mahārāja? Should we remain in that position? Or is it more desirable for us to try for perfect progress? If we choose to make advancement, we will have so many new insights and reject so many of the old.

According to our own progress, devotees cannot but see that some things are to be kept back and others to be invited to the forefront. This is what it means to go nearer, to make progress. We should have some sort of approximate knowledge of what is good, what is bad, what is Kṛṣṇa, what is non-Kṛṣṇa, and that will be realized more and more. "Oh, I could not detect this, but now I feel that this is also a valuable point in the light of the Kṛṣṇa conception."

In this way, realization and advancement come. But one should not leave his former position without being sure of his progress: *sva-dharme nidhanaṁ śreyaḥ para-dharmo bhayāvahaḥ*. We must not take risks for something that is not our own. But when we do find that it is indeed our own, even though it may be a little far, we must take the leap. We will think, "My inner hankering has been searching for that thing alone. Now it is within my reach, so I must take it."

It all depends on our sincerity and proper understanding.

Na hi kalyāṇa-kṛt kaścid durgatiṁ tāta gacchati. Sometimes we may fall down, but we will be able to understand that lower things are not desirable. We will think, "These desires are hunting me; for the time being they have even captured me, but after a while they will vanish." When they do, we will think, "Oh, what suddenly came and overpowered me? My real self-interest has been hampered. I must not allow myself to be affected by them again. I must be very alert."

In this way, sometimes the lower propensities may get the upper hand and so we go backwards, and sometimes we may go forward. We are always in the midst of battle. We are soldiers, always fighting for progress.

Progress is a Living Thing

Progress means elimination of old things and acceptance of the new. Progress means a living, new experience: *bhaktiḥ pareśānubhavo viraktir anyatra ca.* (*Bhāg.* 11.2.42) When we are hungry we are weak. By every morsel eaten we feel satisfaction; the desire for eating diminishes. Weakness is removed and the discomfort of hunger is also removed through eating, morsel by morsel. With every step we shall have to feel whether we are making any progress.

bhaktiḥ pareśānubhavo viraktir
anyatra caiṣa trika eka-kālaḥ
prapadyamānasya yathāśnataḥ syus
tuṣṭiḥ puṣṭiḥ kṣud-apāyo 'nu-ghāsam

"Devotion, direct experience of the Supreme Lord, and detachment from other things—these three occur simultaneously for one who has taken shelter of the Supreme Personality of Godhead, in the same way that pleasure, nourishment and relief from hunger come simultaneously and increasingly, with each bite, for a person engaged in eating." (*Bhāg.* 11.2.42)

We must have a conception of what is Reality and what is progress. We shall have to understand what is imagination or hallucination and what is Reality. Our intensity and attraction for the goal will increase step by step; it won't diminish. It will have to increase if we are following the proper line. We must have some conception of that new goal, and our energy towards the goal will increase.

Progress can be measured by detecting this kind of transformation within. *Pareśānubhavo*: somehow, a conception of the Supreme must grow clearer and clearer in us. What is He? Who is He? *Viraktir anyatra*: indifference to everything that is not related to Kṛṣṇa must grow in us as well. We avoid what does not concern Kṛṣṇa, and when it appears anyway, it produces some apathy or even irritation in us. The negative measure will be how much I am apathetic to everything that is not related to Kṛṣṇa. *Tuṣṭiḥ puṣṭiḥ kṣud-apāyo 'nu-ghāsam*: the inner hunger should be fulfilled as well. "Yes, I am feeling fulfillment." We should have the conviction that we are walking in the right direction. We should have inner sanction of our clear conscience. "Yes, yes, I am doing right." We will feel inner satisfaction.

If we make progress towards the east, the west will be left behind and we shall see new things in our view. If these things are good, our encouragement will increase more and more; we shall make progress—*tuṣṭiḥ puṣṭiḥ kṣud-apāyo 'nu-ghāsam. Anughāsam, puṣṭiḥ,* with every morsel we shall feel stronger. *Tuṣṭiḥ,* satisfaction will come. *Kṣud-apāyaḥ,* our hunger will gradually cease. These three things must be there; then we are in a real, progressive life.

The Only Reliable Agents

We must always be alert to search within, whether we are enticed by any of the agents of *māyā*, misconception. The agents of *māyā* won't leave us for a moment. "Oh, you have so many commitments here. Why are you going? You must first clear these commitments, then we shall allow you to go." In different ways these agents will come and try to take us back. "You have so many commitments here, an incurred debt, and now you are trying to fly away? Absconder! We won't allow you to abscond." In various ways they will come.

One should not believe them. Only believe the scripture, *śāstra*. Only fear the *śāstra* and the *sādhu*. They will plead for us; no one else. The agents of *māyā* are everywhere in our midst. The *śāstra* and the *sādhu* are the only reliable agents. Go to the agent of your ambassador's quarter. Take shelter. When visitors from a foreign land find any danger in their life, they go to their own ambassador's quarter. They will take shelter in that quarter. If their bodies are in danger, they will take shelter with their own. Similarly, in the world of *māyā* and misconception we should try to take shelter of those with the proper devotional conception. The agents of *māyā* will hesitate to enter there.

It cannot be denied that a kind of energy is necessary to maintain one's present position. But when we are determined to push forward, progress becomes all-important. A seeker after the truth will search after newer and newer planes, and that means living and accommodating new experiences. We are to become more and more accommodating, earnest and eager.

sva-dharme nidhanaṁ śreyaḥ para-dharmo bhayāvahaḥ

The advice is given: "Try to maintain your position even at the cost of your life." Then, at the next moment: "Go ahead.

March on." (*Gītā* 3.35) We are first advised to maintain our present position so that we may not fall back. But that does not mean we are not to make progress. *Sva-dharme nidhanaṁ śreyaḥ,* To firmly maintain our position does not mean that we are not to go forward.

sarva dharmān parityajya mām ekaṁ śaraṇaṁ vrāja

"Give up all considerations and take the risk of marching onwards." (*Gītā.* 18.66)

That first advice was given only to reinforce this final order. First, maintain the current position, and then press onward! These are the relative and absolute considerations. A living spiritual conception must be of that nature. The dire necessity is that we address the question of how to maintain and improve our present position.

Dedicated Risk

Die to live, that is the theory to be followed. If we prepare to die a hard death, we shall find that we will gain thereby. In this way we are to measure the quality of our effort: the more dedication, the greater qualitative elevation. No risk, no gain; more risk, more gain. Such is the rule with exploitation and its opposite, dedication. Exploitation is lawless and ruthless, and dedication is risky. But dedication must be to the good, to the Absolute good. Otherwise everything is lost.

Higher knowledge is only allowed when one has this attitude: *Tad viddhi praṇipātena paripraśnena sevāya.* (*Gītā* 4.34) If you have a desire for the higher domain, you must present yourself in this way, with this approach: *praṇipāt,* surrender; *paripraśna,* honest inquiry; and *sevā,* service. You are for Him; He is not for you. He is for Himself. Reality is by Itself, and not for you. Reality cannot be dependent on any other thing for His existence, or to fulfill His purpose. He is independent in the beginning and in the end. He has created the past and the present by Himself, and in the future He is meant to maintain His existence for His own purpose. He is not subservient to any other purpose. Otherwise He is not Reality. Reality is for Itself, Reality is by Itself. If we want to live a proper life, we'll have to die as we are at present with our false ego. That is the basis of Vaiṣṇavism proper.

The Real Spirit

Exploitation and renunciation, *bhukti-mukti-spṛhā*; these two are great enemies of devotion: the tendency to exploit and the tendency to renounce. When one has eaten too much, as a reaction one wants to abstain from eating. Liberation, *mokṣa,* is only a reaction to exploitation. It may appear that we are in a quest for duty, money, sense-pleasure, and liberation (*dharma, artha, kāma, mokṣa*), but this is an external and partial examination of our experience. With a deeper assessment we will find that we are eagerly searching only for *rasaṁ, sundaraṁ,* the fullest satisfaction, the perfect beauty. *Dharma, artha,* and *kāma* cannot satisfy our inner hankering. Even *mokṣa,* liberation from the present hankering is not the goal.

Mere liberation from the negative is artificial. Life must have its fulfillment; everything has its fulfillment and necessary position. Life is not meant for nothing, and zero cannot be the sum total of our existence. The conclusion is infinite, not zero. Mere liberation—to remain in a long, deep slumber—is destructive and inconclusive. It cannot be the object of creation or the object of our existence.

The other side must be researched, the *cid-vilāsa* (the transcendental dynamic plane). And where can we get that? Here in this world is exploitation, and there it is just the opposite, dedication. Both exploitation and renunciation must be eliminated, and we should live in the third plane.

That third plane is the life of dedication. A life of duty, not to any part, but to the whole: "I live for the whole, and that whole is a part of Lord Kṛṣṇa." This is what it means to be a lover of the beautiful. In that way we have to understand, and march onward. And that is full in itself, perfect. Neither of these two—the negative and the renunciation of the negative—can bring real positive gain. The positive is not a mere withdrawal from the negative experience. The positive has its own characteristics. We must come in contact with the positive, *sat-cit-ananda, satyaṁ, śivaṁ, sundaraṁ.* We must commit ourselves in all phases, whatever is possible for us.

It does not matter much whether one is a householder or one is a *sannyāsī.* What is to be seen is how much one has intensely engaged oneself in the service of the Lord. In this vision, a householder may be above a *sannyāsī.* During the time of Mahāprabhu there were many *gṛhastha* devotees, but that was only their external form. Their real spirit was all for Gaurāṅga.

Service is necessary. In whatever position one may be, it does not matter much. *Gṛhasthas* have one position, but when necessity comes they can sacrifice the whole for Kṛṣṇa. Wholesale dedication, reverence for the whole; it does not matter in what position one is living there. The internal hankering, the fire, the dedication within, those are necessary. They may not be found in a *sannyāsī* but may be found in a *gṛhastha, vanaprastha, brahmacārī,* or anyone. We want the substance and not the form: the fire within, the fire burning because of separation from Kṛṣṇa.

Higher Backing is Necessary

When we wander in this world, we acquire so many debts, earn a reaction. Whatever action we undertake, we incur some opposite reaction. They are stored in a very subtle form in our mind, and whenever we find ourselves in this or that situation, they'll be set in motion. Whenever we like to do anything, mostly we do it. Attraction for so many different things will dictate our actions wherever we go. We have taken this loan, now only if we clear the loan, then we can go. So many things in the environment will come and stand in the way. Our previous tendency is always trying to draw us back, the acquired tendency. Hundreds and thousands of debts come to block our way. It is not very easy to make progress. We lack sufficient strength, so above all we must have some divine favor.

Mama māyā duratyayā, it is stated in *Bhagavad-gītā*: "My external potency is hard to overcome." Māyā, the illusory potency, misconception, that is also backed by the Lord. At our sweet will we cannot dismiss her; it is not possible. If we go to fight with her alone, we will be defeated. We will find ourselves outnumbered. But if we have some certificate, some recommendation from the Lord, then Māyā will release us and show us the way out.

Mama māyā duratyayā mām eva ye prapadyante: "This divine energy of Mine, consisting of the three modes of material nature, is difficult to overcome. But those who have surrendered unto Me can easily cross beyond it." (*Gītā* 7.14) If we surrender sincerely unto the Lord, then Māyā will not be courageous enough to give opposition to us. When a *jīva* soul is liberated, Māyā comes with a very submissive attitude, "Why do you leave me, my lord? Please stay with me. I shall try to please you in all respects. Why do you leave me?"

The *mukta-jīva,* the liberated soul, comes to the status of Śiva, Mahādeva, and Māyā offers him all respect. But when we are still under her clutches she plays with us; she won't allow us to get away. So many debts we have incurred here, there. We are roaming eternally, wandering within Māyā's domain and entering death. Wherever we are, we are eating and seeking comfort, and incurring further debt. That loan must be repaid. It is not a very easy thing.

Only when backed by Divinity, by a power higher than Māyā, does she become gentle and not come forward with much disturbance. *Mām eva ye prapadyante māyām etāṁ taranti te,* "Those who have surrendered unto Me can easily cross beyond this *māyā.*" The *sādhaka's* progress depends on the degree of surrender and the degree of acceptance coming from the higher plane. It is not a very easy thing.

We must be fully purged of the enjoying spirit to become members of the Infinite world. No hint of exploitation should be traced in us. We should not run after any type of enjoyment, including the enjoyment of associating with God. We must be fully purged of the enjoying spirit. If a trace of enjoyment remains in us, we shall have to remain in one of the planes of this *brahmāṇḍa,* this universe. And if any tinge of renunciation or retiring spirit is in us, we will not be allowed to enter into the world of Infinity, Vaikuṇṭha.

Kuṇṭha means limitation, and Vaikuṇṭha means the unlimited world. We want to be members of the Infinite world. 'Finite' only refers to the attempt of our separate interest to measure the Infinite. When our ego wants to measure a portion of the Infinite, considering it our personal possession, then whatever we see with our separate interest is *māyā,* misconception and misunderstanding. All such things must be dissolved. And the attitude of renunciation, "If I can't enjoy, I shall stop work; I shall go on strike," that type of reactionary mentality must also be abandoned.

Then we shall be face to face with the positive side only. What is the positive side? It is the wave from the center, *līlā,* the play of the Absolute. That wave is fulfilling the desire of the Supreme Lord, and we will be face to face with that. If the tendency for separate interest or reactionary renunciation remains in us, we cannot come in contact with that eternal flow to satisfy the Absolute. When we are free from these two kinds of whims, we can connect with the eternal flow where all points, everywhere, are active to satisfy the center. Such a plane is not dry; it is happy, constructive, and nourishing. We shall be able to feel it. Only a fleeting contact with it will make us understand that we do not want a particle of anything else. This is our homeward journey, and any other want or demand will keep us in a foreign country filled with birth, old age, infirmity, and death.

Life Nectar of the Surrendered Souls

If you are sincere, you will get a recommendation from above. *Na hi kalyāṇa kṛt kaścid durgatiṁ tāta gacchati,* "One who is engaged in auspicious activities does not meet with destruction either in this world or in the spiritual world. One who does good is never overcome by evil." (*Gītā* 6.40) If one is attempting to advance sincerely, the Lord is omniscient and He sees everything. He can't but give some backing. And then one's way is cleared in accordance with one's sincere surrender. That is *śaraṇāgati,* surrender.

We hear so many stories of the surrendered devotees, and we are encouraged to surrender ourselves. In *Prapanna-jīvanāmṛta,* Life Nectar of the Surrendered Souls, there are many quotations from very dignified *sādhus,* saints. If we read them we can get encouragement from so many devotees in so many different stages. They are speaking like this, their sentiment is like this: by all means, surrender. If we can surrender, encouraged by their example, then according to this surrender, release comes from above. *Śaraṇāgati,* that is the thing.

Judge A Man By His Ideal

One who has a good ideal is in possession of the most valuable wealth. On the other hand, if one hankers only for *kanaka-kāminī-pratiṣṭhā*—money, sense gratification and popularity—they are in animal consciousness. These are properties of animal consciousness. A radical change must be effected in us if we really want a life worth living. This is the singular meaning of our ideal.

We should be judged by our ideal. The greatness of the ideal we are trying to realize should be marked. If our ideal is great, we are great, because if we are sincere, tomorrow, or very soon thereafter, we will attain our cherished objective.

Our ideal is the all-important factor. We may not attain our ideal very easily. It is not inferior merchandise to be disposed of cheaply in the marketplace of *guru* and disciple; it is most valuable. And whatever the cost, it does not matter.

We should feel within us, "I want no less than the highest thing, that *advaya jñāna*, that Autocrat. That all-good Autocrat, the Supreme commander of everything. I want Him and nothing less. And I shall live and move; I shall feel within that whatever I shall do—at every second—I am meant for that. I am meant for my ideal. I have no more time to waste, to hesitate for anything else. If every moment, I move in every way, with the ideal in my heart, I shall always make some progress towards the goal. If I can just stay in touch with my ideal, that will guide and inspire me. In any and every action, whatever I shall do or undo, my ideal will be overhead. And that will gradually take me out of all these entanglements and enticements. One day, I shall be face to face with my desired ideal."

Bhakti Causes Bhakti

Bhakti is its own cause and nothing else. *Nirguṇa* (the spiritual mode) comes from *nirguṇa,* and *saguṇa* (the mundane mode) cannot produce *nirguṇa. Nirguṇa* is *guṇātīta,* beyond material conditioning. *Guṇa* means quality. Disease cannot produce health; removal of the disease is health proper. We must think that *nirguṇa* is health, and *saguṇa* is a diseased condition. *Sattva, rajas, and tamas:* these three modes of material nature are three kinds of disease.

Suppose one is in delirium, the initial treatment must come from the sober section. Those that are in misconception cannot help provide the proper conception. It must come from those with the proper conception. First we must have *sukṛti,* or *ajñāta sukṛti,* accumulated unintentional merit. When *sukṛti* is sufficient, it produces *śraddhā,* faith. And when *śraddhā* emerges, then conscious cooperation begins. Before that, when the patient is helpless, there is some passive treatment. Afterwards, when consciousness has been awakened, the patient can begin to cooperate with the doctor, and the treatment can go on.

When one is fully engrossed in misconception, some intervention from the plane of *nirguṇa* might come to utilize our energy in service, for our *sukṛti. Kṛṣṇa bhakti janma mūla haya, sādhu-saṅga:* "The root cause of devotional service to Lord Kṛṣṇa is association with advanced devotees." (*C.c. Madhya-līlā* 22.83) From the unknown accumulation of *sukṛti,* there is some connection with the *nirguṇa.* That arouses *śraddhā* within us, and *śraddhā* emerges to the surface. Then, we can cooperate with the doctor and the conscious movement towards God begins.

The stages after *śraddhā* may be divided into five. *Śravaṇa* then *varaṇa* then *sādhana,* then *āpana,* then *prāpana;* five stages. The first stage is *śravaṇa,* the stage of hearing. This means hearing from the agents of the Divine, and also includes reading. The *śravaṇa* from the *sādhu* is more powerful. After *śravaṇa-daśā* begins the practical stage. One takes initiation, and attains recognition from the agent of that domain. And then one leads a regulated life. After *śravaṇa* comes *varaṇa,* acceptance. One first has to listen and then to accept the creed practically, to come within the regulated life. *Varaṇa* means acceptance. *Āpana-daśā* is the stage of realization, and *prāpana-daśā* the stage of full self-surrender and distribution to others.

Renunciation Means Yukta-vairagya

Whatever service someone performs on our behalf is not *śuddha-bhakti,* pure devotional service, if we do not do it ourselves. If we give some money to help a *śuddha-bhakta* perform the holy duties, if we supply resources, or ask our students to conduct the worship, but we do not serve directly, it is not *śuddha-bhakti.*

By his own hand, Ambarīṣa Mahārāja cleansed the temple and engaged in other devotional activities, giving the responsibility of the government to the ministers. He did not send any representative to serve in the temple of the Lord. That he did by his own hand, and he delegated to others the government of the country. Similarly, one should practice devotional service directly, not through some representative. That is not recognized as *śuddha-bhakti.* It is laxity, negligence.

Renunciation must always be *yukta-vairāgya,* full dedication of all available energy and resources. According to our present condition, whatever will help us invest our highest energy for the cause, that we should take from this world.

No Spiritual Help From the Mundane

Concentration induced by drugs is artificial. All contributions from the mundane cannot but be artificial and of lower nature. We must not become excited by intoxication, but accept only as much medicine as needed to maintain our normal health. If we believe that with the help of some medicine we shall create more energy, thinking that this is the easy way, it is not only useless, but harmful as well.

This is part of the materialist's conception, the idea that matter has preceded God. The fossil is alleged to evolve to the human species, and the conception of God grows among humans. According to the materialists, the fossil is the cause of our God-conception, the fossil is the father of God.

In the same way, to think that mundane intoxication can give birth to the happy ecstasy of the conception of the Absolute beauty and sweetness, this is atheism.

No material thing can help us to make progress in the spiritual world. They might help to keep the body fit, but material things cannot make any contribution for the improvement of our spiritual position. We should make "the best of the bad bargain." We are already committed to material causes and from that only the negative aspects will be attained. Without food we cannot live, that much we shall have to accept, but we should not think that this will help us spiritually. This will keep our normal health, and from that plane we shall serve.

We shall search for Śrī Kṛṣṇa, take the Holy Name and do some service, all from the normal plane. This is *yukta-vairāgya,* proper detachment—not more, not less. We should take neither more nor less. Either one will be detrimental to our cause. All sorts of temporary excitement and risk should be avoided.

On the normal plane, we have earned our previous *karma,* and from there we should begin. We should not be attached to those things that are detrimental to our normal life. Although presently they seem to be helping, they are not making a real contribution. We should understand that this applies not only to intoxication, but even to money.

dhana-śiṣyādibhir dvārair yā bhaktir upadyate
viduratvād uttamatā hānyā tasyāś ca nāṅgatā

We may think that devotion may be earned by spending money, by using one's son or wife for the cause of devotion. "I am helping my wife to practice devotional activities, so I shall get the benefit," or "I am utilizing my son for devotional purpose, so by virtue of this I shall acquire devotion," or "My *śiṣya,* my disciple, is becoming a good devotee, so as a *guru,* I must get something through him." (*Bhakti-rasāmṛta-sindhuḥ, Purva* 257) These things are not real devotion. *Dāna, śiṣya,* are only bodily thought. By giving money to the devotees, by helping the devotees, we may get some benefit, but it is not *śuddha-bhakti.* It may be *sukṛti,* but not pure devotion. This is because money or these other things do not belong to us. Due to misidentification, we falsely think that we are masters of this or that. Our whole selves should be devoted.

Enter Only for Service

We are to learn the theory and science of gratitude. "I am grateful to you and to everyone in the environment," the very domain is of that character. Everyone thinks himself to be a thief, "I am a trespasser. Only by the grace of the environment can we have a position here. They are all well-wishers except for myself." This should be the temperament. We should sometimes be forgetful of ourselves in the intensity of our service.

We cannot enter that domain as subjects. Even if we approach Him as investigators, we can know Him only as much as He permits. There, all are our masters. We cannot be masters there; we can only be servants. If we want to enter into the highest position, we shall accept the position of the slave of the slave. Only then can we get the chance of entering into that domain. It is not unreasonable.

We are to think, *vaikuṇṭhera pṛthivy-ādi sakala cinmaya* (*C.c. Adi-līlā* 5.53). "The environment of that land in which I aspire to live is made of better stuff than I am." We are to enter into a super-subjective domain. The attitude of all the newly recruited persons there should be: "I am not of subjective character. I am of marginal potency, *taṭasthā*, but I am receiving permission to enter the super-subjective area where everything holds a higher position than I." Everyone there is of that consciousness. "The air, the earth, the trees, everything holds a higher position than I, but still I have been given permission by the Supreme authority to wander here. I have been given some service, and I am eager to render that service to this land." With this attitude in the background, one should live there, and in the foreground one will become accustomed to discharging his particular duty. "I have come and I am treading on a soil whose intrinsic value is really superior."

A child reveres his mother, but he may be taken on her lap. Such is the example of our situation when we enter Vaikuṇṭha and Goloka. "The whole atmosphere is higher than I and is to be revered, but still they have embraced me and taken me in their lap—*svarūpa-śakti*—and I have been asked to do some duty there. The whole environment is to be revered, and I am allowed to live there only as a matter of grace, not as a matter of right."

We are *taṭasthā*, and as a matter of right we may be cast in Brahmaloka, the marginal potency, so we must become conscious of this fact. Before enlisting our name in the Kṛṣṇa consciousness school we must have this primary knowledge. "We have the opportunity to enter a revered land, the land of God's throne. Only for a particular service am I entering the temple that holds a superior position. Wholly for service I am entering, and by their gracious nature they are drawing me there. I am being taken on my mother's lap. I take the dust of her feet upon my head, but she is taking me upon her lap."

Slave of the Slave

We are not independent. Constitutionally we are slaves of the slave, and there we thrive. We are to appreciate that slavery is our fortune. But this is a hard nut to crack, to accept this. How can slavery be for our gain, for our fortune? Kṛṣṇa is so great that His slavery is of a high, noble order. He is so good, so great. Without that sort of disposition it is impossible for us to approach Him, to have any intimate connection. He lives in such a high sphere that it is impossible to meet Him. Only by the acceptance of His intimate slavery can we hope to enter that domain. It is so high for us, so very high. We should really try to understand how slavery is the highest attainment. Just calculate how much higher is the position that Kṛṣṇa holds.

Divine slavery is spontaneous and happy. The very atmosphere is so happy, that if by any means we can enter into that atmosphere, we cannot but be happy, according to our best understanding, our best feeling and conception. It is all-satisfying; slavery is the highest attainment. How high that must be! We are to conceive in that way, what sort of inconceivably higher type of life is possible there: the beauty, the charm, the love. At the same time, the inverse is true.

However much dedication is directed at Kṛṣṇa, a proportional dedication comes from Kṛṣṇa. A finite person gives his whole energy. If the Infinite gives some small portion, that is more than enough. To have the chance of giving and taking in that sphere is desirable, it is a great fortune.

There are other incarnations of Kṛṣṇa that are more or less busy with some official activity, either here in this world of *māyā* or in Vaikuṇṭha. But Kṛṣṇa has no duty. He is always free, always enjoying freedom. He has no definite aim, at His sweet will He moves here and there. He is so free, and with the attitude of a radical. Free temperament, His sweet will playing freely. And

He can give anything and everything at His pleasure.

Svarūpa Dāmodara and Śrīvāsa Paṇḍita had a discussion in Purī. Śrīvāsa Paṇḍita was espousing the cause of Vaikuṇṭha. He was speaking in favor of Lakṣmī Devī, describing Her grandeur, beauty and splendor. "What is there when we cast a glance towards Vṛndāvana? There are only flowers and a creeper and some peacocks tails here and there."

Svarūpa Dāmodara could not contain himself; he could not tolerate this. "Śrīvāsa, you don't remember? You also have some connection with Vṛndāvana. Don't you know that where there is much grandeur one becomes tired of that majesty? But Vṛndāvana is so plain, so humble, so simple. That is the place for the highest realized souls. They are all *kalpataru* (wish-fulfilling). The *kāma-dhenu* (desire fulfilling cow) will supply whatever is necessary. But naturally the residents are rather disgusted with the vanity of the life of grandeur and splendor."

That is *aprākṛta kevala,* the highest stage of existence. It is the display of the Absolute good or beauty. It is His play in the form of this human nature; that reaches the supreme position, the supreme charm there. It includes everything, its amplitude is endless and all embracing.

It is a sin to be culpable, but that is also included in that highest plane, in the highest pastimes. Nothing is neglected. This shows the greatest beauty—the highest having a touch of that which is negligible, that which is hated. We are accustomed to hate, to approach with hate, contempt and apathy. That is also harmonized in such a beautiful way. There is no room for rejecting anything, there it is the fullest play of the Absolute. The play there is fully dressed, dressed to the extreme. Thieving and quarreling, all these apparently mundane and hateful things are beautifully adjusted there. The most ample and deepest essence of harmony has evolved to accommodate and adjust all these things.

So, it is very sweet and very wonderful.

The deepest beauty has been drawn out to make all these beautiful things more beautiful. The best quality things are taken out to allow these blamable things to also play their part, to enhance the beauty. Everything is beautiful. It is beautiful that the Master is stealing. He is quarreling; He is doing so many objectionable things. He is all-enjoyable. All that could take us away from His consciousness, they are utilized there. We have no room to run away. Where should we run? Coming in contact with that, you shall run away from there?

Everything will remind me about my Master. The beauty has flowed to the farthest extremity so as to embrace everything, and we have no place to run away. We are captured, completely captured. In whatever way our attention may be diverted, that possibility is already captured there. Where should we run? There is no room. There is complete dedication, attraction. We are captured wholesale. There is no way out! Mahāprabhu, Gaurāṅga Sundara, Gurudeva, Śrī Gurudeva; all are there.

Saranagati

When I left the mission of my Guru Mahārāja after his disappearance, I came here quite helpless. I had to find my shelter and so I began to search the books that I had. What I received from my Guru Mahārāja, I began to research the references in the scriptures. I tried to dive deep, to collect the very basis of real devotional life. I found that it is *śaraṇāgati*, surrender; and wherever I found the verses recommending and relating to that, I tried my best to collect them and compile the nectar in the life of one who has fully surrendered himself to the feet of the Divine Lord. That is *Śrī Śrī Prapanna-jīvanāmṛtam.*

Paramānanda Brahmacārī was perhaps the seniormost of all our godbrothers. At the age of 13 he came to our Guru Mahārāja.

He was one of the earliest disciples of our Guru Mahārāja, seniormost. Paramānanda said that he read one chapter of *Prapanna-jīvanāmṛta* every day. In *Prapanna-jīvanāmṛta* we have collected many valuable passages from many saints and arranged them according to specific categories. There are so many sayings of so many great devotees and they are all very beautifully arranged and placed there.

In my study I found that *śaraṇāgati* alone is sufficient to produce all sorts of development in *bhakti*. Nothing else is necessary, so try your best to pursue *śaraṇāgati*, and automatically everything will come to you from the other side. Your business will only be to adhere to *śaraṇāgati* to the most intense degree possible.

Śaraṇāgati is enough, but without it devotion cannot stand. The greatness and the substance of *śaraṇāgati* has been sung, praised and appreciated in such a way. The surrendering disposition is the very basis. "I am for You. You may utilize me, or You may neglect me, still I am Yours. You may accept or reject me, but You are my master. You are independent and may deal with me in any way You like. You can put me in eternal hell, or You can take me on Your lap. You have every right over me." With such a heart we must approach our Lord. That is noble, that is divine. We can find the highest degree of divinity in our self-effacement, our self-surrender. That is the real expression of the negative towards the positive.

The negative cannot exist without the positive, and so too the positive cannot exist without the negative. In the words of our Guru Mahārāja, Rādhā and Kṛṣṇa are the predominated and predominating Moieties. Two Moieties—two halves of the one whole. One predominated and one predominating, but both have equal importance in their existence. One cannot stand without the other, and the fullest expression of this principle is Rādhā-Govinda.

Our *mantra,* our *guru-paraṁparā,* the *Rūpānūga-Saṁpradāya,* all point towards this principle. In support of this we find *dāsya-rasa, sakhya-rasa vātsalya-rasa,* and others. But the principal direction is towards *mādhurya-rasa.* They are leading us to the full *rasa.* All others are partial, subordinate and subservient—supplemental to the main *rasa, mādhurya-rasa.* But that supplemental service is also necessary. *Mādhurya-rasa* does not stand alone. It must have its paraphernalia: the friends, the parents, all must be there with this *rasa.* Those who have an inner liking for such *rasa* are so fortunate! Vāsudeva Daṭṭa has said,

yadi gaura na ha'ta, tabe ki haita,
kemane dharitām de
rādhāra mahimā, prema-rasa-sīmā,
jagate jānāta ke?

"If Mahāprabhu had not appeared then how could we sustain our lives? How could we live? What type of ecstatic *rasa* has He imbibed that we have been able to have a little taste? Without this our lives would be impossible. Who else could take us to the acme of realization of the position of Śrīmatī Rādhārāṇī? She is the greatest victim to the consuming capacity of Śrī Kṛṣṇa. She stands as the greatest sacrifice before Kṛṣṇa's infinite consuming power. Rasarāja-Mahābhāva—the *rasa* is there, and She is the drawer of that *rasa* from the storehouse. She has such negative capacity that She can draw out the *rasa* to the highest degree both in quality and quantity."

Śrīla A.C. Bhaktivedānta Svāmī Mahārāja said, "My *guru* is Rādhārāṇī. She will be very gracious to You, Kṛṣṇa, if You help me in discharging the order of my Gurudeva, if You help me in my propaganda work."

kṛṣṇa taba puṇya habe bhāi, e-puṇya koribe jabe
rādhārāṇī khuśi habe dhruva ati boli tomā tāi

"If You seek anything, if You are in want of anything, Kṛṣṇa, then that is the good will of Rādhārāṇī. And She will be pleased with You if You help me, because I am attempting to carry out the order of one whom is none other than Śrīmatī Rādhārāṇī personified. So You must help me."

Kṛṣṇa had no alternative but to come down to him and help in his propaganda work. He had to come. Svāmī Mahārāja was such a great friend of mine! He went away, but he is still with me through you. He is so kind to me! He is forcibly engaging me. Where else shall we get such a good friend, such a kind friend?

Seva Must Originate From Above

If we thrust something on the higher authority then that is *karma-kāṇḍa.* The origin of our motivation must not be within. That must come from Hari, *guru,* or Vaiṣṇava. And we must carry it out. We should not be the creators of the wave of command. We must carry out the news that comes through the wave from above, from Hari, *guru,* or Vaiṣṇava. We are only to carry out orders and not to make any.

When one receives the license from that higher plane, one can issue orders. God gives the license: "Yes, whatever you think, I will be at your back. I have constant connection with you and I supply the wave to your center, instructions of a permanent character. From that capital you will be able to transmit this wave to others."

The command must come from the center, the higher position, and be implemented by those below. The nature of harmony requires this system of control. The center is one, *advaya-jñāna.* He is the Absolute autocrat. *Advaya-jñāna* means the dictation from a particular quarter and carrying out the orders according to the degree of capacity of the different centers. Then the result is connected with the Absolute.

I must not venture to command anything to anybody, but if I have received that sort of order from the upper region, then and then only may I transmit that command. I may be a transmitter but not the absolute creator of any desire of any will. My spoken word may be a sub-center, but not the absolute center. There are many sub-centers, reliable sub-centers.

In Gurudeva, Rādhārāṇī and Baladeva were permanently present, and now also there may be other recognized centers of command. I can communicate with them and carry out their orders. In that way we can keep our connection with the higher authority, the Absolute. We are very eager to keep our connection with the Absolute harmony, eager to have direction from above and act accordingly. By necessity of harmony this sort of conduct is required. A Vaiṣṇava must have this submissive nature.

Whatever power we have, however small, place it at the disposal of the highest beauty, love divine, and it will be distributed. We will also be inundated with the highest quality and degree of joy and fulfillment. Such a life of devotion has been recommended as the key to our progress. Prahlāda Mahārāja, who is a *śuddha-bhakta,* a pure devotee of the primary stage, *śānta-rasa,* has warned us of the contamination of the trading disposition.

We should not attempt to conduct business transactions with God and His agents under pretense of devotion. It is a great danger in our approach to pure devotion *(na sa bhṛtyaḥ sa vai vaṇik*). We must scrutinize ourselves and abandon this trading temperament. At its root is *pratiṣṭhā*—the quest for self-establishment, name and fame. Genuine devotion is devoid of such a tendency.

And we will have to go down sometimes. To go up, carry out the orders of the higher authority. Always maintain that sort of tendency. Setting aside our own sentiment, always look with earnestness towards whatever order we may get from above. That should be our guide, the guide of anyone in the center. And that will maintain harmony and unity in the organization. It is always necessary to maintain the health of the system. When a very elevated Vaiṣṇava speaks like that he is setting the example for us. That should be our attitude, and he is also of that attitude: always hankering, increasing our hunger to get direction from above at every moment. And it is infinite. Every center cultivates that hankering.

There is also *ācārya-abhimāna*: some sum is already deposited with some condition, that it be spent for a particular purpose. Then as if it were his own money, he distributes it—that is *ācārya-abhimāna*. There are so many instructions within a box, some previously deposited direction. The *ācārya-abhimāna* is going ahead with those directions. The inspiration always comes to his heart: do this, do this, do this. Like a soldier he advances further and further, and by doing that he is internally carrying out his orders. He is moving rationally, but internally he is connected with the higher plane: assertion on one side and submission on the other. Begging from the higher power and distributing to the lower section, that should be the duty of every person in the mission. *Yāre dekha, tāre kaha 'kṛṣṇa'-upadeśa.* "If you adhere to this business I will supply the capital to you." Be sincere in your dealings. The current is always there; it is a dynamic thing. The wares, the dynamo must be healthy, wholesome. There is no want of current. The mediator must be all right. The current is infinite.

Dedication Beyond Calculation

The calculation of good and bad in the misconceived area is necessarily all false, completely false. *Dvaite bhadrā-bhadra-jñāna, saba mano dharma.* On the other hand, whatever is good and bad in the plane of Kṛṣṇa consciousness, both are ultimately good. We must try to learn what is the intrinsic value of good and bad. *Sumati* means a good disposition, but good in its fullest conception must come from devotion to Kṛṣṇa, from Kṛṣṇa consciousness.

Exploitation and renunciation, both are bad, and only service, dedication to the central principle of Divinity can really be called good. Service is of two kinds: calculating and surrendered. Surrendered service is the highest type of service, and that is found only in Vṛndāvana. Divine slavery to the extreme. This type of service means to accept slavery as our highest position.

He is so good, that if we can be connected to Him in slavery we will receive infinite good. Whatever degree of slavery we are able to accept, then we may attain such height of goodness. It is quite reasonable. Otherwise we cannot have any entrance into that holiest land. We can gain admission only when we offer our service to the extreme point of slavery. And that slavery must be unconditional.

Slavery in that domain is far, far better than mastery in this land of exploitation, where the reaction can only be very, very bad. And the middle plane, the land of renunciation, is neither good nor bad; it is nothing—zero—a freezing point. It is very hard to conceive of this beneficial divine slavery, but nothing short of that will give us entrance to the holy domain.

Part Three

Higher Talks

Higher Talks

With the stirring of the soul from its identification with the body and the mind, the proper understanding will come gradually in one's spiritual development. As we advance beyond the tendency for renunciation into devotional service, the first decision is whether to aim for Vaikuṇṭha or Goloka. First we must decide that. If we are not satisfied after staying some time in Vaikuṇṭha, we will get the connection of the higher *sādhu*, Kṛṣṇa's agent. And we will be taken on to the higher sphere.

This is clearly depicted in *Bṛhad-Bhāgavatāmṛta*. Gradually one will continue on the way to Ayodhyā, and from there to Dvārakā, and on to Vṛndāvana. According to one's stirring in the heart, the current environment will become gradually tasteless.

In line with one's *sukṛti* and inner adaptability, awakening is accomplished by circumstantial influences. With that stirring, the inner soul derives some taste, and according to that taste one adjusts to the environment. In keeping with the internal taste, we recognize our own: this paraphernalia, these friends, this type of service. These seem to be our own. It is very attractive, very, very attractive. Our appeal is according to taste. In this way we feel attraction for some sort of nourishment.

The awakened souls will be able to select the proper environment. Inner taste will guide us. This is very charming and attracts our hearts. We always seem to be helpless. We can't control ourselves. We feel so much attraction for that particular goal. In that way, we will be directed. Intuition will direct us. That will come to us for selection, for acceptance—elimination and acceptance. With the *sādhana,* with the process of realization, elimination and selection will come gradually.

Why have we come to Kṛṣṇa? For what reason have we come? Why has Kṛṣṇa consciousness attracted our soul, our inner heart? Formerly, we had some conception of religion. But why did we leave that, so many formalities, such association, so many friends within that circle? Why did we leave? Who is to take care of us here in Kṛṣṇa consciousness? Why have we come, taking some risk? The country, the society, the religious conception, why have we left them and come forward for Kṛṣṇa consciousness? That same tendency will again drive us to select different departments of service in Kṛṣṇa consciousness.

That inner tendency, the inner hankering, this sort of service is very pleasing. We can't but associate with this sort of service. That will be the guide: cooperation with *caitya-guru,* the *guru* inside, the dictator inside. Our *guru* is outside and inside. When we cannot catch the dictation of the internal *guru,* we want some guidance from the external *mahānta-guru* and the scripture. And when we reach a certain stage, from there our *ruci* (taste) may guide us. Our inner dictating tendency may guide us, as birds and other creatures are guided by intuition.

Higher Vision of Guru

Although Prabhupāda took initiation from Gaura Kiśora Dāsa Bābāji Mahārāja as suggested by Bhaktivinoda Ṭhākura, still he held Bhaktivinoda Ṭhākura as his real *guru*. He took Gaura Kiśora Dāsa Bābāji Mahārāja as Gurudeva only by the order of Bhaktivinoda Ṭhākura. Bhaktivinoda Ṭhākura selected for him.

We have seen that Prabhupāda took Bhaktivinoda Ṭhākura as *guru* from the internal consideration. His outside and inside was filled with Bhaktivinoda Ṭhākura, not in the physical sense, but in the spiritual sense. He installed Deities of Vinoda-Vilāsa, Vinoda-Rāma, Vinoda-Ānanda, and Vinoda-Prāṇa in many Maṭhas. We saw his attempt also through his Gurudeva, Bhaktivinoda Ṭhākura, to approach Rādhā-Govinda and Mahāprabhu. It was inconceivable, not possible without Bhaktivinoda Ṭhākura's influence in him.

Once I attempted to write something about Bhaktivinoda Ṭhākura, and that became the key to his affection for me. Because I tried to express publicly in a systematic way the greatness and character of Bhaktivinoda Ṭhākura, his attention was drawn to me. It is my own feeling that Prabhupāda will give everything to that lofty spirit who is a little attached to Bhaktivinoda Ṭhākura.

Prabhupāda Sarasvatī Ṭhākura saw Rādhārāṇī and Gadādhara in Bhaktivinoda, the highest ideal of *guru-tattva*: Gaura-Gadādhara in *mādhurya-rasa*, and Rādhārāṇī in *Kṛṣṇa-līlā*. Prabhupāda said that if we raise our head a little higher and look up, then we shall find Rādhārāṇī and Gurudeva. It is Rādhārāṇī who is instrumental in accomplishing the function of Gurudeva from behind. The source of grace for the *guru* is coming from the original source of service and love. He used to see Bhaktivinoda Ṭhākura in that light.

Sākṣād dharitvena samasta śāstrair, we are asked to see Gurudeva not as opaque but as transparent, to such a degree that through him the highest conception of service, the first conception of service can be seen. It can be obtained there. If we are earnest then we shall find the highest link from the original source. We are requested not to see *guru* as limited in his ordinary personification, but as the transparent mediator of the highest function in his line. If only our vision is deep, we can see that according to the depth of our *śraddhā,* our vision, *guru-tattva* is very peculiar, very noble, very broad, wide and very deep.

We are warned against thinking that Gurudeva has mortal qualities. Prabhupāda in his ideal conduct has shown this to us, how much earnestness one may have for Gurudeva. We have seen this in his practice, in his ways and advice. Bhaktivinoda Ṭhākura was completely awakened within him—everything for Bhaktivinoda Ṭhākura.

What high kind of realized conception Bhaktivinoda Ṭhākura has given us! We should not think that he acquired this knowledge in one lifetime. It may seem, from the ordinary events of life, that this was the natural development of *jñāna-śūnya-bhakti.* In his youth, Bhaktivinoda Ṭhākura had some other tendencies. He married twice. Still, that does not negate that he is an eternal servitor of the Lord. Otherwise such intensity and such depth of feeling cannot come abruptly. Prabhupāda saw him as the representation of Gadādhara Paṇḍita. He saw Gaura Kiśora as Svarūpa Dāmodara and Bhaktivinoda Ṭhākura as Gadādhara Paṇḍita.

Gadadhara Pandita

The advent day of Gadādhara Paṇḍita is on *amāvasyā,* on the new moon, the night of the dark moon. Mahāprabhu came in the full moon, *pūrṇimā,* and He drew the entirety of internal wealth from Gadādhara Paṇḍita. Mahāprabhu made him quite empty. He sent Gadādhara Paṇḍita on a black night in the hot summer season. In Mahāprabhu's case, He descended on the night of the full moon during a very good season. Kṛṣṇa descended in the middle of the lunar period. Rādhārāṇī also appeared in the middle. When

They combined as One, They appeared under the full moon. But Gadādhara Paṇḍita appeared under the blackest night.

Gadādhara Paṇḍita appeared and disappeared during the summer season, under the new moon. Mahāprabhu took the fullest advantage from Gadādhara, and sent him to the most negative position. Gadādhara Paṇḍita gave himself voluntarily to Him. His very heart was drawn by Mahāprabhu, *bhāva-kānti.* And he, just like a shadow, gave the entirety of his wealth to Mahāprabhu. Gadādhara Paṇḍita was a shadow, running after Him as if his heart had been stolen. This Person stole all his wealth, and he was fully dependent on Him. Like a shadow, he is moving after Him.

Rādhārāṇī has two corresponding moods: She is Rādhā in *Kṛṣṇa-līlā,* and in *Gaura-līlā,* the mood of distribution, She is Gadādhara. In *Gaura-līlā,* Kṛṣṇa Gaurāṅga appears with the *bhāva-kānti* of Rādhārāṇī as Gadādhara, the man standing by His side like *niṣkiñcana,* one who has lost everything. He is standing there just like a facsimile, only a carcass, only the form without the spirit.

But Gadādhara has so much inner attraction for Mahāprabhu that it surpasses all of His other associates. In Gadādhara we find personified love for Gaurāṅga. No such degree of love for Gaurāṅga can be found anywhere else. Next in affection is Svarūpa Dāmodara. Then comes Rūpa and Sanātana, in the *mādhurya-līlā* connection; then Nityānanda, and Śaci Mātā in the *vātsalya* connection. Advaita Prabhu and Śrīvāsa Paṇḍita also have love for Mahāprabhu, but their devotion is of another type. It is not so deep from the point of view of love, but a respectful attachment.

Gadādhara Paṇḍita tolerated injustice his whole life. All wealth was plundered from his heart. As with Rādhārāṇī, everything is ransacked by Kṛṣṇa to enhance His *līlā.* And the real owner, he is treated as if he were bankrupt. Gadādhara is bankrupt in his own wealth; that is his position.

He is wholly dedicated to Mahāprabhu. Gadādhara Paṇḍita's position, the part he played, was something like that of Rādhārāṇī: Her heart stolen by Kṛṣṇa, the empty body still standing. *Rādhā-bhāva-dyuti-suvalitaṁ naumi kṛṣṇa-svarūpam*, he was fully engrossed in the conception of Śrī Gaurāṅga. Gaurāṅga took everything from him, so he had no other alternative; he was fully absorbed, captured completely by Him.

We find his activity throughout his whole life was like this. Of the other devotees, some were ordered to go to Vṛndāvana, and some were allowed to go there, but though Gadādhara Paṇḍita wanted to visit Vṛndāvana with Mahāprabhu Himself, he was denied. When Jagadānanda Paṇḍita asked to go there, Mahāprabhu, with hesitation, granted him permission, "Yes, go there, but move always under the guidance of Rūpa and Sanātana." He also gave him some special instructions. But Gadādhara Paṇḍita was not allowed to go there.

He was the expansion of Śrīmatī Rādhārāṇī Herself, yet his peculiar position was such: the Queen of Vṛndāvana, but now transferred to Navadvīpa. His position had become just the opposite; he could not enter Vṛndāvana! He prayed for permission, but Mahāprabhu did not give it. He said, "No, stay and live here." And he had to do so. Śrī Gadādhara Paṇḍita represents the predominated Moiety of the Whole. The Whole consists of predominating and predominated Moieties, and he represents the predominated half. He is one half of the Absolute Truth.

Halo of Radharani

Gadādhara Dāsa represents the halo of Rādhārāṇī, but Gadādhara Paṇḍita represents Her mood, Her nature, Her heart. Gadādhara Dāsa is accepted as *kānti, bhāva-kānti. Rādhā-bhāva-dyuti-suvalitaṁ.*

Rādhārāṇī is conceived as divided into two: the inner mood and the outer luster. So Dāsa Gadādhara is conceived as the outer luster, and Paṇḍita Gadādhara is seen as the inner mood. Mahāprabhu has actually assumed both, and the remaining shadow is represented in them.

Dāsa Gadādhara used to stay near Calcutta, in Harisahara. He was a simple and straight-minded man. One day he approached the Kazi (Muslim Governor), "You Kazi, you must take the name of Kṛṣṇa!" "Why, I am a Muslim, why should I take the name of Kṛṣṇa?" "Oh, you have taken already! You have taken the name of Kṛṣṇa!" And he embraced him. "Yes, you have taken." The Kazi was friendly to him.

We find something more important in Gadādhara Dāsa and in his last days he came to take charge of that place in Katwa where Mahāprabhu took *sannyāsa,* and he opened a temple there. Those who are at present in charge of that temple are in the disciplic line of Dāsa Gadādhara. His *samādhi* is also there.

Gadadhara Pandita as Rukmini

We may look to the outer aspect of Gadādhara; his *bhāva* has been taken, emptied. Rukmiṇī means *dakṣiṇa,* not *vāma.* The *vāma* nature is a little aggressive, and fights with the lover. *Dakṣiṇa* tolerates everything, whatever comes, only with a defensive attitude. That is *dakṣiṇa,* that is the mood of Rukmiṇī. So when Mahāprabhu plunders the spirit of Rādhārāṇī, the rebellious *vāma* nature, what remains is comparable to Rukmiṇī—a passive seer, without any power to assert, only an onlooker. An onlooker, tolerating everything, a very pitiable condition that elicits kindness and sympathy from everyone.

Just see what He is and what She is, and what is Her position now. See how Her lover has taken everything from Her, looted everything from Her, leaving Her as a beggar wandering in the street. Rādhārāṇī, when ransacked to such a degree by Kṛṣṇa, becomes Gadādhara, the pitiable figure. But Her wealth cannot abandon Her forever. She is the proprietor; the owner cannot be far off. After a long time, all must come to Her again, someday. And those who serve Her in Her day of distress will receive a great remuneration when She recalls Her property.

Gaura-Gadadhara

Gadādhara is the *āśraya* (shelter) and Gaura is the *viṣaya* (enjoyer). But *viṣaya* has taken the mood, the nature of *āśraya*. That is Gaura, both shelter and enjoyer combined. When Kṛṣṇa assumes the characteristics of Rādhikā, He is Gaura. The inaugurator of *Nāma-saṅkīrtana*, that is Gaura Nārāyaṇa. He is *viṣaya avatāra*, the incarnation of enjoyment. Gaurāṅga is Rādhā-Kṛṣṇa combined; He is Kṛṣṇa in the mood of Rādhikā. He has accepted the nature of Rādhikā.

When He is searching after Himself, trying to taste what sort of ecstasy is in Himself, that self-searching Kṛṣṇa is Gaurāṅga. He is trying to understand Himself, what sort of ecstasy is within Him. Kṛṣṇa in the mood of His devotee, that is Gaurāṅga: introspection, self-seeking, searching for His own wealth.

He is also distributing it to others. He is inquiring about Himself and distributing that personally to the public. That is Gaurāṅga, showing how He should be served by serving Himself. He is demonstrating to the public how He should be served. And for that He took the mood of Rādhārāṇī, to search after Himself. What is there? Why should others come to Him, what is He that so attracts them? And then He is giving Himself to others. Kṛṣṇa is *guru*. When Kṛṣṇa Himself is *guru*, then He is Gaurāṅga. *Guru rūpa hari guru rūpa harim.*

Gadādhara Paṇḍita is *rādhā-bhāva-dyuti-suvalitaṁ*. The entire wealth of Rādhārāṇī's feelings, Her sentiments, mood, and even Her luster were taken by Kṛṣṇa. Rādhārāṇī voluntarily gave all these things. "I can't allow You to roll on the earth with Your body. I shall enfold You." That emptiness we find in Gadādhara Paṇḍita; he is running after Mahāprabhu as His shadow. But he is not poor. It is his wealth that has given Mahāprabhu such a dignified position.

Some even think that He is superior to Kṛṣṇa Himself, that magnanimous Gaurāṅga, the public deliverer of Kṛṣṇa. For our interest, on behalf of the fallen souls, Gaura has come to us for general relief work. We cannot but think that He is greater than Kṛṣṇa. And Gadādhara Paṇḍita's contribution is there in Him. In the high summer, in the darkest night, Gadādhara Paṇḍita appeared. But that does not mean that we should underestimate him. What is his reality, his nature as Rādhārāṇī, we have to inquire, understand, and realize.

Divine Vision

Gadādhara Paṇḍita disappeared on *amāvasyā*, during the dark moon. Bhaktivinoda Ṭhākura also passed away under the dark moon. Prabhupāda has written, *gadādhara din dhāri paiyaca gaurahari.* Prabhupāda noted something common to Bhaktivinoda Ṭhākura and Gadādhara Paṇḍita, that they disappeared on the same day. In this connection Bhaktivinoda Ṭhākura received the grace of Śrī Gaurāṅga. Bhaktivinoda is a favorite of His; Prabhupāda has revealed this.

In another place he wrote that the eternal pastimes are always going on in Navadvīpa-dhāma. Sometimes they are underground, invisible to us, and sometimes on the surface. *Nitya-līlā* always is invisible to us. Now, suddenly, these two personalities have come to the surface, Gadādhara Paṇḍita and Svarūpa Dāmodara. Both have come. Svarūpa Dāmodara came as Gaura Kiśora and Gadādhara Paṇḍita came as Bhaktivinoda Ṭhākura.

This is not to be given expression in any and every place. This is concealed truth, not to be expressed everywhere and anywhere. This is the fact: they are always here, continuing their own function, their participation in the *līlā* of Gaurāṅga. Sometimes it is underground, sometimes over-ground, but it is always difficult to recognize them.

Prabhupāda wrote, "I suddenly found Svarūpa Dāmodara as Gaura Kiśora, and Gadādhara Paṇḍita as Bhaktivinoda Ṭhākura—they most graciously gave me that sort of vision. I could see them as two *pārṣadas,* the eternal companions of Gaurāṅga. I found that." It is mentioned in the conclusion to his *Caitanya Caritāmṛta Anubhāṣya,* "Here, in Navadvīpa-dhāma, the eternal pastimes are going on continuously; only those who have got that deep vision can perceive it."

gadādhara mitra-vara, śrī svarūpa dāmodara,
sadā kāla gaura-kṛṣṇa yaje
jagatera dekhi' kleśa, dhariya bhikṣuka-veśa,
āharābhaḥ kṛṣṇa-nāma bhaje
śrī gaura icchāya dui, mahimā ki kava mui,
aprakṛta pariśāda-kathā
prakaṭa haiya seve, kṛṣṇa-gaurabhinna-deve,
aprakasya kathā yathā tathā

Prabhupāda says, "It is very difficult to perceive the sweet will of Śrī Gaurāṅga, but if we can lift ourselves to that level, we see that Svarūpa Dāmodara Gosvāmī and Śrī Gadādhara Paṇḍita are always engaged in their service here in Navadvīpa. Sometimes it is suppressed and sometimes it is appearing on the surface. In that plane all is going on by the sweet will of Śrī Gaurāṅga, without any restriction. But now I find that those two have appeared on the surface as Śrīla Gaura-Kiśora Dāsa Bābāji and Śrīla

Bhaktivinoda Ṭhākura. I have seen it with my own eye of divine service. But this is not to be advertised, not to be given publicity anywhere and everywhere; people will laugh at it. But this is my heartfelt conclusion."

We are the children of a limited soil, we are children of the limited aspect of the world. Many things are impossible for us. We are accustomed to think that everything is impossible. Only that with which I have acquaintance in my little experience is possible, other things are all impossible. We are trained to think like that. But if we think about the Infinite, it is just the opposite. Anything and everything may be possible, bad or good. In the transcendental world, the goodness, the sweetness has no end. And there are different gradations.

Progress by Grace of the Higher

In this we have to make advancement, progress. That thought comes: *pratyakṣa, apratyakṣa, adhokṣaja, aparokṣa,* and *aprākṛta.* These are the five layers of knowledge. *Pratyakṣa* is where we are awake now. In *parokṣa,* we consider the sense experience of others as part of our knowledge. *Aparokṣa* is independent of all our experience, and there we faint. That is *samādhi.* We cannot feel our low environment, but only our personal consciousness in slumber, deep slumber. Only personal consciousness is present, without any conception of the environment.

And then, by the grace of the higher world, when they take us in there, we wonderfully have some experience of the transcendental world. It is by their grace, by their mercy, not as a matter of right. That is the highest stage, *aprākṛta,* very similar to this, my world of experience, but it will hold the highest position of existence and sweetness in every way: harmony and ecstasy.

"I shall feed you amply; you won't be able to taste it all. Such sweetness is there in an unlimited way. I can say very easily, give up everything you have. What do you have? Nothing. Your experience and the wealth you have, *janma mṛtyu jarā vyādhi*, birth, death, old age and disease—all will pass, they will leave you. They will disappoint you in the next moment. So, you have nothing. Give up the attraction for the present environment. Come, jump desperately to come near Me, and I shall give you shelter. You will be compensated amply." This is the call of Kṛṣṇa in *Bhagavad-gītā*.

Mahāprabhu instructed also, "Give up everything, take the name of the Lord and prepare yourself to go to home. You were not created for trifling in this dishonorable life; your home is there. You are in the midst of the cremation ground and if you like, you can go there, to that honorable land. Save yourself from the cremation ground. Save yourself and try to attain your inner fulfillment and the worth of your existence there."

Gaura-Gadadhara Worship

Bhaktivinoda Ṭhākura was fond of Gaura-Gadādhara worship. They are there in his *samādhi* in Godruma and also in the Nārāsiṅgha Mandira at Yogapīṭha, Māyāpura. Gaura-Gadādhara are established in two places. Prabhupāda also installed Gaura-Gadādhara in Gadai-Gaurāṅga Maṭha at Balihati Dakka. Prabhupāda established Their worship there.

Gaura-Gadādhara represent a complete *madhūrya* conception and more. In Them there is separation, union in separation; Gadādhara Paṇḍita has Rādhārāṇī's *bhāva*. Although he was the possessor of that wealth, Mahāprabhu took it and he stood empty, plundered, following Mahāprabhu as if his heart had been stolen. Yet, he cannot shun Him, nor leave Him. Wherever Mahāprabhu goes, Gadādhara Paṇḍita runs after Him like a poor man. All his wealth has been stolen. With an empty bag, without any vanity, with a vacant heart he is running in pursuance of Mahāprabhu. That is his position.

Prema-vaicittya, separation in union, union and separation. Like *madhūrya-rasa*, but a vow has been taken. In the temple, both husband and wife may be engaged in the worship of the Lord. Though both of them are present, wife and husband together, some vow is taken so they cannot enjoy. What is their attitude? They do not act as husband and wife, but one is engaged in worship, and the other is supplying the materials for worship. They are separated, but still Gadādhara stands in the position of Rādhārāṇī. They have taken a vow together. That sort of *saṁbhoga* is present, spiritual separation in physical proximity. The highest purity is there, without any enjoyment. Still, it is *līlā-vilāsa*, the amorous pastime. It is like that; that is Gaura-Gadādhara.

Sometimes in the case of Rādhārāṇī and Kṛṣṇa, They experience *prema-vaicittya*. They are standing closely together, yet still experience some feeling of separation. So intense is Their feeling. Even though They are together, They are feeling the pain of intense separation. That is *prema-vaicittya*. A pastime is mentioned wherein Kṛṣṇa, Rādhārāṇī, and *sakhīs* are present. Rādhārāṇī sees Her image in the body of Kṛṣṇa. It is so transparent, the body of Kṛṣṇa. Rādhārāṇī's image is reflected there, and Rādhārāṇī thinks, "Oh, there is another lady with a golden colored body." She is very much engaged in jealousy. And Lalitā comes and explains that the reflection of Rādhārāṇī is not another *sakhī*. "That is your reflection on His body." Then She is satisfied.

We are told that service offered when They are in separation has a greater importance than when They are united. When They are separated, They feel great pain, and service at that time is an utmost necessity. Where do we find this greatest necessity? In Gadādhara Paṇḍita, in Rādhārāṇī. Her *bhāva* is plundered by Mahāprabhu and She is bereft of all Her property. Like the poorest of the poor She is standing. It is so pitiable and pathetic that it demands service. Service here will be of the greatest value. In that state, our service will attract the greatest remuneration; even a little service will earn much of the divine compensation.

Vrndavana is for the Shallow Thinkers

In this connection, our Guru Mahārāja once surprised us greatly, "You all know that only the bogus, hollow people and men of shallow thinking like Vṛndāvana." I was very much perplexed to hear this. I had been told that Vṛndāvana is the highest place of spiritual perfection. I had heard that one who has not mastered his senses cannot enter Vṛndāvana. Only the liberated souls can enter Vṛndāvana and have the opportunity of discussing Kṛṣṇa. Vṛndāvana is for the liberated souls. Those who are not liberated from the demands of their senses may live in Navadvīpa, but only the liberated souls may live in Vṛndāvana. Now Prabhupāda was saying that the shallow thinkers appreciate Vṛndāvana, but a man of real *bhajana*, real divine aspiration, aspires to live in Kurukṣetra.

Hearing this, I felt as if I had fallen from the top of a tree. "What is this?" I am a very acute listener, so I was very keen to catch the meaning of his words. The next thought he gave us was that Bhaktivinoda Ṭhākura, after visiting many different places of pilgrimage, remarked, "I would like to spend the last days of my life in Kurukṣetra. I shall construct a cottage near Brahmā Kuṇḍa and pass the rest of my life there. Kurukṣetra is the real place of *bhajana*."

Service Necessity

Why? Service is more valuable according to the intensity of its need. Shrewd merchants seek a market in wartime because in that dangerous situation, money is spent like water, without any care for its value. They can earn more money during war. In the same way, when Śrīmatī Rādhārāṇī's necessity reaches its zenith, service to Her becomes extremely valuable. According to its necessity, service is valued. And in Kurukṣetra, Śrīmatī Rādhārāṇī is in the highest necessity because Kṛṣṇa is so close, but Their *Vṛndāvana-līlā* is impossible.

In a game, if the ball is just inches from the goal, but is driven back, it is considered a great loss. In the same way, after a long separation, Kṛṣṇa is there in Kurukṣetra. The hankering for union felt by His devotees must come to its greatest point, but because He is in the role of a king, they cannot meet intimately. The circumstances do not allow the *Vṛndāvana-līlā* to take place. So at that time, Śrīmatī Rādhārāṇī needs the highest service from Her group, the *sakhīs.*

Bhaktivinoda Ṭhākura says that in that situation, a drop of service will attract the greatest amount of *prema,* divine love. In the pastimes of Rādhā-Govinda, there are two aspects: *saṁbhoga,* divine union, and *vipralambha,* divine separation. When Rādhā and Kṛṣṇa are very near to each other, but can't meet intimately, service at that time can draw the greatest gain for the servitors. Therefore, Śrīla Bhaktivinoda Ṭhākura says, "I shall construct a hut on the banks of Brahmā Kuṇḍa in Kurukṣetra and contemplate rendering service to the Divine Couple. If I can achieve that standard where the prospect of service is so high, then there is no possibility of returning to this mundane plane at any time."

Dvaraka Lila

Rūpa Gosvāmī wrote two books about Mādhava Kṛṣṇa; one is *Vidagdha-mādhava,* the other *Lalitā-mādhava. Vidagdha-mādhava* lives in Vṛndāvana; He is a very clever Mādhava, very clever. And *Lalitā-mādhava* is very submissive, very playful. *Lalitā-mādhava* went to Mathurā and then to Dvārakā, and Rūpa Gosvāmī writes that although externally we find Rādhārāṇī and

Candrāvalī and Their circle of friends, there they are inconceivably transformed into different forms.

Rukmiṇī and Satyabhāmā, the *Mahiṣīs* (Queens), they must have their original *svayaṁ-rūpa* in Rādhārāṇī, Lalitā, Candrāvalī. That is Śrī Rūpa's feeling. They are not independent, their origin is in Rādhārāṇī. And when they come into lawful relation with Kṛṣṇa in *madhūrya-rasa,* they assume a partial form. The fullness is in Śrī Rādhikā, and the partial expansion in all these *mahiṣīs.* Rādhikā and all the other *gopīs* are represented only partially in Dvārakā.

It is peculiar to think that the *Pradhāna Mahiṣī,* the principal queen, is Rukmiṇī. How could she come from Candrāvalī? And the secondary position represents Śrī Rādhikā, Who is the highest in Vṛndāvana, in *madhūrya-rasa.* This is a peculiar thing, and we are to follow in this way. Feeling holds the highest place, the highest value, and in a little lower layer, intelligence gets the better hand.

Candrāvalī's special capacity was her intelligence and patience, along with other general qualifications. Rādhārāṇī's capacity is more emotional. So, in the secondary *līlā,* She obtains the secondary position. Satyabhāmā represents Rādhārāṇī, and Candrāvalī, Her main opposition, has the first class position there in a little lower strata. These things are very abstruse and difficult to understand.

Rukmini Avatara

Rādhārāṇī and Rukmiṇī are of the same line, and that was represented by Gadādhara Paṇḍita in *Gaura-līlā.* In *Gaura-līlā* the peculiarity is this: the *bhāva,* the sentiment, the mood, the emotion of Rādhārāṇī was taken by Mahāprabhu Himself, Kṛṣṇa Himself. So, Gadādhara Paṇḍita is Rādhārāṇī, who was emptied of feeling. His mood is drawn from Him, so only a carcass is left.

Gadādhara Paṇḍita holds a shadow-like position in *Gaura-līlā.*

Rukmiṇī's characteristic was maintained there in Gadādhara Paṇḍita. Sober, considerate, patient; all these things, all these qualities remained there in him. Therefore, sometimes it is said that he is the *avatāra* of Rukmiṇī. But really, his position was that of Rādhārāṇī, who was plundered by Kṛṣṇa, and both combined became Mahāprabhu. That is the peculiar position he holds. Just like a shadow, he cannot leave Śrī Gaurāṅga. Wherever Śrī Gaurāṅga goes, he follows from a distance. He does not know anything but Gaurāṅga. Still, he is not seen to come forward; He is always in the background. In this way he played his role as Gadādhara Paṇḍita.

The Highest Position of Sacrifice

Kṛṣṇa and Rādhārāṇī were born between the new moon and the full moon. But Mahāprabhu took His birth under the full moon, and Gadādhara Paṇḍita under the new moon. New moon means no moon. The full moon was taken by Mahāprabhu, and the new moon was taken by Gadādhara Paṇḍita. He is master of everything, but he has given everything to his Master, and he is empty. He is empty, he is playing in such a way his part, Gadādhara Paṇḍita. He stands in the highest position of sacrifice. This is the ontological perspective.

The History

From the historical perspective we find that he was born in a *brāhmaṇa* family in the place known presently as Bhāratapura. At that time many gentlemen had their homes in the capital, as Navadvīpa was a famous town for the *brāhmaṇas* to cultivate their learning. So they had a home in this place, where Māyāpura is located at present. Mādhava Miśra was the name of his father and Ratnāvalī was his mother's name. They lived here, and he was a student. Gadādhara Paṇḍita was a very meek and modest student, and from his childhood he was devoted to Nārāyaṇa, Kṛṣṇa.

Nimai Paṇḍita, Śrī Caitanyadeva, manifested His character as an impertinent aggressor, and extraordinary genius. Gadādhara Paṇḍita was very much just the opposite. But Gadādhara Paṇḍita had some natural inclination and submission towards Nimai Paṇḍita. And Nimai Paṇḍita also had some special attraction for Gadādhara. Gadādhara Paṇḍita could not face Nimai directly. He felt some sort of shyness around Nimai Paṇḍita. And when Nimai saw that he was trying to remain aloof, He would not let him go, but was always asking him perplexing questions.

Nimai Paṇḍita returned from Gayā as a changed man, as a devotee. Meeting Gadādhara Gosvāmī, Nimai Paṇḍita addressed him, "Your life is fulfilled. From childhood you are devoted to Nārāyaṇa, to Kṛṣṇa, but My whole life is spoiled. I passed My early days in ordinary topics, not cultivating devotion for Nārāyaṇa. I did not know devotion to Kṛṣṇa, to Rādhā-Kṛṣṇa; I passed My whole life uselessly. But you, Gadādhara, from the very beginning you were a pure devotee of Kṛṣṇa. You are fortunate enough. I want your grace, so that I may pass My future days in devotional activity."

Gadādhara Paṇḍita, after taking permission from Nimai Paṇḍita, took initiation from Puṇḍarīka Vidyānidhi, who is acknowledged to be Vṛṣabhānu Rāja, the father of Rādhārāṇī. This Puṇḍarīka Vidyānidhi was a very great devotee of a higher order. Mahāprabhu gave him the name Premanidhi, instead of Vidyānidhi. Mukunda Daṭṭa took Gadādhara Paṇḍita to Puṇḍarīka, and he received initiation there.

When Mahāprabhu took *sannyāsa*, Gadādhara Paṇḍita followed Him. He could not live in Navadvīpa without Nimai Paṇḍita, who was Kṛṣṇa Caitanya. He was so much attached that when he found that Nimai would settle permanently in Purī, he took *kṣetra-sannyāsa* there. *Kṣetra-sannyāsa* is a type of renunciation in which the *sannyāsī* takes the vow of not leaving a particular place for his whole life. So, Gadādhara Paṇḍita came to know that Nimai Paṇḍita would pass the last days of His life in Jagannātha Purī, then he took *kṣetra-sannyāsa* there.

Sometimes it is seen that Nimai Paṇḍita is invited to his *āśrama*, where he has installed Gopīnāthaji. He engaged himself in the worship of Gopīnātha. Nityānanda Prabhu went there also, and was intimately connected with him. Whenever He went to Purī, Jagannātha Kṣetra, He used to stay there.

Gadādhara Paṇḍita used to read the *Bhāgavatam* daily upon the request of Mahāprabhu, Who along with His followers used to hear it from his lips. Mahāprabhu asked Gadādhara Paṇḍita to teach the *Bhāgavatam* to Śrīnivāsa Ācārya, and by His will, Śrīnivāsa Ācārya became the highest exponent of *Śrīmad Bhāgavatam*. Bhaktivinoda Ṭhākura is of the opinion that when Mahāprabhu disappeared, He sat on the *āsana* of Gadādhara Paṇḍita and became one with Gopīnātha, whom Gadādhara worshiped daily.

So, this is what we know about Gadādhara Paṇḍita, who had a most intimate relationship with Mahāprabhu. Svarūpa Dāmodara, Rūpa and Sanātana, Kavirāja, Raghunātha Dāsa, all of them, they could see both Rādhārāṇī and Rukmiṇī in him, in his personality. According to that we can try to understand him, and we shall pray to him.

Other Vaisnava Schools

Vallabhācārya was a worshiper in *vātsalya-rasa*. But when he came in contact with Mahāprabhu's party, he could recognize that *madhūrya-rasa* is the highest devotional disposition. So, he proposed to Gadādhara Paṇḍita, "I do not have *madhūrya-rasa dikṣā*;

please give it to me." And Gadādhara Paṇḍita, who was subordinate to Mahāprabhu, said, "I'm not independent; you must propose this to Him, and by His order I may give you the *mantra*."

Vallabhācārya did so, and getting permission from Mahāprabhu, he took initiation into *madhūrya-rasa*. He attained the service of Kiśora-Kṛṣṇa from Gadādhara Paṇḍita. Nowadays, the party of Vallabhācārya does not admit this. They claim to be independent—worshipers in *vātsalya-rasa*. In this way, their movement follows in that line. And when they come to *madhūrya-rasa*, they give preference to Candrāvalī; they are opposed to Rādhārāṇī.

The Vallabhācārīs are generally worshipers of Gopāla. Gopāla means boy-Kṛṣṇa, who is served in the *vātsalya-rasa* by Nanda-Yaśodā. That is their acme of realization. But they do not deny that He has some connection as a consort to the small *gopīs*, and this Candrāvalī is prominent among them. They do not like Rādhārāṇī. This is the position of the Vallabha school. Vallabhācārya was actually a follower of Gadādhara Paṇḍita. This connection with Candrāvalī came later. That sort of deviation is found in many places in their succession.

The Nimbārka school prefers to worship Rādhā-Govinda, in *svakīya-rasa*, as married husband and wife, not in *parakīya-rasa*, as paramours.

Madhurya and Audarya

Devotees of Gaurāṅga have a twofold internal characteristic: one is participating in *Kṛṣṇa-līlā*, another in *Gaura-līlā*, one in *madhūrya*, another in *audārya*. One is confined in their own *līlā* with Kṛṣṇa, another with the idea of distributing that to the public. Amongst those fortunate souls, *pārṣadas*, servitors, there are three gradations. One is more attracted to *Kṛṣṇa-līlā*, another to *Gaura-līlā*, and some are in the middle position.

When one is in *Gaura-līlā* and a hankering comes to have the *darśana* of *Kṛṣṇa-līlā,* then Gaura-Gadādhara appear as Rādhā-Kṛṣṇa. And when participating in *Rādhā-Kṛṣṇa-līlā,* if one sometimes has any desire for *Gaura-līlā,* Rādhā-Govinda are transformed into Gaura-Gadādhara. In this way, when one has a hankering for service in a particular *līlā,* the Lord manifests Himself with that paraphernalia, that nature, to satisfy the inner will of the devotee, giving facility to that sort of service. A peculiar tendency of service arises at times in the heart of the devotee, and the Lord appears in a way to receive that service.

Sometimes a servant sees his master in a plain dress. Suppose he has some desire to see his master in a gorgeous dress. Then the master, when he comes to know of this desire, will appear before him in a grand and gorgeous dress. Sometimes He may appear as a king, as a lover, as a friend, according to the demand, according to the circumstance and the paraphernalia. But everything is eternal, there is only a change of pace. Some devotees see in one way, others in another way. Bhaktivinoda Ṭhākura says that They are Gaura-Gadādhara and Rādhā-Kṛṣṇa. Another devotee standing by the side, he may not see that.

High Inquisitiveness

To satisfy the inner hankering, the opposite, the relative side also participates. Rāmānanda Rāya wanted Mahāprabhu to show His true self. Observing the nature of Śrī Caitanyadeva's inquisitiveness, Rāmānanda Rāya had some mystic idea in his mind. "Who is He? He is not an ordinary person or *sannyāsī* or a scholar, but something more. Where are these inquiries coming from? His high inquisitiveness is most rare. He must be Kṛṣṇa Himself. All these subtle points are arising in my mind and forcing me to relate all these things."

Then Rāmānanda stated, "Who are You? I don't think You are an ordinary *sannyāsī* scholar. Tell me who You are. You are

Kṛṣṇa Himself. I have a great impression, an inspiration like that. You must not hide Yourself from me. First I saw You as an ordinary *sannyāsī,* preaching about devotion to Kṛṣṇa, but gradually as You rose in a gradual ascending process in Your inquiry, doubt arose in my mind."

"You have come to me. I have not gone to You. You have kindly come to me to purify this nasty person. And now You conceal Yourself from me. I can't understand. But whoever You may be, I am sure that what You are inquiring after, You are that thing. Gradually my vision, my estimation of You is changing, changing, changing. First I saw You as a *sannyāsī,* a *brāhmaṇa,* a devotee. Gradually I am of the opinion that You are *śyāma gopa rūpa,* that cowherd boy, the Absolute in the garb of cowherd boy. What is the peculiar thing I am seeing? That a golden figure is just standing by Your side and the grace of that Lady has covered Your body. I see like that. What is this? What is the mystery? Please divulge it to me. With folded hands I ask You."

Then Mahāprabhu told Rāmānanda that His color is not golden, but by the touch of Rādhārāṇī it appears like molten gold. "Her grace has covered Me, and She never touches anybody but Her Lover, the cowherd Kṛṣṇa. So who am I? Now you see and know for yourself. Rasarāja, the highest ecstasy personified and the highest appreciator of that ecstasy, combined together."

Rāmānanda could not stand any longer there, he could not retain his normal position. Then he again saw that *sannyāsī,* that golden *sannyāsī* sitting in front of him. After a pause, Mahāprabhu said, "Now it is late, I am going." Rāmānanda fainted there and Mahāprabhu went away to the *brāhmaṇa*'s house. Only once did Mahāprabhu show Himself in this way to Rāmānanda, and never anywhere else in His whole *līlā.* There He expressed Himself, showed Himself in that form, "Who am I? Who am I?" Bhaktivinoda Ṭhākura related this.

Pandava Arjuna

Rāya Rāmānanda is more known to us as Viśākhā Sakhī. But superficially he had some aspect of Arjuna, and Mahāprabhu could detect that. Bhāvānanda had five sons, Kalānidhi, Sudhānidhi, Vāṇīnātha, Gopīnātha, and Rāya Rāmānanda. Mahāprabhu told him, "You are My eternal friend. Bhāvānanda is Pāṇḍu and his five sons are the Pañca-Pāṇḍava." Rāmānanda is a very close and intimate friend, like Arjuna. That external impression of Mahāprabhu was given, but Rāmānanda's internal mood is really that of Viśākhā. To see Rāmānanda as Arjuna is temporary and external, a fleeting sentiment of Mahāprabhu. Arjuna is in *sakhya-rasa.* Outwardly Mahāprabhu dealt with Rāmānanda a little respectfully. Outwardly He used to see him with some respect, some deference.

But internally He saw him as a *sakhī.* Svarūpa Dāmodara and Rāya Rāmānanda both would console Him when the great inevitable flow of love in separation arose in the heart of Mahāprabhu, ostentatiously disturbing Him. These two friends tried their best to console Mahāprabhu. Diverting His mind towards different directions, they would read from *śāstra* according to the circumstance, sometimes giving impetus to His own line of thought and sometimes taking Him towards other directions. They tried their best to give Mahāprabhu relief from His outwardly painful gestures and movements. For twelve years, continuously they did this.

A Mystic Poem

Advaita Prabhu almost dismissed Mahāprabhu. "No longer is there any necessity for You to stay in this world." Advaita Prabhu declared to Mahāprabhu,

bāulake kabiha loka ha-ila bāula
bāulake kabiha hāṭe nā vikāya cāula

"Please inform Śrī Caitanya Mahāprabhu, who is acting like a madman, that everyone here has become mad like Him. Inform Him also that in the market-place, rice is no longer in demand." (*C.c. Antya-līlā* 19.20)

In this mystic poem Advaita sent this message to Mahāprabhu through Jagadānanda Paṇḍita. Mahāprabhu read it and became disturbed. Svarūpa Dāmodara, the knower of everything, wondered what was the real meaning of this poem. Mahāprabhu answered in an indirect way, "I don't know what is the real purport of this poem, but I will venture a guess. Advaita Ācārya is very conversant with the ways of the *śāstra* and the conduct of worship of the Deity. In worship we first invite the Deity with an invocation, then for some time the Deity remains to receive our service, and when that is fulfilled, the Deity departs. We cannot keep Him forever. When the purpose for which He descended is accomplished, it is best that He retire. I don't know what is the real meaning, but I guess it is something like that." Then Svarūpa Dāmodara was disturbed. "Advaita Ācārya is bidding adieu to us all."

After that Mahāprabhu stayed for twelve more years, and His mood was not approachable by the ordinary public. Such was the high mood of separation from Kṛṣṇa—to the greatest degree, different manifestations were displayed, physically and mentally. For twelve years He burned continuously like fire. He exhibited the fire of separation.

That is not found elsewhere, such intense feeling of separation from God. It was not known in this world that the spirit of separation from God could be so intense, that it could produce so many symptoms in the body and the mind. We will only find an acquaintance with this in the life of Śrīmatī Rādhārāṇī. But there also we do not find such a complete manifestation of the pangs of divine separation. Such a degree of evolution we do not find anywhere, at any time: continuous, high intensity of divine love, so much sacrifice.

He manifested such intense sacrifice at the altar of the All-beautiful. Such appreciation for the Absolute beautiful, such deep attraction has never been seen anywhere in the history of the world, not even in scripture. No mention is found in any of the oldest scriptures. That was exhibited just the other day, only five hundred years ago. And it is written in the books, it is verified by so many genuine persons, men of standard thinking. There were witnesses: Rūpa, Sanātana, Raghunātha, Svarūpa Dāmodara, Rāmānanda, so many others, all so many eye witnesses.

Gaura-Nagari Rejected

Mahāprabhu's relationship with Viṣṇupriyā Devī and Lakṣmīpriyā Devī as wedded consorts is in the mood of Gaura-Nārāyaṇa, in Vaikuṇṭha mood. That concerns the *yuga-avatāra,* not Rādhā-Kṛṣṇa. It is not of that layer, not of that plane. It is connected with the *yuga-avatāra,* externally. Gadādhara represents the higher plane, while they represent the potency of Vaikuṇṭha. Gaura-Nārāyaṇa is the *yuga-avatāra,* but with a connection with that higher plane. It is mostly in the Vaikuṇṭha conception, His consorthood with Lakṣmīpriyā and Viṣṇupriyā Devī.

So the practice of *Gaura-nāgara* is not accepted by the bonafide school of Śrī Caitanyadeva's followers. There is a controversy. *Gaura-nāgarīs* think that we should see Gaurāṅga as Kṛṣṇa, as He is given in the *Bhāgavatam.* But Vṛndāvana Dāsa Ṭhākura, Kavirāja Gosvāmī, the Gosvāmīs and others have rejected this idea about Gaurāṅga.

The *brāhmaṇa,* the *ācārya,* has come to do the work of a preceptor, not of a *nāgara*, an enjoyer of girls, as we find in Vṛndāvana. It cannot tally; it cannot be proper. There is a hitch. He has taken the position of an *ācārya*, and at the same time He is to play the part of a debauchee? That cannot come together. The law of *rasa* won't allow that.

When a man enters the temple to worship the Deity, he may go there with his wife to help in serving *naivedya* (to prepare offerings) and other things, to assist in the worship. But she may not banter lightly with her husband in the temple. That will be *rasābhāsa*, incompatible. There is a particular mood. When the husband is engaged in worshiping the Deity in the temple, the wife may go there and help him with the materials and other necessary things, but she won't share any light conversation with her husband. No merrymaking is possible there.

Similarly, Mahāprabhu has come in a serious mood to distribute divine love to the world, and with the Holy Name of the Lord He has spread Kṛṣṇa consciousness. He has taken the position of a preacher, a reverent position. So these two things cannot go together.

Bonafide Moods of Devotees

There are three sections amongst the devotees. One is charmed more by *Kṛṣṇa-līlā*, another more by *Gaura-līlā*, and another keeps a balance. The school of Nārāhari Sarakāra is fonder of *Kṛṣṇa-līlā*. They do not recognize Mahāprabhu as a *sannyāsī*. They see only that Kṛṣṇa of Vṛndāvana. He may have put on the garment of a *sannyāsī*, but it is just an external aspect. They don't like this forced identity, and they do not admit it. That is their temperament. Rather they feel great pain. What is the necessity of practicing penance as a *sannyāsī*, enduring so many hardships, not taking proper food and rest? Their heart is aching. How can they tolerate all these things? That is the nature of their complaint to Mahāprabhu.

Jagadananda Pandita

Jagadānanda Paṇḍita has the mood of Satyabhāmā, which is in the Dvārakā conception. In those days it was three hundred miles from Navadvīpa to Purī. He brought a big waterpot filled up with *candana*, sandalwood oil, which is generally applied on the head to keep the brain cool. He brought the sandalwood oil from Bengal to Purī and offered it very modestly to Mahāprabhu, if He would graciously accept it. He appealed to His servant Govinda, "Govinda, keep it there and at times apply this oil to His head. Mahāprabhu cannot sleep, and He talks like a delirious man. This oil will help Him a great deal. I have taken it from Śivānanda and it is a genuine thing."

Govinda told Mahāprabhu, "Jagadānanda Paṇḍita has brought a full pot of *candana* oil, and his request is that You should take it now and then, smear it on the head, then You will have a sound sleep and this may help Your health." "No, no, no. This sandalwood oil will emit a good scent and the people will remark that this *sannyāsī* consorts with a woman. He applies good scented oil to His head. I can't do that. Rather it is My advice that you take it to the temple of Jagannātha and there it will burn, the light will burn with this scented oil and Jagadānanda will receive much benefit thereby. Govinda, remove it from My room."

After Govinda gave it up, Jagadānanda Paṇḍita took it and directly in front of Mahāprabhu smashed it on the floor. All the oil spread there. Then he went straight to his room and took to his bed for three days. After three days, Mahāprabhu heard that Jagadānanda was fasting continuously since breaking the pot. After the fourth day, Mahāprabhu Himself went to him. "Jagadānanda, Jagadānanda, rise, open the door. Today I shall take *prasādam* cooked by your own hand. I will not take any *prasādam* elsewhere. I shall return at the proper time and I shall take My food here today, cooked by your own hand."

What could he do? Jagadānanda had to get up. So he cooked, and Mahāprabhu came with Govinda at the proper time and took *prasādam*. He remarked, "Oh, they are very sweet. Today the dishes are very, very sweet. Cooking with a hot temper makes them sweeter." He remarked like this, "You take your food now, before I go. Before I leave the place, I want to see that you have taken food." "No, no, no, Prabhu, You may go, then I shall take food. Of course, I must take food." Then Mahāprabhu said, "Govinda, you take your seat there and when he has finished eating you will inform Me. You sit there, I am going."

That is the *vāma-bhāva* of Satyabhāmā. Gadādhara Paṇḍita is just the opposite. When Svarūpa Dāmodara tried to incite him by saying that Mahāprabhu was enraged and making harsh remarks about him, Gadādhara said: "No, no, no, how can I react? He is my Lord; toleration would be better for me. I can't venture to react in the same manner. It is not good, and I do not like that. It would be bad to assert myself, to make some remark against the advice and the consideration of Mahāprabhu. I can't do that." In spite of Svarūpa Dāmodara's incitement, Gadādhara Paṇḍita did not dare chastise Mahāprabhu.

Svarupa Damodara

Svarūpa Dāmodara is Lalitā Devī in *Kṛṣṇa-līlā*. He gives permission there to join the service of Rādhārāṇī. He is canvassing to look after the interests of Rādhārāṇī. Such intense attention to the service of Rādhārāṇī is never found anywhere else. Lalitā Devī sometimes even chastises Kṛṣṇa boldly. She takes risks by reproaching Kṛṣṇa, "You do not know the dignity of my Mistress."

Sometimes Rādhārāṇī feels ashamed within Her mind. She thinks, "What does He say about Me?" Lalitā Devī replies, "This shame is very bad. You just sit quietly. You do not know Your own interest. I know what is Your interest, Your position. I cannot tolerate that Your dignity should be minimized in any way, ever." That is the spirit of Lalitā Devī, of Svarūpa Dāmodara.

Svarūpa Dāmodara is the constant companion of Mahāprabhu in Purī. He is a scholar of the highest class and also a very good singer. Without consideration of his elevated social position, he will perform the simplest service. Svarūpa Dāmodara is there always, everywhere with Mahāprabhu. When Mahāprabhu was lost, the devotees inquired after Him the whole night and Svarūpa Dāmodara was there with a lantern, moving along the seashore, looking for Him.

Lalita's Position

Rūpa Gosvāmī composed one stanza in praise of Lalitā Devī, "O! Lalitā Devī, how is she, the first attendant of Rādhārāṇī?" Lalitā Devi is a little aggressive in nature, pushing and meddling in the affairs which are connected with Śrī Rādhā and Kṛṣṇa. She interferes with anything and everything in connection with Rādhā and Kṛṣṇa, thinking that the affairs connecting Them are her responsibility. She is very aggressive in nature and also intolerant. But Rūpa Gosvāmī has justified her character. He writes, "What is the high standard of her love and sacrifice for Rādhā and Kṛṣṇa? Lalitā Devī says that if even a drop of sweat is found on the foot of either Rādhārāṇī or Kṛṣṇa, *rādhā mukunda-pāda,* if she finds even a drop of sweat on the foot of any one of Them, she will come as if with millions of bodies. With such eagerness she will jump to remove that drop of sweat. Lalitā Devī feels such affection for the Divine Couple."

At the source of her aggression and interference in the affairs of Rādhā and Kṛṣṇa we find a great and deep affection. This justifies all her activities as the leader accepted by the associates of Rādhā-Kṛṣṇa. She always veers towards that Couple with such a standard. She can't tolerate a drop of sweat on the foot of the Divine Damsel. On that level she works, as if with millions of bodies she wants to correct it, to remove that drop of sweat. She can't tolerate any trouble, not the least trouble. She is very aggressive and talkative, and goes forward to do anything and everything as if she is mad with leadership. But at the source is her great concern for Them; this justification is there.

Sometimes she chastises Rādhārāṇī Herself, "You do not know how to behave with Kṛṣṇa. I will teach You what to do. Don't make Yourself available to Kṛṣṇa so cheaply. You must be careful of Your own dignity." Lalitā takes the position as caretaker of Rādhārāṇī, always first to look after the cause of Rādhārāṇī, to espouse the cause of Rādhārāṇī. And she is always thinking herself responsible for all the affairs concerning Them.

Sometimes she goes to chastise Kṛṣṇa also, "You don't know the dignified position, what dignified love my friend has towards You. You undermine that. I cannot allow it." From our mundane plane of experience it is not an understandable thing. We are creatures of the plane of lust. Although similar, the difference between the two is great. One is the perverted reflection of the other, the opposite. One is *prema*, the highest sacrifice, and the other is this lust, gross sense pleasure. It is like the North Pole and the South Pole, the distance is like that; just the opposite.

We are mad with this lust, but such madness is only perverted. In the original position it is a noble thing. It is self-forgetfulness, sacrifice, reckless sacrifice for the satisfaction of the Prime Cause, the Autocrat whose extent cannot be calculated. It is noble. Such intensity can never by calculated, it cannot come into our calculation here in this plane. Renunciation, liberation, salvation, these are only the negative aspect of lust. But the positive life, the life of sacrifice, the acme is found only there.

Guardian of the Lila

Lalitā Devī's thinks herself the guardian of Rādhārāṇī. "I am Her guardian, I cannot allow anyone to minimize this great divine love and sacrifice of Rādhārāṇī." Lalitā Devī stands as guarantor, even to Kṛṣṇa, what to speak of other ordinary persons. To Kṛṣṇa this is most valuable and rare; such is Rādhārāṇī's sacrifice in love, the highest intensity and utmost dignity.

It is unthinkable, unknown and unknowable. We may only conjecture as to this ideal. But if we think that we have obtained that position, if we think that we are the masters of that ideal, then it is finished; we have obtained something else. It is such an inconceivable thing, it is *adhokṣaja*. It can never be caught by any force of our mind, or intelligence; *avāṅ mānasa gocara*. Its existence transcends our mental speculation and logical considerations. But still it exists. And Lalitā Devī is of that special temperament; she has a unique importance in the *līlā* of Kṛṣṇa, as the guardian of the *līlā*.

There are other friends of Rādhārāṇī. Some are neutral towards Kṛṣṇa and Rādhārāṇī, some are a little partial towards Kṛṣṇa, but Lalitā Devī is cent-percent partial towards Rādhārāṇī's cause. This is Lalitā Devī. Her birthday, the day of her appearance, is just before that of Rādhārāṇī.

The First Meeting

We are told that Rādhārāṇī was found floating in a lotus. Her father, Vṛṣabhānu Rāja, was childless. He was a *gopa* chief, the cowherd king, the chief cow-keeper. But he did not have any children. Then one day he found a beautiful girl in a lotus flower on the lake. He found Her and took Her home. The girl was very beautiful, perfect, but Her eyes did not open.

Vṛṣabhānu Rāja had a friendship with Nanda Mahārāja. Through Nanda Mahārāja, Yaśodā heard that her friend Kīrtidā, the wife of Vṛṣabhānu Rāja, had found a girl of exquisite beauty in a lake somewhere, but She was blind. She went to visit her, to congratulate Kīrtidā.

Going there, Yaśodā took Kṛṣṇa with her. The ladies were talking and Kṛṣṇa went up to this beautiful girl. Suddenly She opened Her eyes and saw the boy Kṛṣṇa first. The story is told like that: when She first opened Her eyes, Rādhārāṇī saw Kṛṣṇa. This is *līlā,* eternal incidents, events which are repeated in a particular way, like a drama. One drama is repeated many times in the eternal quarter. By Kṛṣṇa's will, some glimpse comes to the current mundane *brahmāṇḍa* as an exhibition, to attract the people of this age. It was in that way. The children's union, interchanging their vision.

Afterwards Vṛṣabhānu Rāja came and Kīrtidā began to nurture the baby girl until She was grown up. *Vṛṣabhānudadhi nava śaśi lekhe,* Rūpa Gosvāmī describes that the family of Vṛṣabhānu is compared to the milk ocean and from this, the moon has arisen as Rādhārāṇī. So beautiful a comparison: as the moon, Śrīmatī Rādhārāṇī has come from the ocean of Vṛṣabhānu's fortune. The fortune of Vṛṣabhānu is compared with the ocean, and from there sprung up Vṛṣabhānu-nandinī Śrī Rādhikā.

Parakiya Rasa

Gradually, Rādhārāṇī grew up and the time came to marry. The marriage was performed ostentatiously. There are different angles of vision about Her marriage. Some say that one day Lord Brahmā married Rādhā and Kṛṣṇa in a jungle. Some say that They were married according to social customs. In different *kalpas,* various versions are known.

But Mahāprabhu accepted *parakīya* to be the highest attainment. They are not married, but each other's heart did not know anyone else as Their lover. Their hearts automatic connection was full. It is not chance coincidence, but rather fulfilled a necessity. Free love, recklessly crossing the directions and the influence of society and the scriptures, crossing the conceptions of religious sentiment, taking so much risk for the union with Kṛṣṇa, this holds the highest position.

There are two very fine points here. One is that it is very rarely possible, it is very hard to get that favorable situation. Another is that at this stage one is taking the greatest risk possible, without caring for anything. This is given the suprememost position, *parakīya-madhūrya-rasa.* In *madhūrya-rasa* these *parakīya* circumstances are necessary to increase the *rasa* to its fullest and most intense capacity.

The highest intensity can be produced by such artificial dearth. If we hide the rice or wheat underground to create a shortage of food, then food becomes very valuable. So also the dearth, the rareness, the impossibility of union has been created in *parakīya-rasa.* To facilitate this relationship, such adjustment is necessary between the two, among the Divine Couple. They are crossing all sort of conceptions of religious sentiments. This is the highest limit. There is no consideration of anything when They meet. At all cost, at all risk They are going to serve each other. The intensity becomes as high as possible. It is managed by Yogamāyā to raise it to the highest level. Yogamāyā manages in such a way that the union will be most fruitful and pleasing. It is necessary to manage in such a way to maximize Their pleasure.

Understand from the Plane of Sacrifice

In *vātsalya-rasa,* Yaśodā is arranging everything, but child Kṛṣṇa does not find satisfaction there. He is satisfied only in stealing foodstuffs. Yaśodā has reserved the very finest stock to feed her child, but He is not satisfied with this. He wants to stealthily take and to feed others also. There He finds great satisfaction.

He does not find satisfaction in the ordinary state. His mother is calling, "Come, my boy, take Your seat here. I have kept many valuable dishes for You. I am serving all these things. You please take." Ordinarily Kṛṣṇa does not find pleasure there; He can't relish it. So stealthily He will go and snatch things and throw them to the monkeys or to some other boys. That is His boyish nature. His satisfaction does not come in the ordinary way.

In *vātsalya-rasa* the Lord is showing autocracy, the autocratic nature of exacting affection from the environment. And autocratic nature is also there extracting the highest form of love from the consort group, in *mādhurya-rasa*. We are to understand all these things in a scientific way.

Everything belongs to Kṛṣṇa. Yaśodā prepares everything for satisfying Kṛṣṇa, to make Him eat, to feed Him. But He is not satisfied to take in that way. Everything belongs to Him; He is the enjoyer of everything, the Absolute. But still *aher iva gatiḥ premṇaḥ svabhāva,* just as a snake naturally moves in a crooked way, so the crooked movement of the waves of love is natural. We are to approach it in this way. If we understand these relationships step by step in a scientific way, then we'll be able to answer any questions that may generally come. "What is the ideal of God, that He is a debauchee? He is stealing! How can such things be adjusted with the ideal of the holiness of God?"

Generally people will come and attack in this way. But they forget that they cannot understand; they cannot follow that first this must be understood from the plane of sacrifice, not from the plane of enjoyment or exploitation. It is beyond renunciation and sacrifice; it is dedication. He is the owner and consumer of anything and everything. He can take it in any way. Everything is for Him. And no one has been given a position to comment on this. It is eternal and irresistible; it is the flow of the divine plane. The highest fundamental flow, the flow of the fundamental plane is of such nature. There is no question of morality, because there is not a second party present there. He is the only party. His movement is such. None may question. It is such by nature.

Prepare Yourself for the Absolute Lila

We have come to rebuke God, but who are we? What is our position that we have become jealous of His activities, which are *advaya jñāna,* Absolute? We are culprits, *nirmatsarāṇāṁ satāṁ.* In the beginning Vedavyāsa says, "What I am going to say here is not meant for malicious people, for the jealous. Such foolish, jealous and malicious people have no entrance into this *līlā* of Kṛṣṇa, which I will describe. Only the sympathetic, the innocent, those who understand His position, what He is, only they may enter." He cannot be questioned. If we question the Absolute movement, then He is wrong. But the Absolute *līlā* can never be wrong. It is causeless and irresistible. It is the sweetest and the purest.

And we, jealous contrarians, will we rebuke Him? We are culpable and are to be punished for that. The universal wave is such. He is the Autocrat. Everything is for Him. He is for Himself. He is not accountable to any person, nor is He required to give explanations to anyone. If that were to be the case, then His Absolute characteristic would be compromised. The Absolute wave is such; it cares for none.

We are represented there. If we can appreciate this, we can have entrance there. In this way we can have a taste of that finest quality of sweetness. We are allowed. If we can adjust, if we do away with all jealousy and maliciousness, we will find in our hearts that it is of the nature of the Absolute sweetness. And then we will be considered bonafide participants in that *līlā.* We will find that we will attain the highest ecstasy in our hearts. We are to prepare ourselves for the Absolute *līlā*.

This is what is necessary for us. We must be open to receive the Absolute wave of sweetness that comes to us; try to understand. Through the divine agent we can prepare ourselves to find this plane of sweetness. This is the background of the *līlā* of Rādhā-Kṛṣṇa. *Śrīmad Bhāgavatam* and Śrī Caitanya Mahāprabhu gave this for us, such a beautiful thing. We must be selfless to the extreme. This is the standard of selflessness, self-effacement, self-forgetfulness, self-surrendering. Then we will be able to participate. The universe, the characteristic, the movement, the sweetness of the Absolute wave, the wave of sweetness Absolute, that is irresistible. It can never be opposed by any force. The ultimate existence of the reality is of such nature. It is not equipoised; it is dynamic. The ecstasy, the happiness is dynamic, and its movement is in such a way.

We can participate if we simply remove all our selfishness, crookedness, and jealous temperament. Then we will be considered fit to connect with that most fundamental wave of Absolute sweetness. This is the background of Rādhā-Govinda *līlā*. We must prepare ourselves in such a way if we wish to approach that highest plane of divinity. This is Vṛndāvana, the characteristic of Vṛndāvana. Mahāprabhu and the *ācāryas*, Bhaktivinoda Ṭhākura and Bhaktisiddhānta Sarasvatī Ṭhākura came with this fact to give it to the world.

Modern Science

What will scientific discovery and invention, or any other partial religious conceptions do for the world? Svāmī Mahārāja (A. C. Bhaktivedānta Svāmī Prabhupāda) took this highest conception to the length and breadth of this world. The world is to come to this thought, at last. To reach there, this is the goal. Svāmī Mahārāja has prepared the groundwork; he called the world to come and see. "This is not un-scientific. It is the most scientific, the most logical, the most obvious, and the happiest goal of our life. Come, all come."

Mahāprabhu came to tell us of this success in life. Know what is our prospect, that our life can come to such a high level. Try to understand what it is. What is it? Generally we are captured by the lust here, even the animals. Everywhere we find that there is a sort of pleasure that can attract us, but what is that? Try to analyze that. And when the outer malicious defective covers are broken and separated, then we shall find the *prīti*. Originally it is that great thing, the divine love, and the perverted reflection of the divine love is acting in this world. Even the animals and the trees are mad for this satisfaction. What is at the source, the ideal of this charm, try to understand that. In the highest play it is so sweet, it is so pure, it is so desirable; and it is the real fulfillment of us all.

It includes the entire animated world and its parts. It is there, the cause and the divinity is there. The perverted reflection is capturing and giving reaction, giving troublesome reaction to this sense pleasure here. But in the original form it is very wholesome. Return home. Home is sweet. The sweetness, the charm of the home is there. In this way it has been described in *Bhāgavatam* and by Mahāprabhu and Gauḍīya Maṭha, and it is given to us as a general call to understand our own fulfillment. We must fulfill our fate and attain the highest fortune.

Beauty Above Power

Power is not the ultimate controller; it is beauty. The control of beauty is very sweet, normal, and natural. Power, awe, reverence, grandeur, these have all become stale when *Bhāgavatam* has presented the Kṛṣṇa conception of Godhead. The Nārāyaṇa conception has become stale. Beauty, and love, and harmony, nothing higher was ever discovered.

Śrī Caitanyadeva gave us that; Vṛndāvana has given us that: Śrī Kṛṣṇa consciousness. Our Guru Mahārāja and Svāmī Mahārāja widely have given it, announced to the wide world that Kṛṣṇa conception, the conception of beauty, harmony, and love. That is at the source, the universal cause, the conception of the Absolute, not anything else. With that fundamental conception we may find relief. We may feel that we are out of danger, we are no longer going to be victims of power.

Affection, beauty, love, harmony is the highest thing ever to come in a conception of this world. In the last scripture of Vyāsadeva, he gave it to the world. The very gist, the highest goal of life is here: to connect with the Kṛṣṇa conception of the Absolute. For those who realize that things are of such a plane, to them even the servitors of Nārāyaṇa in Vaikuṇṭha seem to be of a very lower status.

Thrown Down to Vaikuntha

Raghunātha Dāsa Gosvāmī is called the *ācārya* or distributor of *prayojana-tattva,* the summum-bonum of life. The highest attainment or *prayojana* is supreme. And he is the authority in that department.

He said that if we have too much affinity towards scriptural service, then we will be thrown down to *paravyoma.* We won't be allowed to take our position in the land of freedom, where spontaneous love is the queen and regulates all. The queen of love will throw us down to Vaikuṇṭha. "Go there, do your duty according to scripture, according to calculation, according to the new excitement created by grandeur, awe, reverence, all these things. Go there."

Only the simple, the plain, the spontaneous service, the hearty service of the Lord reigns here, and we are in the midst of that plain thing. We do not care for any other thing, but only for the object of our love. That is our guide, that is our *śāstra,* that is our everything. We do not know anything else, and we do not want to know anything more.

The subtlest power, the power of affection, the power of love, the power of service, that is considered the highest power ever known to the world. We must give up our legal power or any physical power; we should not care for that. *Śakti* is such. An example is given of Asutosh Mukherji, a famous Bengali gentleman. He was asked by the government to go to England several times, but his mother did not allow it. So many instances are there; the mother controls the son. Taking the dust of the mother's feet, he can do anything and everything; he feels like that. Affection and love reign; power fails.

Mahāprabhu says that to give this and that to God is self-deception. Give love, love of Kṛṣṇa, *prema.* That is anything and everything; that is all in all. Instead of spending money, giving our physical force, all these things, love is the real essence of any existence. Offer that to the Lord. Through that, come to the plane of love, the plane of love that Kṛṣṇa has created around Him.

God takes the form of Kṛṣṇa in the plane of love, and that is the most fundamental and most subtle plane. It is behind all this apparent creation of different nature. Come to that plane. Try to penetrate into that plane, where God is Kṛṣṇa and the paraphernalia is Vṛndāvana. Try to have admission there in that plane. The happiest form of life we will find there. Mercy is more beautiful than justice. We cannot blame justice. Justice is justice. We cannot think of blaming the spirit of justice. How can we blame that?

Here, there is mercy over justice. We cannot deny that. Who can extend mercy over justice? He must have such power that He can compensate the demands of justice. He has the power of compensation; therefore, He can give mercy. Such an aspect of the Lord comes through love and affection. We want to live there.

The Emperor is Love

Love is above everything. Love is the only wealth in this world. *Dharma, artha, kāma, mokṣa. Dharma* is duty, our service to society and the environment, without any remuneration. It is like depositing something in the bank, accumulating for later use, perhaps in the afterlife. We deposit in the bank, then use it all for sense pleasure. Nothing else. *Artha* is wealth, which can make sense pleasure possible, and allow us to distribute it to others. In the lowest sense *kāma,* sense experience, is the wealth that everyone is running after; *kāma,* sense pleasure.

Dharma, artha, kāma, and the fourth is *mokṣa.* We know that this wealth is not real wealth; it is only fascination. It is only progress in the wrong way. So we must try our utmost to get out of this game. We are playing in the hand of Māyā, who is fascinating us with these lower things, all this sense pleasure in different forms. We must get out; that is *mokṣa,* liberation.

The power infinite and love infinite, attracting love, self-surrender, that is the highest expression of the Infinite. And that is Rādhā-Kṛṣṇa, the all-attractive Couple; in the words of our Guru Mahārāja, the predominating and predominated moieties. Positive and negative, They may be called. Attraction is the most fundamental element everywhere. All else can be eliminated, ignored, and forgotten, if we come in contact with attraction, love. Everything can be ignored if we are in connection with love.

The fulfillment of our existence, all the existence, everything is love. Love is the principle in the center; it is the only fulfillment of everything, every existence. The very gist of existence is there;

it can't be ignored or challenged by any other form or aspect of our substantial existence. Unchallenged and absolute, the king, the absolute, the emperor is love. None can stand in comparison with that. All will have to accept defeat coming in opposition with the principle of love.

Mahāprabhu pointed out that this is the most substantial thing in this world. Whatever we see and find and experience and come in connection with, love is the most central necessity and fulfillment. *Śrīmad Bhāgavatam* extracts the essence from the whole of the revealed scriptures and says that the most desirable and original thing is love divine. We must not allow ourselves to run hither and thither searching for a base fulfillment. Forcibly focusing our attention, we must concentrate in this direction. This is the highest substance in the creation, meant for us throughout eternity.

Risk Enhances the Mood

Give up your wild goose-chasing habits. Collect and concentrate all your might to progress in this direction, to try to go to the temple of love divine: *āsām aho caraṇa reṇu juṣām ahaṁ syāṁ*. Risk, the background of risk enhances the mood. A necessary part of the highest form of love is to risk the worldly achievement. Risk the so-called purity found in this world for the quest of love divine; that commands the highest position. Very carefully that should be taken.

Newton, the greatest scientist, said "I know nothing." That is the way. The more one is in the midst of purity, the more he thinks that he is impure. That is the nature of infinite measurement. Because the charm is so infinite, it cannot but be estimated in that way. The more they achieve, the more they thirst for more. Realization towards the Infinite is of that characteristic. The more we can advance, the more we think we are helpless to go further. It does not come into the plane of measurement.

One should understand that love is the real essence of life; without that we should not exist. Love is such a precious innate wealth that we would deny our very life if we do not have that most precious inner wealth: love for Kṛṣṇa, for the Absolute.

Search for Krsna

Give the widest shape to your inquiry. Where are you? Who are you? How are you to advance? This is our dire necessity for our own purpose. We can't avoid it. We can't predict the level of thought of that inquiry: Brahman, Paramātma or Bhagavān. Inquiry regarding Bhagavān is the highest, the search for Śrī Kṛṣṇa, Reality the Beautiful. It is a natural necessity within us, for our own interest; we can't avoid it. A sane man, a man who does not want to deceive himself, can't avoid the search for Kṛṣṇa, for his own benefit, his most general necessity.

Search for happiness, *raso vai saḥ*. Search for the best comfort. This is the general question. This should be the only question of the whole world. Search for Śrī Kṛṣṇa. Search, search for love, ecstasy, the highest form of ecstasy. Read and cry. What have I done? What is my necessity, and how am I passing my days? Repent, cry! I have passed my days uselessly; I am a traitor to my own self, I am committing suicide.

Complain against yourself and your so-called friends. We have nothing to do here. Read and cry, do or die! Progress in the right way, or you are inviting your death. The general tenor of life, of all existence will be this. In the most scientific way, search for Śrī Kṛṣṇa, Reality the Beautiful. That is the highest goal of humanity. All problems are solved here. They are all harmonized. There can be no complaint against this attempt. No complaint against this attempt can be normal. Deviation from this general instruction, the general call, is false, unnecessary and injurious. This is the truth, the necessity of everyone, wherever there is life.

The most generalized movement, the most grand and extensive and friendly call is this: "March towards Kṛṣṇa!" All else should be silenced. All other topics should be stopped, and only if this call remains, the real welfare of the world remains. It is a comprehensive call, a non-sectarian call. It is considered sectarian by aberrant persons, but every normal thinking individual understands that this is the most universal ideal.

Search for Śrī Kṛṣṇa, march towards the divine domain; join the universal march towards the divine domain. Free yourself to go back home, back to God, back to Godhead. We are quarreling in a foreign land for fictitious gain. Save them, and take them all home. Only by the grace of that Absolute is it possible. The wave is coming from there to take us home. Only one who knows our home can give us such news, and can take us there. The call comes from home; it originates from home.

Wholesale Satisfaction

In Vṛndāvana we will find that our thirst for any higher change of the environment, any change of association, need no longer be quenched. There is thirst, an eternal thirst for a closer relation with Them. There is no possibility of any higher change of the environment. The only remaining question is how to come into closer connection with that environment. And that becomes the initiative of our movement there, more and more intimate connection with that environment.

The environment is eternal, but in the intimacy of connection with the competition, there is movement. And guidance is given according to that. In this way there is progress. There is some sort of necessity by which the service is moving. And there is repetition, a kind of repetition, but it is ever-fresh and ever-new! In that plane, there is movement of time, but it is eternal. It is managed by Yogamāyā.

And finally, when we come to that plane, we will attain the fullest satisfaction of all the inner parts of our system, the wholesale satisfaction of every atom of every constituent part of our spiritual body. *Prati aṅga lāgi kānde, prati aṅga mora.* "Every part of every limb cries for union with the corresponding part of every limb of the other side." The *sambandha* relationship with the environment may come to such a stage, that every atom constituting our spiritual body and mind, will aspire after union with every corresponding part of the environment.

In this way, in such a friendly way, so many are moving there, and it is adjusted accordingly by Yogamāyā. This is the highest conception. *Prati aṅga lāgi kānde, prati aṅga mora,* "Every atom of my existence is in loving correspondence with the environment, and that is Kṛṣṇa. Kṛṣṇa consciousness has surrounded me. From all sides it has embraced me. I am lost in the world of Kṛṣṇa consciousness. Every atom is feeling as if it is experiencing a separate pleasure in His embrace."

Source of All Other Rasas

This is possible only in the consorthood relationship, where every atom has been embraced, captured, by coming into the most intimate connection with Him. It is *called ādi-rasa,* or *mukhya-rasa.* It is the most original and the source of all other *rasas.* Mahāprabhu came with this gift: *madhūrya-rasa.* It is *anarpita carīṁ cirāt,* that which was never distributed before.

If Mahāprabhu had not appeared in this Kali-yuga, how could we tolerate our life, how could we sustain our very life? What He has given, it is the very gist of life, the very taste, the charm of life. Without that we think it is impossible for anyone to live in this world. Gaurāṅga has revealed such a thing to us. If He had not come, then how could we live? It is impossible to live devoid of such a holy gracious thing as love divine. How could we know that Rādhārāṇī stands above all in the world of love divine? All things we have obtained from Him, and now we think that life is worth living. Otherwise, living was suicidal.

In this human life we have some sort of connection with that, but still we are passing our days in wild goose-chases. How much of our time can we devote for the quest? Many things of scarce importance are encroaching on our time and energy, and we can't concentrate on this holiest prospect. We are not to be blamed any less than those that have no clue. They have their solace; they do not know. But we are more culpable.

Knowing more, we are more responsible. What explanation do we have to give our masters? We knew to a certain extent, but still we used our energy defectively, we wasted our energy. How will we explain? We are more condemned. To serve those that can serve Her, that is the way to approach Her, serving Her servants' servants. Our future is insured if somehow we can be counted in the group of the servitors of Śrī Rādhikā.

Rasa—The Positive Conception of Liberation

For the Vaiṣṇavas, the students of the *Bhāgavata,* the followers of Mahāprabhu, our fate is sealed in search of Kṛṣṇa. We don't want anything else but Kṛṣṇa. The *Bhāgavata* has been described as the ripe fruit of the tree of the *Veda.* The *Veda* has produced the fruit out of its own accord. What is that? *Rasa.* Svayam Bhagavān Kṛṣṇa Vrajendra-nandana. That is the ripened fruit of the tree of the *Veda. Veda* means the embodiment of revealed truth, and this inner current is producing the fruit. And the fruit, when it is ripe, is the *Bhāgavatam.*

But out of our own prejudice, we try to get something from the *Veda,* the tree. The animals try to chew the leaf, someone will cut the root, but the natural product of the *Veda*, the highest revealed truth is Kṛṣṇa. *Raso vai saḥ; śraddhāya mayān lokaṁ.* Through our faith we can get that *rasa* of the highest order. That is the gift of the highest order. That is the gift of all the *Vedas.*

Veda-mātā gāyatrī, she also aims at that pleasure object. I have tried my best to show that sort of meaning from *gāyatrī. Gaṇāt-trāyate,* that which by chanting produces liberation. And what is the definition of liberation? *Svarūpeṇa vyavasthitiḥ*: to engage ourselves in our innermost duty. *Gāyatrī* is directed towards that goal.

The Ripened Fruit

Kṛṣṇa's *vaṁśī,* His flute, is also doing the same thing. In the highest place we find proper adjustment for our service. That is the sound. And Kṛṣṇa's *vaṁśī* is also doing this through its sound. The sound gives impression, inspiration to anyone and everyone. "Come to my sweet service, engage yourself in my sweet service." That is the call of the flute of Kṛṣṇa, and of *Gāyatrī, Veda-mātā.* There in the *Veda* the same thing is said, and that is in the flute.

What is in the *Veda,* is in the flute. And in the middle there is also the *Veda, Śruti, Vedānta, Bhāgavatam. Nigama kalpa taror galitaṁ phalaṁ,* Vyāsadeva says in his introduction to *Śrīmad Bhāgavatam.* What is the necessity of this new book? This is *nigama kalpa taror galitaṁ phalaṁ. Nigama* means *Veda,* and it is compared to a tree. And this *Bhāgavatam,* the natural ripened fruit, comes of its own accord. It is not forced. Of its own accord, the tree gives fruit, and the fruit is ripe, and it is *Bhāgavatam.* So, we drink the juice, *bhāgavataṁ rasaṁ ālayaṁ muhur aho rasikā bhuvi bhāvukāḥ.*

If we have real thinking capacity, this normal hankering, we must come to drink this *rasaṁ.* This is the natural product of the *Veda-kalpataru.* This *gāyatrī gaṇāt trāyate.* If we chant the *Gāyatrī mantra* we will be liberated, emancipated. The positive conception of liberation is *svarūpa-siddhi,* self-determination. And in self-determination we must come in contact with Kṛṣṇa in different *rasas* to get our assured and attached service. And thereby we can imbibe the real juice to make our life fulfilled. Our fulfillment is there. Otherwise, all our attempts are fruitless labor. We must only utilize our energy in the proper way, to make our lives successful.

This advice from the revealed scriptures is meant for all of us. *Śṛṇvantu viśve amṛtasya putrāḥ.* "Oh, you sons of nectar, please listen. You are born for *amṛta,* you were born to taste nectar. And you must not be satisfied with anything but *amṛta.* Awake, arise! Search for *amṛtaṁ,* that nectar, that satisfaction. *Oṁ!* A big Yes! Yes! What you seek, it exists! Don't be disappointed! The revealed scriptures say that it exists. Your thirst will be quenched. You are meant for this by nature; you deserve it. Don't be afraid. Don't be cowed down. In your real being, it is already given, it is there. You can never be satisfied anywhere else. Prepare yourself to receive the result of your long search, the long missing *amṛtaṁ* in the full form, in full quality. We should have no other business, no other engagement, but *kṛṣṇānusandhāna."*

Radha-dasya

When I was in Madras, Prabhupāda's Vyāsa Pūjā took place at the Caitanya Maṭha in Māyāpura. Professor Sannyal had written an article in English for the occasion. He wrote, "I do not know Kṛṣṇa, but because you tell me that I am to worship Kṛṣṇa, I do it." I could not understand the meaning of this statement, the internal meaning. I could not help but wonder why he had said this. Three or four years later, an incident occurred at Rādhā Kuṇḍa that helped me to understand.

Paramānanda Brahmacārī came to Prabhupāda and reported that the Diwan of Bhāratpura State was circumambulating Rādhā

Kuṇḍa by prostrating himself on the ground and slowly advancing by measuring the length of each successive prostration. Paramānanda Prabhu told Prabhupāda with much ardor, "They have so much esteem for Rādhārāṇī!" Prabhupāda then came out from his inner quarters and said, "Yes, but their concern for Rādhārāṇī and our concern for Rādhārāṇī are quite different. They come to Rādhārāṇī because She is Kṛṣṇa's favorite; but our position is the opposite. We worship Kṛṣṇa because He is Rādhārāṇī's favorite. Our interest is in Rādhārāṇī, and Kṛṣṇa is Her favorite. And only because She wants Kṛṣṇa do we have any connection with Him."

At that time I could not understand what Professor Sannyal had written. Then later I read that some *jīva*s are born out of Baladeva's *aṅga-jyoti,* the *brahmajyoti,* the non-distinguishable divine effulgence. That is the source from whence some of us are born. Some have connection with Baladeva's *aṅga-jyoti,* but others originate from the halo of Rādhārāṇī and Her group. These souls have a direct connection with Rādhārāṇī. She is their Mistress and they necessarily follow whatever She does.

Prabhupāda told us that we are really *śaktas,* worshipers of God's potency; not *śaktas* like the worshipers of Durgā, but *śuddha-śāktas.* The real, original potency, Kṛṣṇa's dedicating Moiety, is in Vraja. Both direct and indirect connections with Kṛṣṇa come through Her. This is Rādhā's position. We heard all these things from Prabhupāda.

This is also the significance of the *sannyāsa-mantra.* In ordinary *mantras,* a direct connection with Kṛṣṇa is established, but in the *sannyāsa-mantra,* our spiritual connection is shown to be with the *gopīs.* That is *Rādhā-dāsya,* the service of Rādhikā. It is above *Kṛṣṇa-dāsya.* The purport, the gist of the *sannyāsa-mantra,* is *gopī-dāsya.*

Meeting at Kuruksetra

In both Navadvīpa and Vṛndāvana, the background is similar. In Navadvīpa, to gain victory over the opposition party, Mahāprabhu left His household life. And in *Vṛndāvana-līlā* it is also similar. The opposition in *Vṛndāvana-līlā* came from Mathurā in the form of Agha, Baka, Pūtanā, Tṛnāvarta, and other demons who were sent by King Kaṁsa. To uproot the opposition, Kṛṣṇa had to go to Mathurā. And when He went there, He found that the opposition was widespread.

Kaṁsa's father-in-law, Jarāsandha, Kālayavana, Śiśupāla, Dantavakra, and many others were inimical to Kṛṣṇa. Kṛṣṇa promised the *gopīs* that after finishing His enemies, He would return to Vṛndāvana to play peacefully with them. To uproot the opposition party, Kṛṣṇa had to go away. And He told the *gopīs* in Kurukṣetra, "I have some other enemies; after finishing with them, I will be reunited with you." That sort of hope was given to the *gopīs* in Kurukṣetra.

In Samanta-pañcaka, Kurukṣetra, Kṛṣṇa met the residents of Vṛndāvana after a long separation, perhaps a hundred years. The *gopīs* prayed to Kṛṣṇa, "We are not *yogīs* that will be satisfied with abstract thinking about You. Do You think that we are *yogīs* that will be satisfied with our imagination? We are not a party to that. Neither are we *karmis,* incurring so much debt from nature. Shall we come to Your door to get relief? We do not belong to any of these two sections. We want to live with You as a family; not to use You for any other purpose. We want to have a direct family life with You. Don't You know that? And You came first by Uddhava and now You have avoided us for so long. Are You not ashamed?"

This is their inner meaning. Mildly they are making the case that they won't be satisfied by anything else. "You know it for certain, You know it better. If You kindly come, if we had You completely in our midst, our prayers would be answered. We are not satisfied with anything less than that. Anything less than that cannot satisfy us. We are not talking of abstract thinking, nor do we wish to utilize You to relieve us from the entanglement of this material nature. We have no conception of bodily consciousness. We do not want relief from the reactionary suffering of this material life. We don't care for that. We are unconscious of that. What is our real need? We want to serve You directly in our loving relationship. Please try to do that."

And Kṛṣṇa's answer to them also has an inner meaning: "You know, all the people want Me. Through devotion, they want Me to help them to acquire the highest position in the eternal world, the world of eternal benefit. If they attain such a connection with Me, they consider themselves fortunate. But I consider Myself fortunate because I have your affection. I have such valuable affection, which I found in your heart. I consider Myself fortunate."

Rādhārāṇī could see the inner meaning of Kṛṣṇa's answer. She became satisfied. Wherever He may be in the physical sense, at heart He is Hers alone. Very soon He cannot but come to join Her party again. Kṛṣṇa is coming closer to Rādhārāṇī, coming near the *gopīs,* after such a long separation. He finds Himself very culpable; He has committed a great crime.

Coming to the *gopīs* and remembering their qualities of love and surrender, Kṛṣṇa feels most criminal. He bends His body to touch the feet of Rādhārāṇī. *Kiṁ pādam te nutasi vipaṇa*. One poet has represented this scene in this way, and that poem was collected by Rūpa Gosvāmī in his *Padyāvalī*. Kṛṣṇa is coming in touch with the atmosphere of Vṛndāvana. He is a king, a paramount king in the whole of India, but when He came in contact with the *gopīs,* He found Himself a criminal.

Kṛṣṇa fell at Her feet: "Your position is so high, so very

high. For so long I was away from You, increasing My duties. Without trying to satisfy You, I engaged Myself in different duties." Bending His body, He was about to touch the feet of Rādhārāṇī. Stepping back, She remarked, *kiṁ pādam te nutasi...*

"Why are You coming to touch My feet? I think You have lost the balance of Your mind. But You are master of the situation; no explanation can be called from You. You are as pure as anything. You have not done anything wrong. You are *Svāmī,* You are My husband, You are My Master, and I am Your maidservant." *Svāmīno hi tantryā.* This is the arrangement of the Vedic scripture. We find in the scriptures that the male has such freedom, but not the female.

"There is no offense in leaving Me to attend to so many duties. For some time You were engaged in some other quarter, what is the harm? What is the fault in You? That does not matter, this right is given to You by scripture and by society. There is no crime, no sin. Already You have that liberty, so You have not committed any wrong. You have so many duties to discharge, but I am only for Your service. I could not keep up the standard. I am really the criminal, the culprit. The meanness is with Me, the defect rests with Me entirely.

You are not responsible for this separation. Why do You consider that You are at fault, that You have committed wrong? The positive proof is that I sustain My life. So great an affection I have experienced, and yet I am still alive. I did not die from the pangs of Your separation. I am showing My face to the world, but I am not faithful to You. I could not uphold the standard of faith that I should have maintained for Your love. Therefore, I am a criminal, and You are not so.

"It is written by the saints in all the scriptures that the wife should be thankful and exclusively devoted to the husband as her Lord. In this meeting, I should fall at Your feet and beg for

Your forgiveness, because I really have no love for You. I am maintaining this body, and showing My face to the world. I am not a proper partner for You, so please forgive Me. But You are doing the opposite. Don't touch My feet!"

This is the ideal of our affection towards Kṛṣṇa. We, the finite, should have this attitude in our connection with the Infinite. Whatever little connection or attention we may have at any time, we should be all attentive towards Him. There is no other alternative. Mahāprabhu says *eka bhakti*, exclusive devotion towards the autocrat Kṛṣṇa; the Absolute good. Absolute love is autocratic, and our disposition must be of this kind, being so small. If we want such a great thing, then this is not injustice, that our demand should be like this. Our prospect, our adjustment, our understanding must be of this type. Such was the meeting at Kurukṣetra.

No Love for Krsna

Mahāprabhu also said something similar, *na prema gando'sti*. "I do not have an iota of divine love for Kṛṣṇa. Why am I shedding tears profusely, uninterruptedly, day and night? Why am I shedding tears for Kṛṣṇa? For show, to pretend that I have *Kṛṣṇa-prema*, divine love for Kṛṣṇa. Only for show, to get some fame as a servant of Kṛṣṇa, to deceive the people. I am a hypocrite. The positive proof is here. I'm still alive. I did not die. If I had real love, in this separation I should have died. That is the positive proof that I don't have even the scent of *Kṛṣṇa-prema* in Me."

Kṛṣṇa-prema is so high, so attractive, that once in contact with that, none can maintain his life without further connection. It is impossible. It is so high, so enchanting, so attracting, so beautiful, and so heart-warming. It is impossible. That divine love for Kṛṣṇa is not to be had in this mundane world. It is impossible that a human being can come in contact with that sort of divine love. If anyone by chance comes in contact with that, no separation from it is possible. He can't forget that. He cannot live separately without that connection.

If by chance there is any contact followed by separation, one will die instantly. It is so attractive, so high, one will die instantly, being without that vital devotion of the higher, noble life. It is so great, so noble, so beautiful, so magnanimous. We are out to search for that goal in the world. Mahāprabhu came to inform us that there is such a vital thing, the life of our life. It is impossible to go on living without that love. There is such a prospect for us all. Mahāprabhu came to distribute it to the world.

Karttiki-Srimati Radharani

Kārttika *māsā* is known as *niyama-sevā māsā*. During this period the devotees try to follow some fixed program to enhance their devotion. Slothfulness is not encouraged. We have to fix a particular program of devotional attempts like reading the *śāstra*, doing some *kīrtana* or some particular devotional activity that may be useful for advancement towards our goal. *Niyama* means to regulate our life to a particular schedule of service.

We must regulate *sevā*, leading to *aṣṭa-kālīya-sevā*, the 24-hour service to the Lord. During all times this should be the tenor of our disposition, especially in Kārttika, and Kṛṣṇa will be very pleased. If we do this in connection with Rādhārāṇī, it will be much favored by Kṛṣṇa Himself, because it is harmonized with His highest beloved.

Kārttika *vrata* is popular among the Vaisnavas, and especially the Gauḍīya Vaiṣṇavas, whose ultimate goal is *Rādhā-dāsya*. They observe this month conscientiously. Whatever has been mentioned in the *śāstra*, we observe it. Gauḍīya Vaiṣṇavas have much regard for Kārttika *vrata*, the vow of special service during the month of Kārttika.

There are many rules and regulations mentioned in the scriptures, and those who are very much fervent in this matter follow those rules and customs, cultivating the favor of Rādhārāṇī. She is pleased with this Kārttika *vrata*. Some restriction should be there in our daily movement. Drawing all of our energy to one point, we should try to cultivate some affection for Her, Who is Kārttikī.

Asta-kaliya-lila

In Navadvīpa we generally recommend the chanting of the *aṣṭottara śata-nāma* of Mahāprabhu and Kṛṣṇa, Their 108 Names. Their whole *līlā* is given there. One can come in touch with the whole *līlā* of Mahāprabhu as well as Kṛṣṇa. Morning and evening, repeat the eight *śloka*s of Mahāprabhu. Our Guru Mahārāja used to make us sing *aṣṭa-kālīya-līlā.* The day is divided into eight periods, and we chanted about the *līlā* during those eight times. *Aṣṭa-kālīya-līlā*: it has been recommended in Bhaktivinoda Ṭhākura's song, to come in connection with the entire *līlā*.

The eight *śloka*s of Mahāprabhu, the *Śikṣāṣṭaka,* contain all the developed ideas in a nutshell. *Bhajana,* the whole of *Kṛṣṇa-līlā* is covered in these eight *śloka*s. Especially in his Bengali translation, Bhaktivinoda Ṭhākura has composed certain songs giving deeper meaning, which bring us into close touch with those lofty ideas for our highest realization.

Kārttika is a special month in which we try our best to cultivate all of our feelings and regulate them for the attainment of our intimate connection with Kṛṣṇa. By investing our energy even in a small way during the *Kārttika mahinā,* we can get better results, just as in times of war capitalists may find more opportunity for earning profit. In a short time they can earn more; that sort of arrangement is everywhere. Here also there are particular points of time, when using our energy in a focused way can be more beneficial. Such is the time in Kārttika *mahinā*. Purity of purpose is almost guaranteed, because the object is to satisfy Rādhārāṇī, the Divine Potency.

In his last years, our Guru Mahārāja used to pass the Kārttika month sometimes in Vṛndāvana and sometimes in Purī, with a special group of devotees. In his last year he observed this month in Purī. We were with him. Previously he was in Vṛndāvana, and from Purī he came back and that year he disappeared in the month of Māgha. We passed this last month in Purī with him, in 1936. On January 1st, 1937 he disappeared.

Svayam Bhagavan and Svayam Rupa

Svayaṁ Bhagavān is always with Rādhārāṇī, and others are of lower order. Svayaṁ Bhagavān is always with Svayaṁ Rūpā. Svayaṁ Bhagavān and Svayaṁ Rūpā, Rādhārāṇī. In *rasa,* Svayaṁ Bhagavān is always by the side of Rādhārāṇī, and Svayaṁ Prakāśa is by the side of the other *gopīs.* It is the first-class double, or facsimile, of Kṛṣṇa. There is first-class double, then second-class double, and so on.

In *rasa,* only Svayaṁ Bhagavān is at the side of Rādhārāṇī, and at the side of other *gopīs* is Svayaṁ Prakāśa. In this way the gradation is there. So, *rādhā-kiṅkarā* has been settled for us to be the highest achievement. Through Rādhārāṇī we can taste the service of Svayaṁ Bhagavān. Svayaṁ Bhagavān and Svayaṁ Rūpā. The qualitative current that passes among Them, that we want. Our maximum, highest *proyojana* is there.

When Svayaṁ Bhagavān and Svayaṁ Rūpā are connected and performing *līlā,* that is of the highest order. However minor the contact, we want that quality only, *rūpānuga-dhara.* That is available in quantity to those younger devotees, the *mañjarīs.* They have free entrance to the deepest *līlā.* The more mature friends, the *sakhīs,* cannot approach. They may not approach, but the

Rūpa Mañjarī class may do so freely. These are very high talks. We are not eligible to speak about all these things.

You are helping me to take out from my inner heart so many beautiful and valuable things. It is through your help that these old memories are coming again fresh to me. I am forced to take out those things of the inner nature of my previous life that I received from my Gurudeva as wealth. Again I have the chance of seeing that treasury. I am given the opportunity by this recapitulation of what I heard at the divine feet of Gurudeva. I just sincerely repeat it to you. It is such. This is our education, what I received from the divine feet of Gurudeva.

Index

The Krsna conception 1
Necessity of a Real Agent 3
A Proper Guardian Assures Our Future 4
Measuring the Infinite 6
Earnest Desire Is The Only Price 7
Vaisnava is Higher than Sastra 8
Pure Spiritual Attraction 10
Real Taste for the Truth 11
Nama-Seva 12
Nama: More Than Mundane Sound 13
It Is Not So Cheap 13
Serve the Name through a Genuine Agent 15
Necessity of True Humility 16
Potency within the Name 19
Mayavada Nama is like Thunder 20
Gradations of the Holy Name 21
Name Proper from a Bonafide Guru 22
Advantage of Kali-yuga 24
Sraddha is the Minimum Demand 25
Qualifications for Chanting the Name 28
Krsna is Everywhere 30

Hankering In Surrender Is Our Wealth 31
Accept Slavery to Its Perfection 32
The Power of the Holy Name 34
Who Is A Brahmana 35
How Sound Enters the Disciple's Heart 36
Bhakti Under the Higher Agent Only 39
Connection with Divinity 42
Subjective Vision 43
Deep Engagement in Responsible Service 45
Under Our Affectionate Guardian's Hand 46
Distributing Their Inner Wealth 47
Cast Ourselves to the Infinite's Whim 48
Better to Serve in Heaven 50
Power of Affection 51
Infinite Touches the Finite 52
Easy Grant to Your Appeal 53
Highest Criterion of Lila 55
Guru Is Servant of His Disciples 58
Approach Guru through Sraddha 59
Search for Our Heart's Fulfillment 60
Acquired Taste 62
Descending Humility 63
The Knot of Material Existence is Slashed 64
Sraddha is More than Calculation 65
Truth Is Hidden in the Hearts of Great Souls 66
Duty of a Vaisnava 68
Revolutionary Preaching 70
Scientific Progress is Not Progress 73
Strong Preaching 75
Preaching Requires Organization 76
Real Progress is Soul Progress 78
Real Dedication 80

Enter the Land of Dedication 83
Active Dedication 85
Beauty, Charm and Sweetness 86

Follow The Angels 91
Do Not Approach Directly 93
My Ideal Is Always to Serve Him 95
Do Not Discuss Higher Lilas 95
Preach the Basics 96
Intimate Connection is Rejected 97
Not To Live at Radha Kunda 97
Not to Interfere with the Higher Lilas 98
Not to Listen to Rasa-Lila Katha 99
Follow the Will of Our Gurudeva 100
Smarana Subservient to Kirtana 101
Imaginary Perfection is Self-deception 104
The Death Blow to the Sahajiyas 105
Entering the Land of Gurus 106
Cheap Imitators and Pseudo Devotees 107
Love and Lust 108
Exploitation, Renunciation and Dedication 110
I Have No Love For Krsna 110
Sacrifice Our Mundane Experience 111
Tangible Dedication 112
Tangible Depth in Divinity 114
Effective Bhajana 116
Approach Nityananda Prabhu 117
Real Humility 117
Our Duty 119
Angels Fear To Tread 120
Do Your Duty in Your Plane 120

Not an Academic Endeavor 122
Defect of the Intellect 123
The Finite Cannot Know the Infinite 123
Reject Your Knowledge 124
Approach the Guru 125
Become an Angel 126
Die To Live 127
Not an Ornamental Thing 128
Systematic Knowledge is Knowledge Proper 130
Relative and Absolute Considerations 130
Try To Go Ahead 132
Risk Means Progress 133
Progress is a Living Thing 134
The Only Reliable Agents 136
Dedicated Risk 137
The Real Spirit 138
Higher Backing is Necessary 139
Life Nectar of the Surrendered Souls 142
Judge A Man By His Ideal 143
Bhakti Causes Bhakti 144
Renunciation Means Yukta-vairagya 145
No Spiritual Help From the Mundane 145
Enter Only for Service 147
Slave of the Slave 149
Saranagati 151
Seva Must Originate From Above 154
Dedication Beyond Calculation 157

Higher Talks 161
Higher Vision of Guru 162
Gadadhara Pandita 164
Halo of Radharani 166

Gadadhara Pandita as Rukmini 167
Gaura-Gadadhara 168
Divine Vision 169
Progress by Grace of the Higher 171
Gaura-Gadadhara Worship 172
Vrndavana is for the Shallow Thinkers 174
Service Necessity 174
Dvaraka Lila 175
Rukmini Avatara 176
The Highest Position of Sacrifice 177
The History 177
Other Vaisnava Schools 179
Madhurya and Audarya 180
High Inquisitiveness 181
Pandava Arjuna 183
A Mystic Poem 183
Gaura Nagari Rejected 185
Bonafide Moods of Devotees 186
Jagadananda Pandita 187
Svarupa Damodara 188
Lalita's Position 189
Guardian of the Lila 191
The First Meeting 191
Parakiya Rasa 192
Understand from the Plane of Sacrifice 193
Prepare Yourself for the Absolute Lila 195
Modern Science 196
Beauty Above Power 197
Thrown Down to Vaikuntha 198
The Emperor is Love 200
Risk Enhances the Mood 201
Search for Krsna 202